CHINA

and U.S. Foreign Policy

SECOND EDITION

CONGRESSIONAL QUARTERLY

1735 K STREET, N. W., WASHINGTON, D. C.

Congressional Quarterly Inc.

Congressional Quarterly Inc., an editorial research service and publishing company, serves clients in the fields of news, education, business and government. It combines specific coverage of Congress, government and politics by Congressional Quarterly with the more general subject range of an affiliated service, Editorial Research Reports.

Congressional Quarterly was founded in 1945 by Nelson and Henrietta Poynter. Its basic periodical publication was and still is the CQ *Weekly Report,* which is mailed to clients every Friday. The *Weekly Report* is cross-referenced quarterly in a cumulative *Index.*

The CQ *Almanac,* a compendium of legislation for one session of Congress, is published every spring. *Congress and the Nation* is published every four years as a record of government for one presidential term. Congressional Quarterly also publishes paperback books on public affairs.

CQ Direct Research is a consulting service which performs contract research and maintains a reference library and query desk for the convenience of clients.

Editorial Research Reports covers subjects beyond the specialized scope of Congressional Quarterly. It publishes reference material on foreign affairs, business, education, cultural affairs, national security, science and other topics of news interest. Service to clients includes a 6,000-word report four times a month bound and indexed semi-annually. Editorial Research Reports also publishes paperback books in its fields of coverage. Founded in 1923, the service was merged with Congressional Quarterly in 1956.

China and U.S. Foreign Policy, 2nd edition was edited by William B. Dickinson Jr.

Book Service Editor Robert A. Diamond. Contributors: Arlene Alligood, Peter A. Harkness, Robert A. Barnes, Helen B. Shaffer and Stanley L. Williams. The cover was designed by Art Director Howard Chapman. Editorial Assistant: Robert E. Healy.

Library of Congress Catalog No. 73-83474
International Standard Book No. 0-87187-045-2

TABLE OF CONTENTS

Between the people of China and the people of the United States there are strong ties of sympathy, understanding and mutual interest. Both are essentially democratic and individualistic. Both are by nature peace-loving, non-aggressive and non-imperialistic.... There must not and cannot be any conflict, estrangement or misunderstanding between the Chinese people and America.

—Mao Tse-tung, talk with U.S. diplomat
John Stewart Service, March 13, 1945

Now what do the Chinese Communists want? They don't want just Quemoy and Matsu. They don't want just Formosa. They want the world.

—Richard M. Nixon, television debate with
John F. Kennedy, October 13, 1960

...I am planning a journey to mainland China. The purpose of that journey involves not just peace for my generation, but even more, it affects peace for generations to come because looking far to the future we cannot have a peaceful world if 800 million of the most creative, able people in the world, one-fourth of all the people in the world, are isolated from the rest of the world.

—President Richard M. Nixon
July 31, 1971

NIXON TRIP TO CHINA OPENS NEW ERA IN RELATIONS

The United States and the People's Republic of China have set aside more than two decades of mutual hostility and are searching together for means of normalizing their relations. President Nixon's historic 1972 trip to Peking, the first state visit by a U.S. President to mainland China, gave an initial push to the effort. Both sides seem determined not to lose the momentum built up by that visit and by subsequent contacts.

The opening of "liaison offices" in Washington and Peking in May 1973 was seen as an initial step toward the eventual establishment of full diplomatic relations. Sino-U.S. exchanges in a number of fields—science, technology, culture, sports and journalism—continued to form the base for better understanding. Another important measure of progress was the expansion of U.S.-China trade from less than $5 million in 1971 to $92.5 million in 1972.

Whatever the eventual course of the cautious search for a reconciliation, historians are likely to date the new era from February 1972. That was the month President Nixon journeyed to the People's Republic of China, proclaimed in 1949 after Communist forces drove the Nationalist Chinese government of Chiang Kai-shek from the mainland to Taiwan. For 22 years thereafter the United States had pursued a policy of isolating Communist China from the family of nations.

Nixon in China

Led by Premier Chou En-lai, Chinese officials gave Nixon a restrained welcome upon his arrival at Hung Chiao Airport in Peking on Feb. 21, 1972. Later that day, however, the President met with Chairman Mao Tse-tung —an indication of the importance the Chinese leadership assigned Nixon's visit.

The hour-long Nixon-Mao meeting took place at Mao's residence somewhere in the old Forbidden City and was described afterwards only as "frank and serious." The President was accompanied by Henry A. Kissinger, his adviser for national security. Mao was accompanied by Premier Chou and by Wang Hai-jung, deputy director of protocol, and Tang Wen-sheng, an interpreter.

At a banquet that evening in the Great Hall of the People, Chou offered a toast to the Nixon party, including Mrs. Nixon, in which he said that the visit was a "positive move." President Nixon responded by noting that "more people are seeing and hearing what we say than on any other occasion in the whole history of the world." Nixon was referring to television coverage, beamed to the world via communications satellite. *(For the text of the toasts, see p. 2)*

Other highlights of the Nixon trip, by date:

• **Feb. 22**—Nixon and Chou met for four hours of policy discussions. Accompanying the President were Kissinger and John H. Holdridge and Winston Lord of the National

Trade Restrictions Eased

On Feb. 14, 1972, three days before departing on his trip to the People's Republic of China, President Nixon ordered a further loosening of U.S. trade policy toward Peking. *(Trade policy, p. 59)*

The decision placed China under the same trade restrictions (labelled Group Y) as the Soviet Union and most of the Soviet bloc. China had previously been classified a Group Z country, with whom no U.S. trade was allowed. Other Group Z countries are North Vietnam, North Korea and Cuba.

In addition, the President decided to modify remaining Foreign Assets Control Regulations pertaining to the People's Republic of China. He directed removal of the requirement that U.S. controlled firms in countries (including Western Europe, Canada, and Japan) which are members of COCOM—the international coordinating committee on strategic trade with Communist countries—obtain a Treasury license in addition to a host country license for the export of strategic goods to the People's Republic of China. He also directed elimination of the requirement that U.S. controlled firms abroad obtain prior Treasury licensing for the export of foreign technology to the People's Republic of China.

Security Council. Secretary of State William P. Rogers and Foreign Minister Chi Peng-fei held a separate conference. After a private dinner, the Nixons, accompanied by Chou and his wife, attended a special performance of "Red Detachment of Women," a revolutionary opera.

• **Feb 23**—Chou and Nixon met for four more hours of talks. An evening of exhibitions of gymnastics and table tennis followed. Mrs. Nixon visited an agricultural cooperative near the capital, and the Peking Glassware Factory.

• **Feb. 24**—Nixon spoke informally to reporters for the first time during his visit while on an excursion to the Great Wall of China. "As we look at this wall, we do not want walls of any kind between peoples," the President said. The President also visited the Ming Tombs, constructed by members of a dynasty that ruled China from the 14th to the 17th centuries. Nixon and Chou met again for three hours, followed by a private dinner.

• **Feb. 25**—In his last full day in Peking, the Nixon party visited the Forbidden City to view the palaces and courtyards of ancient Chinese emperors. That afternoon, Nixon and Chou met for an hour of private talks. That night in the Great Hall of the People, Nixon gave a banquet for Chou at which the President remarked that the two countries had "begun the long process of removing

(Continued on p. 3)

Chou En-lai, Nixon Toasts in Peking, Feb. 21, 1972

Chou En-lai. *Mr. President and Mrs. Nixon, ladies and gentlemen, comrades and friends:*

First of all, I have the pleasure on behalf of Chairman Mao Tse-tung and the Chinese Government to extend our welcome to Mr. President and Mrs. Nixon and to our other American guests.

I also wish to take this opportunity to extend on behalf of the Chinese people cordial greetings to the American people on the other side of the great ocean.

President Nixon's visit to our country at the invitation of the Chinese Government provides the leaders of the two countries with an opportunity of meeting in person to seek the normalization of relations between the two countries and also to exchange views on questions of concern to the two sides. This is a positive move in conformity with the desire of the Chinese and American peoples and an event unprecedented in the history of the relations between China and the United States.

The American people are a great people. The Chinese people are a great people. The peoples of our two countries have always been friendly to each other. But owing to reasons known to all, contacts between the two peoples were suspended for over 20 years. Now, through the common efforts of China and the United States, the gate to friendly contacts has finally been opened. At the·present time it has become a strong desire of the Chinese and American peoples to promote the normalization of relations between the two countries and work for the relaxation of tension. The people, and the people alone, are the motive force in the making of world history. We are confident that the day will surely come when this common desire of our two peoples will be realized.

The social systems of China and the Unites States are fundamentally different, and there exist great differences between the Chinese Government and the United States Government. However, these differences should not hinder China and the United States from establishing normal state relations on the basis of the Five Principles of mutual respect for sovereignty and territorial integrity, mutual nonaggression, non-interference in each other's internal affairs, equality and mutual benefit, and peaceful coexistence; still less should they lead to war. As early as 1955 the Chinese Government publicly stated that the Chinese people do not want to have a war with the United States and that the Chinese Government is willing to sit down and enter into negotiations with the United States Government.

This is a policy which we have pursued consistently. We have taken note of the fact that in his speech before setting out for China President Nixon on his part said that "what we must do is to find a way to see that we can have differences without being enemies in war." We hope that, through a frank exchange of views between our two sides to gain a clearer notion of our differences and make efforts to find common ground, a new start can be made in the relations between our two countries.

President Nixon. *Mr. Prime Minister and all of your distinguished guests this evening:*

Mr. Prime Minister, I wish to thank you for your very gracious and eloquent remarks. At this very moment, through the wonder of tele-communications, more people are seeing and hearing what we say than on any other such occasion in the whole history of the world. Yet, what we say here will not be long remembered. What we do here can change the world.

As you said in your toast, the Chinese people are a great people, the American people are a great people. If our two people are enemies the future of this world we share together is dark indeed. But if we can find common ground to work together, the chance for world peace is immeasurably increased.

In the spirit of frankness which I hope will characterize our talks this week, let us recognize at the outset these points: We have at times in the past been enemies. We have great differences today. What bring us together is that we have common interests which transcend those differences. As we discuss our differences, neither of us will compromise our principles. But while we cannot close the gulf between us, we can try to bridge it so that we may be able to talk across it.

So, let us, in these next 5 days, start a long march together, not in lockstep, but on different roads leading to the same goal, the goal of building a world structure of peace and justice in which all may stand together with equal dignity and in which each nation, large or small, has a right to determine its own form of government, free of outside interference or domination. The world watches. The world listens. The world waits to see what we will do. What is the world? In a personal sense, I think of my eldest daughter whose birthday is today. As I think of her, I think of all the children in the world, in Asia, in Africa, in Europe, in the Americas, most of whom were born since the date of the foundation of the People's Republic of China.

What legacy shall we leave our children? Are they destined to die for the hatreds which have plagued the old world, or are they destined to live because we had the vision to build a new world?

There is no reason for us to be enemies. Neither of us seeks the territory of the other; neither of us seeks domination over the other; neither of us seeks to stretch out our hands and rule the world.

Chairman Mao has written, "So many deeds cry out to be done, and always urgently. The world rolls on. Time passes. Ten thousands years are too long. Seize the day, seize the hour."

This is the hour. This is the day for our two peoples to rise to the heights of greatness which can build a new and a better world.

In that spirit, I ask all of you present to join me in raising your glasses to Chairman Mao, to Prime Minister Chou, and to the friendship of the Chinese and American people which can lead to friendship and peace for all people in the world.

(Continued from p. 1)

that wall between us." Chou noted that "whatever zigzags and reverses there will be in the development of history, the general trend of the world is definitely toward light and not darkness."

• **Feb. 26**—The Nixons journeyed to Hangchow, a resort city 100 miles southwest of Shanghai, where they were the guests of Nan Ping, chairman of the Revolutionary Committee of Chekiang Province.

• **Feb. 27**—In the company of Chou En-lai, the Nixons flew to Shanghai. A joint communique was released indicating that their talks had resulted in agreement on the need for increased Sino-U.S. contacts and for eventual withdrawal of U.S. troops from Taiwan. The 1,800-word communique, concluded after several nights of intensive negotiation, stated that progress toward "the normalization of relations" between the two sides was "in the interests of all countries." *(For text of communique, see p. 6)*

Henry A. Kissinger held a news conference in Shanghai on aspects of the communique. Asked what features of it indicated significant steps by China since its 1971 invitation to the U.S. table tennis team *(p. 10)*, Kissinger replied: "The formalization of exchanges encouraged by the two governments, the opening of trade encouraged by the two governments, the establishment of a diplomatic mechanism for continued contact, the joint statement of some general principles of international relations, the joint statement of some basic approaches to the view of the world with respect to, for instance, the section which includes the reference to hegemony—these, I believe, are matters that most of us would have considered unthinkable at the time of the invitation to the ping-pong team."

• **Feb. 28**—President and Mrs. Nixon were greeted by crowds and a military band at Andrews Air Force Base in Maryland. The presidential homecoming followed a nine-hour stopover near Anchorage, Alaska, to allow a period of rest after the flight from Shanghai. Vice President Spiro T. Agnew welcomed Nixon and remarked, "We feel easier tonight because of the trip you took." In a nationally-televised address to the crowd, the President declared: "We did not bring back any written or unwritten agreements that will guarantee peace in our time." *(For excerpts of Nixon's homecoming address, see p. 100)*

Congressional Reaction

Nixon was met by a rising chorus of praise for establishing contacts with the Chinese communist government.

The praise was not unanimous, however. Nixon's agreement that Taiwan was a part of China and that its future was a matter to be determined by the Chinese, evoked bitter criticism from some sources.

The statement was interpreted by some conservatives as meaning the abandonment of the Nationalist Chinese government. Criticism came from such disparate candidates for President as Rep. John M. Ashbrook (R Ohio), Nixon's conservative opponent for the Republican nomination, and Sen. Hubert H. Humphrey (D Minn.), the Senate's most articulate liberal in the years when U.S. policy on China was dominated in Congress by pro-Chiang forces, which included Nixon as a representative, as a senator and as vice president.

"For over two decades," Ashbrook said, "it is we who have fostered and supported, both by words and deeds,

Taiwan Disclaimer

Just a week before President Nixon embarked on his trip to Peking, the Ministry of Foreign Affairs of the Republic of China (Taiwan) on Feb. 17, 1972, issued the following statement:

"President Richard M. Nixon of the United States of America has decided to proceed to the Chinese mainland for a visit from February 21-28, 1972.

"The Government of the Republic of China hereby solemnly declares that it will consider null and void any agreement involving the rights and interests of the Government and people of the Republic of China which may be reached between the United States and the Chinese Communist regime as a result of that visit, because the regime now occupying the Chinese (mainland) has no right whatsoever to represent the Chinese people.

"The Chinese Government believes that President Nixon is cognizant of the unscrupulous nature of the Chinese Communist regime and its notorious wiliness of using negotiation as a means to carry out its intrigues of infiltration and subversion vis-a-vis free nations, and that he will not lower his guard against such intrigues. Since the announcement of his intention to visit the Chinese mainland on July 15, 1971, President Nixon has, on numerous occasions, reassured the Republic of China of his desire to maintain existing Sino-American friendship and to honor all the treaty commitments. The Chinese Government trusts that the American President will live up to the solemn assurances that he has repeatedly made.

"The fact that the Government of the Republic of China has been prevented from exercising its jurisdiction over all of its territory is mainly due to the Communist armed rebellion. This is a situation which is totally different from that of some other nations brought about by international agreements. Insofar as the Republic of China is concerned, the so-called question of unification is a question as to how to destroy the Chinese Communist rebel regime and thus enable our people on the mainland to regain their freedom. On this point, there is absolutely no room for compromise or negotiation. Under no circumstances will the basic national policy of the Government of the Republic of China to recover the Chinese mainland brook any change."

James C. H. Shen, Nationalist Chinese ambassador to the U.S., said in Washington March 2, 1972, that Secretary of State William P. Rogers had assured him that day of the U.S. commitment to the 1954 Taiwan defense treaty. Shen, who had gone at Rogers' invitation to a special briefing on President Nixon's visit, remarked: "I understand a little more now but I have no comment on my personal feelings."

On Feb. 28, 1973, a Peking spokesman proposed a meeting between Communist Chinese and Nationalist Chinese officials to discuss uniting the two Chinas. The Taiwan government on March 1 rejected the invitation as "a Communist trick" designed to damage relations between Taipei and the United States.

the concept of an independent Republic of China on Taiwan. Now, in a single week, we have abandoned that position—and in so doing we have set up the framework to abandon 15 million people to the tender mercies of a regime that during its tenure in office—its 23 years of enlightenment and progress—has managed to slay, at conservative estimate, 34 million of its own citizens."

Humphrey's concern was more for the native Taiwanese, as distinct from the Nationalist Chinese who came from the mainland.

"It is now clear," he said, "that the rug has been pulled out from under the Taiwanese, though the people of the island of Formosa once aspired to determine their own destiny."

Humphrey also took issue with Nixon's statement (in his arrival speech) that no other nation's fate was negotiating behind its back in the talks with Chou and that no American commitment to another country was given up.

"It is apparent from the communique as I read it," Humphrey said, "that concessions were made by the President and by Dr. (Henry A.) Kissinger (Nixon's national security adviser), but not any, insofar as I have been able to interpret, were made by the Chinese."

Ashbrook's view was echoed by four House conservatives, Representatives Philip M. Crane (R Ill.), John R. Rarick (D La.), John G. Schmitz (R Calif.) and Robert L.F. Sikes (D Fla.).

Panda-Plomacy

Two giant pandas given to the United States by the People's Republic of China arrived at their new home in Washington's National Zoo on April 16, 1972. Zoos throughout the nation had competed for the animals, Ling-Ling and Hsing-Hsing, but President Nixon decided on the Washington location because they were given by Chinese premier Chou En-lai "in behalf of the American people."

Two musk oxen presented to China by the U.S. arrived in Peking April 9, 1972. The National Zoo prepared special air-conditioned quarters for the pandas. Attendance soared when the animals went on display.

Ling-Ling

Further criticism came from two other candidates for the presidency, Rep. Paul N. McCloskey Jr. (R Calif.) and Sen. Henry M. Jackson (D Wash.). McCloskey welcomed the limited renewal of relations with China but said that, despite Nixon's trip, "we did not progress one inch toward settling the major problem of today, ending the Vietnam war." Jackson expressed disappointment that Nixon had not gained concessions on Vietnam from the Chinese government.

Sen. James L. Buckley (Cons-R N.Y.), said that relaxation of the U.S. commitment to defend Taiwan would "vastly diminish" his regard for Nixon. But he said he still would support Nixon for re-election.

Sen. George McGovern (D S.D.), the eventual Democratic nominee for President, praised the Nixon trip, as did Sen. Edward M. Kennedy (D Mass.). Chairman J.W. Fulbright (D Ark.) of the Senate Foreign Relations Committee, a persistent critic of Nixon's Vietnam policy, indicated he was satisfied with the results of the trip. So did Sen. Barry Goldwater (R Ariz.), the unsuccessful Republican presidential candidate in 1964. Goldwater said he was satisfied that "we have not given away one single thing to the Red Chinese" and that "we will uphold our treaty commitments to the Taiwan government."

During Nixon's visit, U.S. officials arranged for high-level visits to China by congressional leaders. Senate Majority Leader Mike Mansfield (D Mont.) and Minority Leader Hugh Scott (R Pa.) visited six Chinese cities, from April 19 to May 3, and House Majority Leader Hale Boggs (D La.) and Minority Leader Gerald R. Ford (R Mich.) followed June 23-July 8.

Other 1972 Developments

Despite President Nixon's statements that no secret deals had been made in Peking, some of the closest allies of the United States feared that the Nixon visit might presage a U.S. withdrawal from Asia. Marshall Green, the assistant U.S. secretary of state, was sent on a tour of reassurance early in March. Green meet with leaders in South Korea, Taiwan, the Phillippines, South Viet Nam, Laos, Cambodia and Thailand.

On March 13, 1972, the U.S. and Chinese ambassadors to France met in the Chinese embassy in Paris for the first of a series of private discussions on matters of interest to the two countries. Arthur K. Watson represented the United States, and Huang Chen represented the People's Republic of China. In announcing the talks three days earlier, White House Press Secretary Ronald L. Ziegler had said Paris was chosen as a "mutually convenient location." He said the problems to be discussed in the Paris meetings would be "far broader than anything ever taken up in Geneva and Warsaw," where previous Sino-U.S. ambassadorial contacts had taken place.

Returning from his May visit to the Soviet Union, President Nixon on June 1, 1972, told a joint session of Congress that his trips to Peking and Moscow were "part of a great national journey for peace" and were a move away from "perpetual confrontation" and toward "better understanding, mutual respect, point-by-point settlement of differences."

On June 19, 1972, Henry A. Kissinger, the President's adviser on national security, arrived in Peking and held four hours of talks with Premier Chou En-lai. Another four hours of discussions on the Indochina war took place June 20 between Kissinger and Chou, with Foreign Minister Chi Peng-fei and other officials in attendance. After four days of meetings, an official joint statement was issued simultaneously in Washington and Peking June 24. It stated that the Kissinger Chou meetings "consisted of concrete consultations to promote the normalization between the two countries."

On July 30, 1972, the Associated Press and Hsinhua, the official Chinese press agency, agreed to an exchange of news and photographs. It was the first regular news contact with mainland China for a U.S. organization since December 1949, when the last Associated Press correspondent left the country. Late in 1972, a group of American newspaper editors under the auspices of the American Society of Newspapers Editors visited China.

1973 Developments

A major barrier to improved U.S.-Chinese relations was removed early in 1973 when Chinese authorities released a CIA agent shot down over China in 1952, as well as two U.S. airmen imprisoned after being shot down during missions in the Indochina war.

Downey Release. The White House announced on March 9 that the last three Americans held prisoner in China would be set free, one of them at the personal request of President Nixon to Premier Chou En-lai. Chou agreed to commute the sentence of John T. Downey, the CIA agent, and allow him to leave China. President Nixon had sent word to Chou that Downey's mother was critically ill in New Britain, Conn.

The White House also announced that two American pilots, Maj. Philip E. Smith of the Air Force and Lieut. Comdr. Robert J. Flynn, would be freed. They were captured in 1965 and 1967 when they strayed over China during raids on North Vietnam.

Downey, 42, had been imprisoned by the Chinese since 1952. He and Richard Fecteau disappeared on a plane in 1952 during the Korean war. No word of the fate of the plane or its passengers was received until China announced in November 1954 that Downey had been sentenced to life imprisonment on espionage charges. Fecteau, who had received a 20-year sentence, was released on Dec. 12, 1972, after having served most of his sentence.

At a news conference on Jan. 31, 1972, President Nixon said that Downey's release was more difficult to obtain than the two other prisoners captured in 1965 and 1967 because Downey had been a CIA agent. It was the first time that the United States had admitted that Downey was a spy. In fact, the Defense Department had contended for years that Downey and Fecteau were "authorized passengers on a routine flight from Seoul, South Korea, to Japan in a plane which was under contract to the Far East Air Force."

Downey was set free at the Hong Kong border on March 12, 1973, and was flown to his mother's bedside in New Britain, Conn. Three days later Flynn and Smith crossed the border into Hong Kong and were flown to Clark Air Force Base in the Philippines. At a March 13 news conference in New Britain, Downey said he looked on his 20-year imprisonment "to a large extent wasted," and added: "I don't see that it benefited anybody."

(Continued on p. 7)

Liaison Office Statement

Following is the text, as made available by the White House Feb. 22, 1973, of a communique between the United States and the People's Republic of China.

Dr. Henry A. Kissinger, Assistant to the U.S. President for National Security Affairs, visited the People's Republic of China from February 15 to February 19, 1973. He was accompanied by Herbert G. Klein, Alfred Le S. Jenkins, Richard T. Kennedy, John H. Holdridge, Winston Lord, Jonathan T. Howe, Richard Solomon, and Peter W. Rodman.

Chairman Mao Tse-tung received Dr. Kissinger. Dr. Kissinger (and) members of his party held wide-ranging conversations with Premier Chou En-lai, Foreign Minister Chi Peng-fei, Vice Foreign Minister Chiao Kuan-hua, and other Chinese officials. Mr. Jenkins held parallel talks on technical subjects with Assistant Foreign Minister Chang Wen-chin. All these talks were conducted in an unconstrained atmosphere and were earnest, frank and constructive.

The two sides reviewed the development of relations between the two countries in the year that has passed since President Nixon's visit to the People's Republic of China and other issues of mutual concern. They reaffirmed the principles of the Joint Communique issued at Shanghai in February 1972 and their joint commitment to bring about a normalization of relations. They held that the progress that has been made during this period is beneficial to the people of their two countries.

The two sides agreed that the time was appropriate for accelerating the normalization of relations. To this end, they undertook to broaden their contacts in all fields. They agreed on a concrete program of expanding trade as well as scientific, cultural and other exchanges.

To facilitate this process and to improve communications, it was agreed that in the near future each side will establish a liaison office in the capital of the other. Details will be worked out through existing channels.

The two sides agreed that normalization of relations between the United States and the People's Republic of China will contribute to the relaxation of tension in Asia and in the world.

Dr. Kissinger and his party expressed their deep appreciation for the warm hospitality extended to them.

Liaison Offices. Returning from a five-day visit to China on Feb. 22, 1973, Henry Kissinger announced that the two countries would establish liaison offices in each other's capitals. In a press briefing in Washington, Kissinger said the liaison offices would be established in the "nearest future" and would "cover the whole gamut of relationships."

Asked if the move was a prelude to establishing diplomatic relations between China and the United States, Kissinger said America "had no further steps in mind" and that "this is as far as we can go at this point."

COMMUNIQUE STRESSED NORMALIZATION OF RELATIONS

Following is the joint U.S.-China communique issued at Shanghai, Feb. 27, 1972, at the conclusion of President Nixon's trip to the People's Republic of China:

President Richard Nixon of the United States of America visited the People's Republic of China at the invitation of Premier Chou En-lai of the People's Republic of China from February 21 to February 28, 1972. Accompanying the President were Mrs. Nixon, U.S. Secretary of State William Rogers, Assistant to the President Dr. Henry Kissinger, and other American officials.

President Nixon met with Chairman Mao Tse-tung of the Communist Party of China on February 21. The two leaders had a serious and frank exchange of views on Sino-U.S. relations and world affairs.

During the visit, extensive, earnest and frank discussions were held between President Nixon and Premier Chou En-lai on the normalization of relations between the United States of America and the People's Republic of China, as well as on other matters of interest to both sides. In addition, Secretary of State William Rogers and Foreign Minister Chi Peng-fei held talks in the same spirit.

President Nixon and his party visited Peking and viewed cultural, industrial and agricultural sites, and they also toured Hangchow and Shanghai where, continuing discussions with Chinese leaders, they viewed similar places of interest.

The leaders of the People's Republic of China and the United States of America found it beneficial to have this opportunity, after so many years without contact, to present candidly to one another their views on a variety of issues. They reviewed the international situation in which important changes and great upheavals are taking place and expounded their respective positions and attitudes.

The U.S. side stated: Peace in Asia and peace in the world requires efforts both to reduce immediate tensions and to eliminate the basic causes of conflict. The United States will work for a just and secure peace: just, because it fulfills the aspirations of peoples and nations for freedom and progress; secure, because it removes the danger of foreign aggression. The United States supports individual freedom and social progress for all the peoples of the world, free of outside pressure or intervention. The United States believes that the effort to reduce tensions is served by improving communication between countries that have different ideologies so as to lessen the risks of confrontation through accident, miscalculation or misunderstanding. Countries should treat each other with mutual respect and be willing to compete peacefully, letting performance be the ultimate judge. No country should claim infallibility and each country should be prepared to re-examine its own attitudes for the common good. The United States stressed that the peoples of Indochina should be allowed to determine their destiny without outside intervention; its constant primary objective has been a negotiated solution; the eight-point proposal put forward by the Republic of Vietnam and the United States on January 27, 1972 represents a basis for the attainment of that objective; in the absence of a negotiated settlement the United States envisages the ultimate withdrawal of all U.S. forces from the region consistent with the aim of self-determination for each country of Indochina. The United States will maintain its close ties with and support for the Republic of Korea; the United States will support efforts of the Republic of Korea to seek a relaxation of tension and increased communication in the Korean peninsula. The United States places the highest value on its friendly relations with Japan; it will continue to develop the existing close bonds. Consistent with the United Nations Security Council Resolution of December 21, 1971, the United States favors the continuation of the ceasefire between India and Pakistan and the withdrawal of all military forces to within their own territories and to their own sides of the ceasefire line in Jammu and Kashmir; the United States supports the right of the peoples of South Asia to shape their own future in peace, free of military threat, and without having the area become the subject of great power rivalry.

The Chinese side stated: Wherever there is oppression, there is resistance. Countries want independence, nations want liberation and the people want revolution—this has become the irresistible trend of history. All nations, big or small, should be equal; big nations should not bully the small and strong nations should not bully the weak. China will never be a superpower and it opposes hegemony and power politics of any kind. The Chinese side stated that it firmly supports the struggles of all the oppressed people and nations for freedom and liberation and that the people of all countries have the right to choose their social systems according to their own wishes and the right to safeguard the independence, sovereignty and territorial integrity of their own countries and oppose foreign aggression, interference, control and subversion. All foreign troops should be withdrawn to their own countries.

The Chinese side expressed its firm support to the peoples of Vietnam, Laos and Cambodia in their efforts for the attainment of their goal and its firm support to the seven-point proposal of the Provisional Revolutionary Government of the Republic of South Vietnam and the elaboration of February this year on the two key problems in the proposal, and to the Joint Declaration of the Summit Conference of the Indochinese Peoples. It firmly supports the eight-point program for the peaceful unification of Korea put forward by the Government of the Democratic People's Republic of Korea on April 12, 1971, and the stand for the abolition of the "U.N. Commission for the Unification and Rehabilitation of Korea." It firmly opposes the revival and outward expansion of Japanese militarism and firmly supports the Japanese people's desire to build an independent, democratic, peaceful and neutral Japan. It firmly maintains that India and Pakistan should, in accordance with the United Nations resolutions on the India-Pakistan question, immediately withdraw all their forces to their respective territories and to their own sides of the ceasefire line in Jammu and Kashmir and firmly supports the Pakistan Government and people in their struggle to preserve their independence and sovereignty and the people of Jammu and Kashmir in their struggle for the right of self-determination.

There are essential differences between China and the United States in their social systems and foreign policies. However, the two sides agreed that countries, regardless of their social systems, should conduct their relations on the principles of respect for the sovereignty and territorial integrity of all states, non-aggression against other states, non-interference in the internal affairs of other states, equality and mutual benefit, and peaceful coexistence. International disputes should be settled on this basis, without resorting to the use or threat of force. The United States and the People's Republic of China are prepared to apply these principles to their mutual relations.

With these principles of international relations in mind the two sides stated that:

• progress toward the normalization of relations between China and the United States is in the interests of all countries:

• both wish to reduce the danger of international military conflict;

• neither should seek hegemony in the Asia-Pacific region and each is opposed to efforts by any other country or group of countries to establish such hegemony; and

• neither is prepared to negotiate on behalf of any third party or to enter into agreements or understandings with the other directed at other states.

Both sides are of the view that it would be against the interests of the peoples of the world for any major country to collude with another against other countries, or for major countries to divide up the world into spheres of interest.

The two sides reviewed the long-standing serious disputes between China and the United States. The Chinese reaffirmed its position: The Taiwan question is the crucial question obstructing the normalization of relations between China and the United States; the Government of the People's Republic of China is the sole legal government of China; Taiwan is a province of China which has long been returned to the motherland; the liberation of Taiwan is China's internal affair in which no other country has the right to interfere; and all U.S. forces and military installations must be withdrawn from Taiwan. The Chinese Government firmly opposes any activities which aim at the creation of "one China, one Taiwan," "one China, two governments," "two Chinas," and "independent Taiwan" or advocate that "the status of Taiwan remains to be determined."

The U.S. side declared: The United States acknowledges that all Chinese on either side of the Taiwan Strait maintain there is but one China and that Taiwan is a part of China. The United States Government does not challenge that position. It reaffirms its interest in a peaceful settlement of the Taiwan question by the Chinese themselves. With this prospect in mind, it affirms the ultimate objective of the withdrawal of all U.S. forces and military installations from Taiwan. In the meantime, it will progressively reduce its forces and military installations on Taiwan as the tension in the area diminishes.

The two sides agreed that it is desirable to broaden the understanding between the two peoples. To this end, they discussed specific areas in such fields as science, technology, culture, sports and journalism, in which people-to-people contacts and exchanges would be mutually beneficial. Each side undertakes to facilitate the further development of such contacts and exchanges.

Both sides view bilateral trade as another area from which mutual benefit can be derived, and agreed that economic relations based on equality and mutual benefit are in the interest of the peoples of the two countries. They agree to facilitate the progressive development of trade between their two countries.

The two sides agreed that they will stay in contact through various channels, including the sending of a senior U.S. representative to Peking from time to time for concrete consultations to further the normalization of relations between the two countries and continue to exchange views on issues of common interest.

The two sides expressed the hope that the gains achieved during this visit would open up new prospects for the relations between the two countries. They believe that the normalization of relations between the two countries is not only in the interest of the Chinese and American peoples but also contributes to the relaxation of tension in Asia and the world.

President Nixon, Mrs. Nixon and the American party expressed their appreciation for the gracious hospitality shown them by the Government and people of the People's Republic of China.

(Peking Summit continued from p. 5)

A day earlier Sen. Edward M. Kennedy (D Mass.) had introduced in the U.S. Senate a resolution calling for "prompt establishment of full diplomatic relations" with China. He said the U.S. should end its diplomatic recognition of the Nationalist government on Taiwan and announce a unilateral guarantee for Taiwan's security.

Envoys Appointed. On March 15, 1973, President Nixon announced at a news conference that he had selected Ambassador David K. E. Bruce to head the U.S. liaison office in Peking. Bruce, 75, was called from retirement after exercising diplomatic functions under four Presidents. Nixon said he chose Bruce "because I thought it was very important to appoint a man of great stature to this position." The President said the liaison office would be opened about May 1, 1973, and would be staffed by 20 persons. China experts Alfred Jenkins of the State Department and John H. Holdridge of the National Security Council were assigned to that staff.

Bruce arrived in Peking May 15 officially opening the U.S. liaison office. On May 29, 1973, the chief of the Chinese liaison mission, Huang Chen arrived in Washington to resume official contact with the United States after what he called a "20 year detour."

A NEW CHINA POLICY: DOCUMENTS FROM THE PAST

President Nixon's efforts to normalize U.S. relations with mainland China constitute a remarkable reversal in American foreign policy.

The President has overturned a policy—considered axiomatic by four preceding administrations—whereby the proper posture for Washington to assume toward Peking was one of military containment and diplomatic isolation. And Mr. Nixon's journey to China in February 1972 was the first state visit in U.S. history to any country with which Washington had no diplomatic relations.

The President's overtures to Communist China hopefully will bring an end to a 25-year period of Chinese-American hostility, a timespan which has included two American wars on the Asian mainland (Korea and Vietnam) and two other occasions when Washington and Peking came to the brink of war (the Formosa* strait crises of 1955 and 1958).

Nixon's attempt to break with the past has been welcomed in Peking. He has been described by Premier Chou En-lai as a man of "courage."

Bibliographic Breakthrough

These dramatic moves on the diplomatic front have been matched in recent years by some equally striking developments in the documentation of U.S.-Chinese diplomatic history. The State Department in 1967 and 1969 published two volumes of previously classified documents on U.S. contacts with the Chinese Communist leaders in 1944 and 1945.**

The documents provide a prophetic backdrop to the Nixon administration's decision to normalize relations with Peking. They disclose that the Roosevelt and Truman administrations rebuffed efforts by Mao Tse-tung and Chou En-lai to establish friendly relations with Washington in the postwar world.

Dixie Mission. The documents cover the activities of an 18-man U.S. military and diplomatic mission, code-named "Dixie," which flew from Chiang Kai-shek's wartime capital in Chungking to the Communist Chinese headquarters in Yenan in the summer of 1944. Invited to Yenan by the Communists, the Americans looked upon the trip as an opportunity to assess the value of the Communist guerrillas as military allies and as recipients of U.S. aid in the war against the Japanese.

Chief political officer on the mission was John Stewart Service, a 36-year-old diplomat born in China of missionary parents and fluent in Chinese. In his talks with the Communist leaders—as well as from other documents appearing in the two volumes—three Communist objectives emerged: establishment of a U.S. consulate in Yenan, a personal visit by Chairman Mao and Chou to Washington for exploratory talks with President Roosevelt and long-term U.S.-Chinese economic cooperation.

Mao, in his March 13, 1945, talk with Service, said: "America and China complement each other economically; they will not compete....America is not only the most suitable country to assist this economic development of China; she is the only country fully able to participate."

Service recommended that Washington avoid taking sides in the impending civil war and remain flexible to accept the reality of Communist power. The Dixie Mission concluded that the Communists were a more effective force against the Japanese than the Nationalists.

These views were rejected by U.S. Ambassador to China, Maj. Gen. Patrick J. Hurley, who supported Chiang's veto of U.S. aid to the Communists. Hurley resigned in November 1945 and testified before the Senate Foreign Relations Committee that Service and other U.S. diplomats in China were harming American interests.

Leaning to One Side. The immediate goal of the Communists' appeal for U.S. aid, reported Service, was to weaken U.S. support for Chiang. A second motive was their desire to avoid too heavy a dependence on the Soviet Union.

"Already in 1945 the Chinese Communists leadership anticipated that potential conflicts with Stalin argued for striking a balance with Washington," China analyst Allen S. Whiting told the Senate Foreign Relations Committee in June 1971. According to Whiting, in 1946 Chou En-lai gave U.S. envoy George C. Marshall, who had replaced Hurley, a terse analysis of the Communists' attitude toward Washington and Moscow: "Of course we will lean to one side. But how far we lean depends on you."†

Who 'Lost' China?

Marshall's efforts to mediate differences between the Communists and Nationalists failed in 1946. In the ensuing civil war, the Nationalists were routed and fled to Formosa in 1949.

In the summer of 1949, the Truman administration responded to the mounting Republican charge that the Democrats had been responsible for the "loss" of China. A 1,054-page State Department White Paper on U.S.-China relations published in August placed responsibility for Chiang's defeat on the ineptitude of the Nationalists. Secretary of State Dean Acheson declared that "the only alternative open to the United States was full-scale intervention in behalf of a government which had lost the confidence of its own troops and its own people." Neither Acheson nor the voluminous documentation of the White Paper mentioned the Dixie Mission.

"Formosa" is the name given to the island by Portuguese explorers. Taiwan is the Chinese name.

**Foreign Relations of the United States (1944), Vol. VI and (1945), Vol. VII, Washington, D.C. 1967 and 1969.*

†*Quoted to Whiting by John F. Melby, a member of Marshall's staff.*

In January 1950, President Truman announced that the administration would not give the Nationalists military support to defend Formosa. But the outbreak of the Korean war in June brought an abrupt end to Washington's hands-off policy on Formosa. Peking's entry into the war in November cemented U.S. support for Chiang. Washington and Taipei signed a defense treaty in 1954, and in 1955 Congress gave the President authority to use U.S. forces to defend Formosa.

Scapegoats. Throughout the 1950s, the Republicans repeatedly charged that the Democrats had lost China. Running for Vice President in 1952, Richard Nixon declared: "China wouldn't have gone Communist—if the Truman administration had had backbone."

The principal victims of the charge that China had been lost were the foreign service officers who had recommended in the 1940s that Washington keep a dialogue open with the Chinese Communists.

Service, ousted as a security risk from the State Department in 1951 under the pressure of Senator Joseph R. McCarthy (R Wis.), was vindicated in 1957 by the U.S. Supreme Court in an 8-0 decision. He returned to the State Department and served until retiring in 1962.

Less fortunate was John Paton Davies, who had served in China in 1943-1944. In one of his cables in November 1944, he had written: "We must make a determined effort to capture politically the Chinese Communists rather than allow them to go by default wholly to the Russians." This message was presented in 1951 before the Senate Internal Security Subcommittee as evidence of Davies' alleged communist sympathies.

Dismissed from the State Department in 1954, Davies spent the next ten years as a furniture manufacturer in Peru. He returned to Washington in 1964 to initiate a legal effort to clear his name. The State Department cleared him in January 1969.

Sino-Soviet Bloc

The Democratic and Republican participants in the debate over the loss of China disagreed sharply on one point—the quantum of U.S. aid Chiang Kai-shek should have received in the 1940s. But they agreed on a more fundamental issue: neither party recommended improved relations with Peking.

'More American than Oriental'

"In meeting and dealing with these men, one is struck by their being straightforward and frank. There is no 'beating around the bush.' If they do not know something, they say so. If they promise something, you feel sure that it can and will be done....It is not surprising that they have favorably impressed most or all of the Americans who have met them during the last seven years: their manners, habits of thought and direct handling of problems seem more American than oriental."

John Stewart Service on the Chinese Communist leaders, Yenan, September, 1944.

Critics of this policy, such as Davies, contended that Washington's unwillingness to deal with the Chinese Communists forced them into the hands of the Soviets. In more recent years, analysts have pointed to the Communists' reaction to the publication of the White Paper in August 1949.

In issuing the document, Acheson accused the Communists of "having foresworn their Chinese heritage by becoming instruments of Soviet imperialism." At the time he spoke, Peking and Moscow were not yet allies; the Soviets were still signatories to a 1945 defense treaty with Chiang.

Acheson's remark prompted the sharpest public attack on U.S. policy Mao Tse-tung had ever made. In October, Moscow broke diplomatic relations with the Nationalists and recognized Peking. In February 1950, Mao went to Moscow to sign a 30-year treaty of mutual assistance. Chou En-lai said the treaty "welded together the two countries into a force of 700 million people which it is impossible to defeat."

Security and Classification

The surfacing of Sino-Soviet tensions in the 1960s led American policymakers ultimately to re-examine the assumptions of their China policy. It also provided a favorable climate for publication of the story of American relations with the Chinese Communists during World War II.

The documents concerning U.S. contacts with the Chinese Communist leaders in 1944-45 are not the only classified materials on U.S. diplomacy to have emerged in the past several years. In 1969-70, the persistent efforts of the Senate Foreign Relations Committee obliged the executive branch to introduce into the public record a wealth of information concerning U.S. military commitments abroad. It was in this manner that the American public received in April 1970 the first official confirmation that U.S. forces had been engaged since 1961 in a clandestine war in Laos.

Highly critical of the executive branch's delays in declassifying information on U.S. commitments abroad, Senators J. W. Fulbright (D Ark.) and Stuart Symington (D Mo.) have repeatedly claimed that national security was not at stake in the government's decision to delay release of material. Symington's subcommittee charged in 1970 that the classified information was well known to foreign governments and suggested that the principal reason for delaying declassification had been to "avoid embarrassing either...past administrations, present government officials or...other governments."

Questions of National Security. The State Department's decisions in 1967 and 1969 to publish the record of the Dixie Mission have provided diplomatic historians with a welcome addition of primary source material. Less charitable critics of the government's information policy, however, are likely to raise some questions—would U.S. national security have been endangered by earlier publication in the 1950s—or for that matter, in the 1949 White Paper? And, more fundamentally, was national security ever a consideration in delaying release of the documents for over two decades?

Mr. Nixon has not set out to "regain" the China that was "lost" in the 1940s. Rather, he is seeking to reopen a dialogue with the China with which American diplomats were talking in 1944-45.

RECONCILIATION WITH CHINA: THE HISTORICAL PRECEDENTS

No recent news has been more evocative of the past—and more prescient of the future—than the accounts of the American ping pong team's tour (April 10-17, 1971) of Mainland China. For this unexpected visit, undertaken at Peking's invitation, cracked the barrier of hostility that has existed since 1949 between that country and the United States.

When ping pong diplomacy was followed by President Nixon's announcement July 15 that he would visit the People's Republic of China before May 1972, it was clear that a breakthrough had occurred portending a likely end to the 21 years of American non-recognition of Mao Tse-tung's Communist government.

Mr. Nixon's visit obviously could signal a new configuration of world global relationships. For many it raised hopes for a speedier end to the war in Vietnam and a lowering of tension that threatened new wars; however, fear and distrust, based on two decades of hostility, persisted.

At first it seemed that the two decades of icy hostility had begun to melt down into a mutual willingness to let bygones be bygones. China's leaders spoke of renewing old friendships with Americans. Memories of the past of what had been called America's long love affair with China began to flood the American consciousness.

Sober second thoughts made it clear that the spring thaw had barely begun and that new freezes might lie ahead. On both sides hard truths were reasserted about issues that bar reconciliation. One requiring immediate consideration was the future status of the other China—the Nationalist government of Chiang Kai-shek, known as the Republic of China, which governs only Taiwan and a few neighboring islands but claims all of China as its rightful domain. *(U.S. relations with Taiwan, p. 19)*

Since 1949 the only official contacts between the United States and China had been the "Warsaw talks." The talks between ambassadors of the two countries, 136 in all, began in Geneva in 1955 but had been held in Poland since 1958. They were secret by mutual consent. The talks were barely resumed early in 1970 after a two-year hiatus when China broke them off again—this time in protest of the U.S. invasion of Cambodia. No talks were scheduled after the 1970 break-off, although liaison officers of the two embassies in Warsaw continued to maintain contact.

'Ping Pong Diplomacy'

"The ping heard round the world," as *Time* magazine put it, was first sounded on April 6, during the international championship table tennis competition in Nagoya, Japan, when the team from China invited members of the American team to visit the mainland before returning to the United States. No group of Americans had been allowed into China since the Communists took control in 1949. "We have...extended the invitation for the sake of promoting friendship between the peoples of China and the United States," the spokesman for the Chinese team, Sung Chung, said.

The invitation was accepted and on April 10, the 15 Americans—nine players, four officials, and two wives—walked across a bridge from Hong Kong into Communist territory, where they were greeted by a delegation of smiling Chinese officials who escorted them to a train that took them to Canton. During the week of their visit, the Americans were kept on a full schedule of sightseeing, playing and entertainment.

They visited Peking, Shanghai, the Great Wall, a university and a rural commune. They participated in an exhibition Ping Pong match before a cheering audience of 18,000, attended a ballet staged by the wife of Party Chairman Mao Tse-tung, and were guests at a party April 14 at which Premier Chou En-lai engaged the visitors at length in good-humored chitchat. Chou impressed the visitors as a surprisingly genial host. In his formal greetings to them, he said: "You have opened a new page in the relations of the Chinese and American people. I am confident that this beginning again of our friendship will certainly meet with the majority support of our two people."

Equally significant with the invitation of the players, Peking permitted five American newsmen to enter China to report the trip. Chou said at the April 14 party that more American journalists would be granted visas to come to China, although "they cannot all come at one time." Since then other journalists were allowed to enter, and it was reported that American applications for visas were being received cordially at the newly opened Chinese embassy at Ottawa, Canada. Tillman Durdin, a veteran *New York Times* reporter in the Far East who was allowed a 30-day visit, reported on his return to Hong Kong in mid-May that China's leaders said they favored a regular flow of visitors from the United States. He said that a "trickle" had already begun. Capping these improved relations with American journalists was the August 5 interview Chinese Premier Chou En-lai accorded James Reston, vice president and columnist for the Times, during his six-week visit to China.

Trade and Travel Barriers

Peking's "ping pong diplomacy" was recognized as a serious and planned step in the formulation of a new foreign policy rather than merely an impromptu gesture of good sportsmanship. A State Department spokesman, Charles W. Bray III, described Peking's invitation to the team as an "encouraging development...clearly consistent with the hopes expressed by the President and Secretary of State that there could be greater contact between the American and Chinese peoples." There were indications that the State Department had encouraged Graham

B. Steenhoven, president of the U.S. Table Tennis Association, to reciprocate with an invitation to the Chinese players. Steenhoven announced on April 20, after his return to his home in Detroit, that he had extended such an invitation and that it had been accepted. White House Press Secretary Ronald L. Ziegler said that the U.S. government would welcome a visit by a Chinese team.

On the day that Chou talked with the American players, April 14, the White House announced that a 20-year embargo on trade with China would be relaxed. The announcement stated:

• Visas for visitors from the People's Republic of China would be expedited.

• U.S. currency controls (imposed in 1950) would be relaxed so that China could use dollars to pay for exports.

• American oil companies would be allowed to provide fuel to ships or planes going to or from China ports (except on Chinese-owned or chartered craft going to or from North Viet Nam, North Korea, or Cuba).

• U.S. vessels would be permitted to carry Chinese cargo between non-Chinese ports; U.S.-owned foreign flag carriers would be allowed to call at Chinese ports.

There followed on June 10 a further relaxation of trade restrictions when the White House announced a long list of goods that American businessmen could export to China. The items included farm, fish and forestry products; tobacco; many kinds of fertilizers and chemicals; coal; rubber and textiles; some metals; agricultural, industrial and office equipment; household appliances; some electrical appliances; automobiles; consumer goods; roadbuilding and construction equipment, and some relatively unsophisticated computers. The inclusion of construction equipment was regarded as significant because it was known that the Defense Department wanted to keep it off the list. The department's opposition to the sale of locomotives was also known, and they did not appear on the list.

Few Public Protests

Perhaps the most significant aspect of the thaw in relations was the weakness of the outcry against it. In view of the political blood that had been spilled in the United States in years past over the question of who was responsible for China's "going Communist," the equanimity with which most Americans accepted the prospect of a reconciliation was a sure sign that the times—and public opinion—had changed. Senate Minority Leader Hugh Scott (R Pa.) observed that less than a decade ago such overtures as the administration had made toward China would have sent "shock waves" over Congress.

Senate Majority Leader Mike Mansfield (D Mont.) told the Senate that "the change is long overdue." Sen. Edward W. Brooke (R Mass.) professed to see the "first steps toward removing the fears and prejudices which have...distorted our visions of each other." The Assistant Senate Majority Leader, Robert C. Byrd (D W. Va.), said the United States "must accept" the fact that a Communist government rules all of mainland China. Sen. Robert Dole (R Kan.), chairman of the Republican National Committee, said that ping pong diplomacy could hasten the ending of the war and help re-elect Nixon.

There were some dissents from expected sources, but with little effect on the course of events. Leading figures in the so-called China Lobby that for years has supported Nationalist China's claims expressed displeasure. Former Rep. Walter Judd (R Minn.), chairman of the Committee of One Million Against the Admission of Communist China to the United Nations, charged on April 12 that "powerful forces" were bringing pressure "in the hope of forcing President Nixon to accept Mao on Mao's terms." Anna Chennault warned against the hazards of trade dealings with a poor and Communist China. Judd, a former medical missionary in China, had long been identified with a hard-line anti-Communist policy in the Far East. Mrs. Chennault is the Chinese-American widow of Maj. Gen. Claire L. Chennault, who headed the U.S. Air Force in China during World War II. Though Mrs. Chennault holds no official position, she is influential in Washington. *(China lobbies, p. 38)*

Meanwhile, the new possibility of travel to China stirred interest among businessmen, scholars and inveterate tourists. As applications for visas from Americans began to rise, major U.S. airlines sought authority to fly to leading Chinese cities. The president of Trans World Airlines, Forwood C. Wiser, said on May 8 in Hong Kong that TWA would operate charter flights to China if the Peking government granted permission. United Air Lines also has applied for flight authority. Najeeb E. Halaby, president of Pan American World Airways, told shareholders in Miami on May 4 "we see a real possibility of resuming service" on the China route Pan Am served in 1947-49. He said Pan Am had been "quietly" seeking an approval from Peking for three years.

The president of Xerox Corporation, C. Peter Mc-Colough, told stockholders on May 20 that a London subsidiary had missions in Peking exploring market possibilities. In Washington, a Committee on Scholarly Communication with the People's Republic of China, an adjunct of the National Academy of Sciences, was trying to communicate with a counterpart science academy in Peking in order to arrange for the exchange of persons, journals and invitations to international meetings. Among members of the committee were leading China specialists A. Doak Barnett of the Brookings Institution, Jerome A. Cohen of Harvard and Alexander Eckstein of the University of Michigan. The desire of Americans to go to China was nothing new. There are still many Americans who remember it well as it was in the old days and are curious to see what 22 years under communism have done.

Historical Ties

Americans have long had strong sentimental ties with China. They were forged by generations of American traders, missionaries, businessmen and teachers, many of whom lived for years in China and raised their families there. The influence of these ties on U.S. foreign policy in Asia has been pervasive. It helped account for the great swell of sympathy for the Chinese during the Japanese invasion in the 1930s and it sharpened the bitterness when China went Communist.

Over the years the American feeling about China has been a composite of good and bad. Former Secretary of State Dean Acheson called it a "love-hate complex," but it had many shades in between. Affection for the Chinese was genuine, but it did not necessarily include an appreciation of Chinese sensibilities. American altruism and philanthropy were mixed with avarice and bigotry, and admiration was tinged with condescension. Doubtless the Chinese had similarly ambivalent feelings about Americans, who came to them as friends and benefactors, but also as exploiters. So today the building of a new relationship must deal with both a tradition of friendship and a large residue of distrust and ill will.

In a lecture in March 1968, Senator Mansfield described the two American images of China: One is "the image of the China of wisdom, intelligence, industry, piety, stoicism, and strength,...of Marco Polo, Pearl Buck, Charlie Chan and heroic resistance to the Japanese during World War II"; the other is "the image of the China of cruelty, barbarism, violence, and faceless hordes...the China of drum-head trials, summary executions, Fu Manchu, and the Boxer Rebellion." Felix Greene, another long-time China watcher, wrote in *A Curtain of Ignorance:* "From our earliest contacts, China has exerted a peculiar fascination for Americans, a fascination compounded both of highest admiration and the deepest suspicion."

America's first contact with China was in search of trade. Even before the first Yankee clipper set sail under the American flag for Canton in 1784, the China trade had figured in the life of the American colonies. The tea of the Boston tea party had come from China. In the early years of the nation, trade with China was highly profitable. "There was a kind of China craze in those years. Wealthy matrons bought Chinese porcelain from returning skippers.... Today, in the elegant reception rooms of the Department of State (in Washington) there are proud displays of Chinese export porcelain. These are regarded as pieces of Americana." [1]

China had traded with the West since ancient times, but the traders had always been received as inferior suppliants or vassals, subject to the pleasure of the emperor, and their contacts with the Chinese were narrowly confined to designated representatives of the ruler. Trade in goods was mostly one-way. Europe craved the silks and spices of the East but China had little use for Europe's goods and demanded pay—tribute—in good or silver.

This situation changed in the 19th century when the imperialist nations of Europe, pressing for trade concessions, broke down China's carefully guarded barriers against foreign penetration. In so doing, they irreparably damaged the power and prestige of the Manchu dynasty. The British took the lead, the others followed. The change began with the Opium War of 1839-42, which was essentially a show of British naval power to force the dynasty to open up the country to foreign exploitation and to grant Britain trade concessions.

These concessions were extended after another unequal contest between China and the combined British and French forces in 1856-60. Coastal and river cities became "treaty ports available to foreign ships. British settlements—enclaves subject only to English law—were established. The entire country was opened to travel, trade, missionary work, investment and settlement. Other nations—Belgium, France, Germany, Japan, Russia, the United States—gained similar privileges in the course of the century.

"Throughout the process of the opening of China, the United States followed through portals cut by the British, avoiding the aggression and inheriting the advantages." [2] U.S. "extra-territorial rights," equal to those granted other foreign nations, were first established in a U.S.-China treaty signed in 1844. The United States could reap the rewards of an open China with an easy conscience for it had taken no military action to gain them nor did it seek to win outright possession of Chinese territory for colonial purposes. American power was nevertheless there to protect commercial interests.

These interests lay in the background of decisions that led to the Spanish-American War and the acquisition of the Philippines. "American businessmen feared that European aggression against China would rob them of their investment there," Marvin Kalb and Elie Abel said in tracing the evolution of U.S. policy in Asia. "They looked upon the Philippines as a fine fallback position." Albert Beveridge, a Republican senator from Ohio at that time, summed up the prevailing view. "Just beyond the Philippines," he said, "are China's illimitable markets. We will not retreat from either."

By this time the United States had come to regard itself as protector of China against the threat of partition by the colonizing nations. China, for its part, was eager to modernize in the western manner. A bond of friendship grew up between the American and Chinese peoples." "It was, a strangely symbiotic relationship. Its strength lay in the promise each people held out for the other. Its mortal weakness (was) that this friendship concealed ulterior motives on one side and repressed deeply felt humiliations and grievances on the other," said author Felix Greene.

Missionary Influence

The opening of China came at a time when the proselytizing zeal of American churches was at a high level. China became an irresistible magnet for missionary work. "China's vastness excited the missionary impulse; it appeared as the land of the future whose masses, when converted, offered promise of Christian and even English-speaking dominion over the world." The first American missionary arrived in China as early as 1811 but the main growth came later in the century. By 1925, there were 8,000 missionaries in China, most of them American. Their influence far outweighed their number and the number of their conversions. By the eve of World War II there were no more than 2.25 million Christians in China (1.5 million Roman Catholic and 750,000 Protestant). But the missionaries and their converts held favored positions in the western-dominated parts of China and they provided major channels, through their schools, hospitals and other establishments, for the promulgation of western ideas.

Of particular importance was the influence of the missionaries on the minds of Americans back home and indirectly on foreign policy. "Hardly a town in our land was without its society to collect funds and clothing for Chinese missions...and to hear the missionaries' inspiring reports," Dean Acheson wrote. "Thus was nourished the live portion of the love-hate complex that was to infuse so much emotion into our later China policy." [3] The author of

---

1 Marvin Kalb and Elie Abel, *Roots of Involvement: The United States in Asia 1784-1971* (1971), p. 22.

2 Barbara W. Tuchman, *Stilwell and the American Experience in China 1911-45* (1971), p. 29.

3 Acheson, Dean, *Present at the Creation* (1969), p. 8.

another account said: "It would be hard to over-emphasize the extent of the influence of the missionaries in shaping and directing the Far Eastern policies of the United States.... Beginning with President McKinley, they received...special recognition from the executive branch....For many years missionaries, businessmen and government officials collaborated in the movement to implant American social and economic institutions in China; and of the three the missionaries were by far the most powerful."[4]

Their view of China became the American view. They sympathized with the privations of the people in an industrially backward, strife-torn country and took the view that America was obligated to help them. "Congregations all over the United States listened to the returned missonary...tell of the deserving qualities of the Chinese people and of the great reservoir of future Christians. The public impression was that America had saved China's integrity by the doctrine of the Open Door—a policy which called for equality of commercial rights in China among foreign interests. Missionary propaganda helped to create the image of China as protege, an image which carried an accompanying sense of obligation toward the object of one's own beneficence."[5] Undetected by most Americans for many years was the undercurrent of resentment and sense of humiliation in China over its subservience to the foreign intruder.

American friends of China sincerely believed they could help China by leading it to adopt American ways. The revolution of 1911 that wiped out the Manchu dynasty and established a nominally republican government was accepted as a sign that China was on the way to becoming another western-style democracy, potentially strong and, of course, a true friend of the United States. This image of China contributed greatly to the shaping of America's policy on Asia as World War II drew to its close. Memoirists of Franklin D. Roosevelt's presidency (1933-45) recalled that his sympathy for China was profound, that he was fond of recounting anecdotes of his trader-ancestors in their dealings with the Chinese, that his mother had spent considerable time as a girl in China, and that his home contained many mementos of the family's China ties.

"Out of this background," Dean Acheson wrote, "came a notion of President Roosevelt's which seemed quixotic to Churchill and Stalin: that China, with our help and under our tutelage, would rise from its ashes to the position of a great power and play a benificent role after the war in bringing stability to Asia." At the Yalta Conference in February 1945, Roosevelt bargained for China's future. Through his efforts, (Nationalist) China became one of the five permanent members in the United Nations Security Council when such recognition could not be justified in terms of any objective standards of power.

But China was divided. The forces of Chiang and Mao fought to a showdown, despite American efforts to reconcile them in the interest of a unified China. American support had long been committed to Chiang, a Christian convert. He and his Wellesley-educated wife were familiar figures and had come to symbolize the China that Americans knew and liked best.

Mao's triumph set the stage for one of the most vindictive periods in American political history. Its theme was: "Who lost China to the Communists?" Americans returning from China, who had witnessed the victory of Mao's People's Liberation Army, brought home stores of severe disillusionment. "The great shock...was that their beloved Chinese liberals, the Americanized university professors and their students, went over to the revolution...."[6]

McCarthy Era

Disillusionment over China helped to split the bipartisan support of foreign policy that had prevailed during the war. It gave the Republican Party an effective battle cry: the charge that the Democrats were "soft on Communism." The outbreak of war in Korea in June 1950 and the intervention of 200,000 Chinese "volunteers" in that war five months later magnified the import of the charge. President Truman, Secretary of State Dean Acheson, and Gen. George C. Marshall were among those charged with having given away America's Chinese birthright.

During the McCarthy era the "soft on communism" attack often centered on the "loss" of China. For five years, 1950-54, Sen. Joseph McCarthy (R Wis.) carried on a highly effective vendetta against the State Department and other federal agencies that he said were riddled with Communists and their dupes. The "old China hands"—Foreign Service men and scholars with long experience in China—were major targets. The State Department was virtually drained of its China experts; some were drummed out of government service.

James C. Thomson Jr., an East Asian specialist in the State Department from 1961 to 1966, believes that American involvement in Viet Nam is a legacy of the McCarthy era. The department's Bureau of Far Eastern Affairs was "purged of its best China expertise, and of farsighted, dispassionate men, as a result of McCarthyism." Those who remained, Thomson feels were committed to the containment and isolation of China. "Career officers in the department, and especially those in the field (in Viet Nam), had not forgotten the fate of their World War II colleagues who wrote in frankness from China and were later pilloried by Senate committees for critical comments on the Chinese Nationalists."[7]

"We interpreted the advent to power in China of Mao Tse-tung's Communist regime...as the conquest of China by Moscow," Louis J. Halle wrote in *The New York Times* magazine on June 6, 1971. "There were those among us who knew the historical, geographical and strategic circumstances that, in the long run, made anything but conflict between Mao's China and Moscow virtually inconceivable, and who knew as well the long record of conflict between Mao and Moscow. They were, however, intimidated into silence, or if they tried to speak out their careers and reputations were ruined by accusations of treason."

The policy toward mainland Chinas, as cast in Cold War terms, remained fixed during the Eisenhower years

---

4 Richard Van Alstyne, *The Listener* (1961), quoted by Greene, *op. cit.*, p. 4
5 Tuchman, *op. cit.*, p. 32.

6 Tom Engelhardt, "Long Day's Journey: American Observers in China, 1948-50," in *China and Ourselves* (1965), edited by Bruce Douglas and Ross Terrill), p. 105.
7 James C. Thomson Jr., "How Could Viet Nam Happen? *Atlantic Monthly*, April 1968, pp. 47, 53.

(1953-60). Early in 1955 the United States and China stood on the verge of a military showdown over the tiny islands of Quemoy and Matsu lying in the Taiwan Strait a few miles off the China mainland. At Eisenhower's request, Congress authorized the use of American forces to defend the islands which, occupied by Chiang Kai-shek's forces, had come under Communist artillery attacks from the mainland. As it turned out, American forces were not sent to the islands; by April of that year Chou En-lai said "the Chinese people do not want to have war with the U.S.A." and expressed a willingness to negotiate the issue.

In the midst of the Quemoy-Matsu crisis, the Senate ratified a mutual defense treaty with Chiang's government in which the United States pledged to defend Taiwan, the offshore islands and "such other territories as may be determined by mutual agreement" against attack from China. The United States regarded China as the aggressor trying to impose international Communism on Aisa. As recounted by Sen. Mansfield: "It was assumed that if the endorsement of the free nations were withheld, this regime...would wither and eventually collapse. On this basis, recognition was not extended to Peking. The official view was that the National Government...(on Taiwan) continued to speak for all of China."

Even as a more realistic view of the situation developed, few politicians dared challenge the established position. President Kennedy, according to Arthur Schlesinger Jr., in *A Thousand Days* (1965), considered the state of our relations with Communist China as "irrational" but thought "the international gains (if any) of admission (to the United Nations) would be far outweighed by the uproar it would cause at home." Eisenhower had warned Kennedy privately, Schlesinger added, that he would consider it necessary to return to public life if there was a threat of China's admission to the United Nations. Kennedy, with his slim majority, "felt that he could not take on the China problem"—not during his first term at least.

Johnson Policy

The atmosphere began to change during the Johnson years. The Senate Foreign Relations Committee held hearings in March 1966 to which a number of scholars were called to participate in a forum on "China and American attitudes toward China." The problem, as presented by A. Doak Barnett, then of Columbia University, was "how to reestablish a reasonable basis for contact and discourse between the United States and mainland China." In that year the United States eased restrictions on the travel of scholars to Communist countries, and President Johnson said in a televised speech that eventual reconciliation with China was necessary. He said the United States would seek to reduce tensions between the two countries. As a presidential candidate in 1960, Nixon strongly opposed admitting China to the United Nations. As a candidate in 1968, he said: "We simply cannot afford to leave China forever outside the family of nations." As President, he took a series of steps to invite more contact. *(Details p. 16)*

There is evidence to suggest that China began to reassess its position of hostility toward the United States near the end of the past decade. The reassessment came at a time when the Sino-Soviet dispute over Communist ideology had led to a bitter rivalry between Mos-

cow and Peking which flared, in March 1969, into a series of armed skirmishes along the Manchurian-Siberian border. And it came after the turbulent Cultural Revolution of 1966-67 had subsided. The upheavals wrought by five or six million Chinese students—the "Red Guards"—were aimed at purifying life in China. An unwanted side effect was to make Peking's relations with other countries extremely abrasive. According to one count, by Oct. 1, 1966, the 17th anniversary of the People's Republic, China had picked quarrels with no fewer than 32 countries. Only five foreign governments sent delegations to the Oct. 1 observances in 1967. President Johnson said in his State of the Union message to Congress, Jan. 17, 1968: "The radical extremism of their government has isolated the Chinese people beyond their borders."

However, a change may already have been in the making. Robert S. Elegant, who watches China from Hong Kong, had written the previous autumn: "Amid the turmoil of the last days of the Great Proletarian Cultural Revolution, there are signs that a profound change in the Chinese approach to the outside world is now in train. The Chinese pragmatists are being forced toward recognition that China is not so powerful—morally or materially— that she can impose her own order upon mankind." [8] The outer world did not receive confirmation of change—or even that a response would be elicited from Nixon's conciliatory gestures—until the American table tennis team received its invitation. "That a response from Peking finally came was not a surprise to President Nixon," Senate Assistant Minority Leader Robert P. Griffin (R Mich.) told the Economic Club of Detroit on May 17, 1971. "But I can tell you that no one was more surprised than he when Ping Pong became the vehicle for delivery."

Taiwan Question

The chief obstacle to normal relations between the United States and the People's Republic of China is the existence of the other China—the Republic of China with its capital in Taipei on Taiwan. The United States has never wavered in its support for the latter's claim to represent China in the United Nations and for its hold on China's permanent seat in the U.N. Security Council. So far the United States has succeeded in defeating perennial efforts to supplant Taipei delegates with Peking delegates in the United Nations. But support for the American position has been shrinking. In 1970, for the first time, a majority voted in favor of the switch, but the vote was short of the two-thirds majority required for action on an "important question. The vote on a resolution to unseat the Taipei delegation and replace it with one from Peking, taken on Nov. 20, 1970, was 51 for, 49 against, with 25 abstentions, the resolution failing by 16 votes. The vote to declare the matter an "important question" requiring a two-thirds majority was 66-52 with seven abstentions. In 1965 the vote to admit Peking was 47-47. The issue came up again when the General Assembly convened on Sept. 15, 1971. *(Details p. 24-25)*

China Trade

Segments of American business have shown keen interest in the potentiality of a new market of about 760 million consumers, few of whom possess washing ma-

---

8 Robert S. Elegant, "China's Next Phase," *Foreign Affairs*, October 1967, p. 140.

chines, electric refrigerators, automobiles, or other American necessities of life. But China is a poor country, consumer buying power is barely at subsistence and the economy is tightly controlled. So a suddenly booming export market for American consumer goods can hardly be expected. But China has real needs for other goods that the United States could supply. *(Far East trade p. 59)*

In a study prepared for the National Committee on U.S.-China Relations, Robert F. Dernberger, a University of Michigan economics professor, projected that under favorable conditions for growth and under the same terms that apply to U.S.-Soviet trade, China's purchases of American goods might reach $900 million by 1980, an amount equal to about 2 per cent of the current level of American exports. China's foreign trade, estimated at $4.3-billion a year and about equally divided between imports and exports, is small for a country of its size. It contrasts with America's 1970 total of $42.7-billion in exports and $39.9-billion in imports.

One expert on trading with China, Stanley Lubman of the University of California, has concluded that U.S.-China trade "would symbolize the intent of the two nations to improve their relations...." Lubman, however, in testimony before the Senate Foreign Relations Committee June 29, 1971, stressed some of the problems that trade with China might present for U.S. businessmen. Lubman said that most Western businessmen are permitted entry to China only for the semi-annual Canton Trade Fairs at which the Chinese conclude most of their foreign trade transactions. The Westerners deal with representatives of trading corporations, not with the ultimate end-users of Western imports. The result is that Westerners have found it almost impossible to introduce new products at the trade fairs. The Chinese negotiators come to Canton with a "shopping list," from which departures are extremely difficult. Another difficulty is that the Chinese are "reluctant to give a Western seller the full information he may need to assure himself that his product will perform up to specifications. The Chinese are...concerned to avoid disclosing 'economic intelligence.' Yet when particular operating conditions cause less than fully satisfactory performance of a Western product...the Chinese may press a claim for alleged defects."

Despite these difficulties in trading with China, Lubman stressed that "Sino-Western trade has flourished. Relationships of mutual trust and confidence have developed over the years...." *(Lubman's testimony p. 86)*

Under recent easing of trade restrictions, foreign-based subsidiaries of American companies have already sold to the People's Republic. General Motors dealers overseas, for example, recently sold China earth-moving equipment. China wants commercial aircraft, not necessarily new planes. They want plants to make fertilizers, chemicals and synthetics.... They lack spare parts (for communications and transport systems) that we could supply," Samuel Pisar, East-West trade expert, told an interviewer with the *Wall Street Journal.* "In return they have some mercury, some silver, furs, silks, tapestries and even supplies for Chinese restaurants."

If the United States is interested in tapping this market, it must compete with other developed nations— not only of the Communist bloc but America's friends and allies. Japan has now replaced the Soviet Union as China's main trading partner. Among the other leading China traders are West Germany, Britain, Australia, Canada and France. Canada, which established diplomatic relations with Peking in 1970, has sold vast quantities of wheat to China since early in the 1960s. Competition from rival traders may be less a limiting factor for America's trade with China than self-imposed restraints due to fear of building up a hostile power.

Efforts to expand the China trade may well lead to a major debate on the benefits versus the hazards. Proponents of more trade complain that the Pentagon tends to slap the "strategic" label on almost any kind of export goods destined for a country outside the Western orbit, and this can delay or prevent the granting of export licenses for shipping particular items. China may well look upon American decisions on trade as a key to American sincerity in wishing to reduce tensions between the two countries.

Old Fears About Peking

A new image of China is unfolding in the American mind, replacing the image of the outlaw nation—sullen, unreasonable, unpredictable and bent on revolutionary conquest. The new image is hardly ideal in the American scheme of things, but it does describe a nation possessing at least some of the sturdier virtues, certainly a nation with which the United States may be able to deal in the normal way.

The most important change of American viewpoint, expressed by leading Asia scholars and "China hands" in the government, concerns the menace China presents to world peace. In simplest terms, the United States no longer believes China presents an immediate threat of military conquest in the name of world revolution. As expressed by Assistant Secretary of State Marshall Green before the Senate Foreign Relations Committee, Oct. 6, 1970: China "is not today considered to pose a 'juggernaut' type of threat to its neighbors and has been prudent in facing United States power in the area."

Altered circumstances accounted for the "evolution in our perception of the intentions of the People's Republic of China," Green said. In the early 1950s, what appeared to be close collusion between Russia and China implied a threat to enlarge Communist spheres of control "by force of arms if necessary." Today, he added, it is apparent that "world power...is polycentric and becoming more so." The deep schism between China and Russia, the rise of a strong Japan and the declining appeal of China as a model for developing countries in the Far East alleviate earlier fears. Even the achievement of nuclear capability "will not necessarily make the Chinese more aggressive," Green said. "I believe they will continue to be deterred by overwhelming U.S. and Soviet power."

Some China-watchers believe that country will be too deeply concerned with internal matters for the foreseeable future to take on any outside military adventures. The recent news stories that have let the West glimpse the strange world of inland China tend to confirm the picture of a reasonably content, hard-working people with miles to go to catch up with the industrial West. They also depict a people ready to be friends despite two decades of propaganda portraying Americans as imperialist devils. A moratorium on the devil theme in international relations should be salutary for both sides.

DRAMATIC SHIFT ACHIEVED IN RELATIONS WITH PEKING

"Any American policy toward Asia must come urgently to grips with the reality of China. This does not mean...rushing to grant recognition to Peking, to admit it to the United Nations and to ply it with offers of trade.... It does mean recognizing the present and potential danger from Communist China, and taking measures designed to meet that danger...this means a policy of firm restraint, of no reward, of a creative counterpressure...I would not recognize Red China now and I would not agree to admitting it to the UN...."

Richard M. Nixon, campaign, 1968

"A significant change has taken place among the members of the United Nations on the issue of admission of mainland China. We are now analyzing that situation...."

President Nixon, June 1, 1971

"The United States...will support action at the (United Nations) General Assembly this fall calling for seating the People's Republic of China. At the same time the United States will oppose any action to expel the Republic of China or otherwise deprive it of representation in the United Nations."

Secretary of State William P. Rogers,
August 2, 1971

The Nixon Administration has been credited with bringing about the first stage of a momentous diplomatic revolution in United States' policy toward Communist China.

After two decades of hostility and nonrecognition of the People's Republic of China—the world's largest country with one-fourth of the earth's total population—the U.S. Government in mid-1971 announced a complete shift in policy:

● After 22 years of opposition, the United States would support the admission of Communist China to the United Nations.

● President Richard M. Nixon would personally go to China Feb. 21-28, 1972, becoming the first American President to visit the mainland and the first to deal face-to-face with the Chinese Communist government.

And, on Oct. 25 the People's Republic of China was admitted to the United Nations. The Republic of China (Taiwan) was expelled despite U.S. opposition and efforts at dual representation. *(United Nations action, p. 23)*

Although the shift in policy was a dramatic one, it was not sudden. The Administration's efforts seeking to expand contact with Mao Tse-tung's Communist government had been spread over two-and-a-half years beginning in early 1969 and could best be described as a series of slow and cautious moves toward rapprochement with Peking.

During that period the Nixon Administration had:

● Lifted a 21-year embargo on trade with China permitting free export of a wide variety of nonstrategic U.S. products and permitting commercial imports.

● Removed the $100 limit on purchases of Chinese goods which tourists were permitted to bring into the United States.

● Terminated all restrictions on the use of American passports for travel to China.

● Terminated in November 1969 the regular U.S. naval patrol in the Taiwan Strait.

● Announced the United States would reduce its military presence on the Asian mainland.

● Announced that it would remove all nuclear weapons which had been installed on Okinawa as a deterrent against Communist China.

● Suspended American air intelligence-gathering missions over mainland China.

The changes in U.S. policy toward Communist China reflected the view expressed by Mr. Nixon in his January 1969 inaugural address: the United States had passed the era of "confrontation" and was entering a period of "negotiation" with the Communist world.

And, two years later, in his second annual report on foreign policy, President Nixon forecast the U.S. acceptance of China's growing role in world affairs:

"It is a truism that an international order cannot be secure if one of the major powers remains largely outside it and hostile toward it. In this decade, therefore, there will be no more important challenge than that of drawing the People's Republic of China into a constructive relationship with the world community, and particularly with the rest of Asia....

"We are prepared to establish a dialogue with Peking. We cannot accept its ideological precepts, or the notion that Communist China must exercise hegemony over Asia. But neither do we wish to impose on China an international position that denies its legitimate national interests."

Remaining Problems

Despite efforts made in both Washington and Peking to begin a new chapter in Sino-American relations in mid-1971, it was evident that there remained serious complications. Among them:

● Settlement of the war in Indochina.

● American involvement in the Chinese Communist-Nationalist civil war through continued recognition of the Chiang Kai-shek government on Taiwan.

● Efforts to ease tensions with the Soviet Union, such as the strategic arms limitation (SALT) talks.

● The guarantee of Nationalist Chinese security under the 1954 mutual defense treaty and the Formosa Reso-

• The deep Sino-Soviet ideological rift and the frequent military clashes along their common border.

While the consequences of Mr. Nixon's initiatives to ease the rigid U.S. policy of isolating and ostracizing China could not be foreseen, his moves had definitely affected the domestic political arena. He had clearly staked out his claim as the peace candidate in the 1972 Presidential elections.

In 1966, Mr. Nixon was publicly warning that within five years the United States would be at war with China "if we reward aggression in Vietnam." His position had evolved by 1971 to the following, stated in an April 29th news conference:

"...the long-range goal of this administration is a normalization of our relationship with mainland China, the People's Republic of China, and the ending of its isolation from the other nations of the world."

It was thought ironical that Richard M. Nixon, who made his early reputation as a Communist-hunter, should be the very man credited with putting the United States back on speaking terms with 800 million Communist Chinese.

President Nixon actually became the beneficiary of two factors: general acceptance that world peace requires the normalization of relations with the People's Republic of China; and "pro-Communist" charges would not be hurled at Mr. Nixon the way they were at previous Democratic administrations.

President Nixon's efforts in the China-thaw were regarded as a remarkable achievement, whether viewed in the context of national security implications or domestic political impact.

Previous Administrations

Following the October 1949 Communist takeover of mainland China and the flight of the Nationalists to Formosa soon after, the Truman Administration assumed a wait-and-see posture toward Peking. But, with the outbreak of the Korean War and China's entry into the war in October 1950, U.S. policy and American opinion congealed into firm opposition of the mainland regime. *(p. 27)*

Thereafter, the U.S. Government focused on ostracizing Peking from the international community, containing Communist aggression and cementing the U.S. commitment to Taiwan. Anti-Communist sentiment reached a peak during the early 1950s.

The Eisenhower years (1953-1961) saw the continued hard-line position toward Peking.

Despite some expectations that the Administration of President John F. Kennedy would effect a major policy shift, the U.S. position remained basically unchanged during the Kennedy Administration. By the mid-1960s, however, there were indications that previous policy was being reappraised by the Johnson Administration in accordance with the President's overtures toward a general East-West detente. At the same time, however, the President and his advisers emphasized the need for vigilance against a continuing Communist Chinese military threat, with particular reference to the potential Chinese role in the Vietnam war and the country's potential nuclear capability.

Changed Climate

Immediately after the Nixon Administration took office, James C. Thomson Jr., a former East Asian specialist at the State Department, suggested that President Nixon was in a particularly favorable position to effect a change in U.S. policy. Democratic Presidents, Thomson wrote in the February 1969 *Atlantic,* "were acutely gun-shy on China policy; in the late forties and fifties Republicans had a political field day with the issue of the 'loss of China'.... A Republican President, and pre-eminently this Republican President, brings to the China problem some very special assets. Who, for instance, can pin the label of 'softness on Communism' on Richard M. Nixon when he makes overtures to Peking?"

Turning to the climate in Congress, Thomson observed, "Today much of the old so-called 'China Lobby' is either dead or retired. Equally important, the leadership of the new Congress lies with the relatively flexible Democrats, many of whom have been restive under the rigidity of (former Secretary of State) Rusk's China posture.... (They are joined by an) increasing number of moderate Republicans who have urged a review of China policy...." *(China lobbies p. 38)*

Even before elected, Mr. Nixon, during his 1968 campaign for the Presidency, clearly outlined the need for a reversal in U.S. China policy.

"...We simply cannot afford to leave China forever outside the family of nations, there to nurture its fantasies, cherish its hates and threaten its neighbors. There is no place on this small planet for a billion of its potentially most able people to live in angry isolation...," he said.

Stressing what was to later become the Administration's Asian policy, Mr. Nixon said that "Only as the nations of non-Communist Asia become so strong—economically, politically and militarily—that they no longer furnish tempting targets for Chinese aggression, will the leaders in Peking be persuaded to turn their energies inward rather than outward. And that will be the time when the dialogue with mainland China will begin." He maintained that the world could not be safe until China changed and that the long-range goals of the United States would best be served by "pulling China back into the world community."

Speaking also in 1968 on China as a nuclear threat, Nixon said "At the end of this century, Communist China will have a billion people that will have unlimited atomic weapons and it can be exporting them all over the world, and it is essential that whoever is the next President of the United States develop policies now that will get Communist China to change so that we can open a dialogue with them."

On Jan. 27, 1969, Mr. Nixon stated in his first Presidential news conference, "Until some changes occur on their side...I see no immediate prospect of any change in our policy" toward Communist China.

Yet, by the end of the year, the Administration had made several cautious overtures toward increasing U.S. contacts with the Chinese People's Republic, despite the fact that at first Peking showed little interest in reciprocating.

Sino-Soviet-American Relations. A long-term relationship with Peking—drawing it into a constructive role in international affaris—appeared to be particularly necessary, not only for peace in Indochina but to give the Soviet leaders some pause for thought and reason for moderation in their own diplomacy. Mr. Nixon believed that China's continued isolation would be more dangerous to peace than their gradual involvement in world diplomacy.

One consequence of the deep Sino-Soviet idelogical rift and the frequent military clashes along their common border was that both Peking and the Soviet Union view improved U.S. relations with either as collusion. Peking for its part has repeatedly attacked the collusion of U.S. "imperialism" and Soviet "revisionism" in arms control efforts, has interpreted the U.S. position in the Sino-Soviet conflict as being pro-Soviet, and has expressed fears of a pre-emptive Soviet nuclear attack.

Summarizing the U.S. position in a major foreign policy speech in 1969, then Under Secretary of State Elliot Richardson acknowledged the danger of the situation:

"In the case of Communist China, long-run improvement in our relations is in our own national interest. We do not seek to exploit for our own advantage the hostility between the Soviet Union and the People's Republic. Ideological differences between the two Communist giants are not our affair. We could not fail to be deeply concerned, however, with an escalation of this quarrel into a massive breach of international peace and security. Our national security would in the long run be prejudiced by associating ourselves with either side against the other. Each is highly sensitive about American efforts to improve relations with the other. We intend, nevertheless, to pursue a long-term course of progressively developing better relations with both. We are not going to let Communist Chinese invective deter us from seeking agreements with the Soviet Union where those are in our interest. Conversely, we are not going to let Soviet apprehensions prevent us from attempting to bring Communist China out of its angry, alienated shell."

Nuclear Threat. In addition to the benefits to be derived from a Sino-Soviet-American detente, another need for improved relations with China was that country's eventual nuclear capability. China detonated its first nuclear device in October 1964.

Supporting the overtures to Peking, Sen. Stuart Symington (D Mo.) said in 1969 "Now that all peoples are beginning to realize the true implications of a nuclear exchange, it would appear that a change in our China policy is long overdue." The reaction of other Members of Congress to the growing Chinese nuclear capability has been to suggest involving Peking in international disarmament talks. Sen. Henry M. Jackson (D Wash.) made such a proposal as early as Nov. 5, 1969.

Vietnam. Would improved relations with China and a change in U.S.-China policy help hasten an end to the Vietnam war, or at least United States participation therein?

There was little doubt in the United States that American involvement in Vietnam was another factor which had had a significant impact on U.S.-Communist Chinese relations. As long as the war continued, a major source of tension between the two countries would remain.

From the American viewpoint, there was continued uncertainty and apprehension about Chinese Communist actions in Vietnam. From the Communist Chinese viewpoint, U.S. assurances that its aims were limited to ensuring self-determination for the South Vietnamese were

China Policy and the ABM

In Defense Secretary Melvin R. Laird's fiscal 1972 defense posture statement, one paragraph of the 191-page report was devoted to the Chinese missile threat.

Although China has clearly arrived in the nuclear age, emphasis on the country's threat to the United States as a nuclear power has been played down since early 1971.

In a Jan. 20, 1970, news conference, President Nixon focused on China as a threat requiring the deployment of a massive second phase of the anti-ballistic missile (ABM) system. Nixon argued that the second phase of the program was "absolutely essential against any minor power, a power, for example, like Communist China." Congress refused to authorize the expanded version of the ABM system later in 1970 and headlines warning of China's missile threat to the United States stopped appearing over stories quoting the ubiquitous, nameless "high Administration official."

In 1971 Dr. John S. Foster Jr., director of defense research and engineering, outlined for the Senate Armed Services Committee Chinese advances in weaponry:

"The Chinese have been testing since 1967 a thermonuclear device in the three-megaton class. The fourth such device was successfully detonated October 1970. They have continued to progress in propulsion and control is shown by their having launched a space satellite in April 1970 and another in March 1971."

Foster told the committee that China would probably have 10 to 25 intercontinental ballistic missiles (ICBM) in operation by mid-1977.

greeted with extreme suspicion, particularly on those occasions when U.S. combat activities were escalating.

Against this background, the Nixon Administration's policy of withdrawing U.S. troops from Vietnam may have had a positive effect on Peking's willingness to negotiate with the United States.

The Chinese also sent out signals suggesting they would back a new Geneva conference on Indochina and support the idea of a neutralized South Vietnam. And, American troops continued to leave Vietnam at a rate of several thousand a week. Thus, it appeared that improved relations between the United States and China would permit the United States to make a graceful exit from Vietnam.

Asian Policy. The Administration's intention of altering the U.S. role of "global policeman" also required a change in U.S. relations with Peking. The first detailed expression of this policy was contained in the Guam Doctrine enunciated by Mr. Nixon on the eve of his trip to Asia July 25, 1969. Henceforth, he said, the United States would seek to reduce its military presence on the Asian mainland, while providing Asian countries with the economic and military assistance they might need in assuming responsibility for their own defense.

The Chinese saw the Nixon Doctrine as contradictory in that while the United States proposed to reduce its commitments in the Pacific, it encouraged Japan and other countries to assume a larger military role. That, in turn could lead to greater anxiety on the part of China.

In an Aug. 5, 1971, interview with *New York Times* vice president and columnist James Reston, Premier Chou En-lai said that he found the Doctrine "indeed a contradiction." "There should be an effort at relaxation by all parties concerned," he said.

In order to implement the Guam Doctrine, the Administration would need to seek a mutual agreement with Peking on the renunciation of force. In light of a future reduced U.S. military posture in Asia, Peking may be more willing than it was previously to come to some sort of accommodation with the United States.

Some China experts in the U.S. government and the academic community are convinced that China, as it emerges from the chaos of the Cultural Revolution, is thinking politically beyond the Indochina war. Both Mr. Nixon and Secretary of State William P. Rogers are known to be tailoring the China policy to what they believe will be the realistic needs of Washington as well as Peking when the Indochina war has ended and new Asian security arrangements have to be worked out.

Trade. Peking is reported to be particularly interested in increasing trade with the United States. Yet, neither the Administration nor American business executives anticipate meaningful commerce with China in the foreseeable future despite the relaxation in 1971 of the two-decade embargo. *(Far East trade, p. 59)*

In theory, substantial trade could develop if Peking chose to shift some of its imports from Western Europe and Japan to the United States. Last year China imported some $2-billion worth of goods, 75 per cent of which came from non-Communist countries. Peking exported an equal amount of goods.

The United States has had no trading experience since 1950 with Communist China. And, during that year, China bought only $50 million worth of American goods and sold $150 million worth of her products to this country. *(Testimony on trade with China p. 86)*

A "China Trade Association," representing small manufacturers, was organized in Washington in March 1971.

The growth of trade between the two nations is apt to be limited by many factors:

• China is short of the things it could sell in quantity to the United States.

• Some raw materials it has in quantity the United States does not need.

• Doing business with the Chinese—as with any state-run economy—is difficult and time-consuming.

• Japan's closeness to China has given it a distinct competitive edge over Europeans wanting to trade there. The United States will likely encounter the same situation.

• Those in Europe who have traded with the Chinese have found them hard bargainers. The negotiations have taken a long time and profit bargins have been low.

Speaking on the trade issue, scholar Alexander Eckstein urged unilateral steps toward the People's Republic of China. Eckstein, a professor of economics at the University of Michigan, told the Joint Economic Committee Dec. 9, 1970: "Seventeen years after the end of the Korean War it is about time to lift the embargoes pure and simple. It is an anachronism, a monument to

bureaucratic rigidity and a symbol of a bankrupt China policy we have been pursuing for the last 20 years."

Nixon Administration and China

During its first year, the Nixon Administration took three cautious, but unilateral and unconditional, steps to improve U.S.-Communist Chinese relations:

• On July 21, 1969, the State Department announced a slight easing of travel and trade restrictions. (A total embargo had been in effect since President Truman invoked the 1917 Trading with the Enemy Act against Peking in 1950.) American tourists and residents abroad were allowed to bring into the United States $100 worth of Chinese Communist origin goods for noncommercial purposes. In addition, scholars, professors, journalists, university students, Members of Congress, scientists, physicians and Red Cross representatives were automatically entitled to have their passports validated for travel to mainland China.

• In November 1969, the Administration quietly ended the regular two-destroyer patrol (of the Seventh Fleet) in Taiwan Strait. The U.S. Navy had maintained a presence in the Strait since June 1950. *(p. 27)*

• Dec. 19, 1969, the government announced that subsidiaries and affiliates of U.S. firms abroad would be permitted to sell nonstrategic goods to Communist China and buy Communist Chinese products for resale in foreign markets. Individuals would be able to bring products of Communist China origin into the United States for noncommercial purposes without limit on their value. The announcement followed negotiations early in the month on renewing the Warsaw sessions.

Warsaw Talks. The Warsaw talks between U.S. and Chinese representatives in Poland were the only official contacts between the two countries for 16 years. Despite the increasingly numerous and critical issues facing the two nations, the frequency of the ambassadorial talks had steadily decreased from 73 meetings between Aug. 1, 1955, and Dec. 12, 1957, to five meetings each in 1964 and 1965, three meetings in 1966, two in 1967, and one—the 134th—in 1968.

A meeting scheduled Feb. 21, 1969, was abruptly canceled by Peking—a little more than one month after Mr. Nixon took office. The meeting finally took place one year later, on Jan. 20, 1970, two years after the last previous session in Warsaw. The resumption of the talks and the announcement that another meeting would be held only one month later, on Feb. 20, was viewed by many observers as signalling possibly significant shifts in both Washington's and Peking's policies. But no one in the Nixon Administration publicly predicted what was likely to result from the discussions.

When the State Department announced March 15, 1969, that the annual extension of the general travel ban to Communist China, North Korea, North Vietnam and Cuba would be extended for only six months instead of the usual year, some observers speculated that a change of policy was in the offing; but the ban was extended another six months on Sept. 15, 1969.

Despite the Administration's policy of seeking to expand contacts with Peking, the President and Pentagon officials during Mr. Nixon's first year continued to emphasize Peking's aggressive intentions and pointed to the potential Chinese nuclear threat as a major justification for deploying the antiballistic missile system (ABM). *(Box p. 18)*

Administration statements about the People's Republic of China—most particularly those of Secretary of State William P. Rogers and Under Secretary Elliot Richardson, both of whom are leading advocates of increased contacts with Peking—seemed to have shed much of the cold-war vocabulary. Throughout 1969, both officials made it clear that the United States remained willing, and even eager, to renew the Warsaw discussions.

In an interview with *U.S. News and World Report* Jan. 17, 1970, Secretary Rogers said it was difficult to forecast what the Warsaw talks would accomplish. "We hope that we can open up some channels of communication," he said. "For example, we would hope that there might be reciprocal visits of journalists, educators and others. We hope that there might be more steps on trade matters...."

When the long-postponed 135th session was finally held Jan. 20, 1970, the topics remained confidential by mutual agreement. Caution was the watchword of U.S. officials. Peking was reported to be particularly interested in increasing trade with the United States. On the U.S. side, the Administration's unilateral actions in 1969 indicated receptiveness to a slight easing of the embargo.

The Taiwan Issue. The Taiwan issue during 1969 proved to be the major obstacle to a U.S.-Communist Chinese accommodation, even in the fields of trade and travel. Both Taipei and Peking insisted that Taiwan remain part of China; each firmly rejected any suggestion of a "two-China" solution, since both claimed to be the sole legitimate representative of the Chines people. *(Taiwan p. 26)*

The United States was committee to defend Taiwan against armed attack by the Mutual Security Treaty of 1954 and the Formosa Resolution (H J Res 159—PL 84-4) passed by Congress Jan. 28, 1955. *(Texts p. 21, 22)*

The possibility of discussing a mutual Washington-Peking renunciation of force was raised Feb. 18, 1969, by Secretary Rogers, who said U.S. participants had been instructed to suggest at the Feb. 20 meeting (which Peking canceled) "consideration of an agreement on peaceful coexistence consistent with our treaty obligations in the area."

Some State Department advisers were wary of immediately bringing up the matter of peaceful coexistence or mutual renunciation of force, unless both sides construed it to entail some kind of modus vivendi outside the Taiwan area.

The Nixon Administration during 1969 had ruled out any "two-China" policy. It continued to reaffirm the existing U.S. commitment to Taiwan's autonomy, but refrained from restating the previous U.S. position that the Nationalist government was the sole legitimate government of all China.

The gradual reduction of U.S. forces in the Taiwan area during the first year of the Nixon Administration led Fox Butterfield to conclude (Jan. 18, 1970, *New York Times* magazine) "Curiously, these changes have the cumulative effect of bringing the U.S. closer to meeting the Chinese Communists' demand that we withdraw from Taiwan and the (Formosa) Strait before any discussions of other issues, such as trade or visits by journalists." *(U.S. troop reductions on Taiwan p. 32, 33)*

But observers generally agreed in early 1970 that solution of the Taiwan issue was a long way off. Any easing of U.S.-Communist Chinese tension was likely to come about, they said, by very small steps in the areas of trade and cultural exchanges. Each government was in a transitional stage of developing policies toward the other.

1970

During 1970, the United States continued to relax trade and travel restrictions toward Peking.

Despite the official nonrecognition policy, the following tentative steps toward normalization between the two nations were undertaken in 1970 by the Nixon Administration:

● The U.S.-Chinese ambassadorial talks resumed in Warsaw after a two-year lapse.

● The selective licensing of goods for export to Communist China was authorized by the United States.

● The President noted that in 1970, 270 Americans had their passports validated for travel to the People's Republic of China. This brought the total number to nearly 1,000 though only three Americans had been permitted entry.

In his foreign policy speech in early 1971, Mr. Nixon said that these unilateral efforts would continue. Although Peking had made no new overtures to the United States and had given no indication of resuming the Warsaw ambassadorial talks, it had moderated its tone in foreign policy and had established diplomatic relations with Canada, Italy and Chile.

1971: Dramatic Shift

In his second annual State of the World report, President Nixon on Feb. 25, 1971, forecast U.S. acceptance of the growing role Communist China—the People's Republic of China—would play in the international arena.

The President repeated the U.S. commitment to the government of Nationalist China on Taiwan. But, he said, "The United States is prepared to see the People's Republic of China play a constructive role in the family of nations."

For the first time, the President referred to Communist China by its formal name, the People's Republic of China. Although his message to Congress and the nation did not include substantive changes in U.S.-China policy, it revealed a trend toward increased dialogue and contact with the Chinese people.

"The 22-year-old hostility between ourselves and the People's Republic of China is another unresolved problem, serious indeed in view of the fact that it determines our relationship with 750 million talented and energetic people," the President said.

He continued: "For the United States the development of a relationship with Peking embodies precisely the challenges of this decade: to deal with, and resolve, vestiges of the postwar period that continue to influence our relationship and to create a balanced international structure in which all nations will have a stake. We believe that such a structure should provide full scope for the influence to which China's achievements entitle it."

Presidential Visit

In April 1971, President Nixon raised the possibility of paying a visit to the long-forbidden land of Communist China.

At a meeting with the American Society of Newspaper Editors in Washington April 16, Mr. Nixon expressed the hope that he could visit China someday. A few days later on April 29, he returned to the theme at a news conference saying: "I hope and, as a matter of fact, I expect to visit mainland China sometime in some capacity...." Edgar Snow, an American writer who has had access to Chinese leaders for years, wrote in *Life* (Arpil 30, 1971) that Chairman Mao told him in December 1970 that Mr. Nixon would be welcomed in China, whether as a tourist or as President of the United States.

Snow said that during his six-month stay in China in the fall and winter of 1970-71, he learned that "foreign diplomats in Peking were aware...that messages were being delivered from Washington to the Chinese government by certain go-betweens" to assure Chinese leaders that Nixon had a "new outlook" on Asia and wanted to end the impasse in Sino-American relations. It was believed there, Snow said, that Mr. Nixon had offered to send personal representatives to Peking.

It was during this period, the spring of 1971, that the Nixon Administration took what appeared to be a sudden shift in policy toward Communist China. The Administration:

• Terminated all restrictions on the use of American passports for travel to China on March 15.

• Terminated a 21-year-old embargo April 14 on trade with Communist China and announced that a long list of goods eligible for export to China would soon be released.

Nixon Announcement. On July 15 Mr. Nixon revealed to a nationwide television audience that his assistant for national security affairs, Henry A. Kissinger, had been diverted secretly from a round-the-world fact-finding mission to meet with Chinese Premier Chou En-lai in Peking July 9-11. Mr. Nixon said that he had been invited by Chou "to visit China at an appropriate date before May 1972," and he had accepted the invitation.

No American President has ever visited China. White House sources were quored as saying the May 1972 deadline was the date before which the visit would have to occur to avoid becoming involved in the 1972 political campaign.

The President's planned visit changed the potential for the rapprochement sought by both Mr. Nixon and the government of the Chinese People's Republic almost instantaneously from a remote possibility to a practical prospect. The purpose of the trip, Mr. Nixon said, was "to seek normalization of relations between the two countries and also to exchange views on questions of concern to the two sides."

The President described the event as "a major development in our efforts to build a lasting peace in the world." It was clearly a breakthrough portending a likely end to 21 years of American nonrecognition of Mao Tse-tung's Communist government.

He stressed that his move would not be "at the expense of our old friends." This was interpreted as primarily reassurance for Nationalist China. But the Nationalist government was not assuaged. Premier C.K. Yen issued a statement of surprise and regret on July 16. Mr. Nixon assured Nationalist President Chiang Kai-shek, in a letter revealed July 20 in Taipei that the United States would honor its mutual security treaty commitment to the government on Taiwan.

The Issues. White House sources said U.S. recognition of Communist China was not likely before Mr. Nixon's trip, indicating that recognition was not a precondition posed by the Chinese. But recognition seemed the logical next step in the series of Administration initiatives which included rescission of travel restrictions and the April 14 termination of the 21-year U.S. embargo on trade.

The opening with China forecast a broadening of the focus of U.S. Asian policy from a settlement in Vietnam to a more general Far Eastern rapprochement.

Vietnam. Speculation arose immediately after the announcement of the President's trip that rapprochement with China would improve the chance of a negotiated peace in Vietnam. The White House tried to discourage this linking of China with Vietnam. Press Secretary Ronald L. Ziegler said that Mr. Nixon had declined to speculate on the Vietnam effect of the China journey and that such speculation would not be helpful.

Mr. Nixon's announcement reduced pressure on him to respond favorably to the North Vietnamese-National Liberation Front proposal, made in Paris July 1, to return all American prisoners of war by Dec. 31 if all U.S. troops were withdrawn by that date. But Chou, speaking in Peking July 19, said withdrawal of U.S. troops from Indochina must take precedence over other efforts to improve Chinese-American relations. In his Aug. 9 interview with columnist James Reston of *The New York Times,* Chou said: "(F)irst of all the question of Vietnam and Indochina should be solved, and not the question of Taiwan or other questions."

Members of Congress were divided as to whether the President would withdraw all U.S. combat troops from Vietnam before the trip and on Sept. 30 the Senate declared it U.S. policy that a withdrawal of U.S. troops from Indochina would be completed within six months. The Administration opposed the action. House conferees opposed the "six months" deadline and on Nov. 11 Congress cleared the amendment leaving it to the President to set a withdrawal date.

Soviet-U.S. Relations. Interpretations of the affect of the President's proposed trip on U.S.-Soviet relations differed, though they did not necessarily conflict.

In one view, the warming in U.S.-Chinese relations was a setback for the Soviet Union. It was an historic event in which the Russians had no part and dramatic evidence that Soviet efforts to improve its own relations with both the United States and China had failed to forestall rapprochement which excluded Moscow.

According to other opinion, the trip to Peking posed possible difficulties for U.S.-Soviet relations.

Reaction from Congress. President Nixon's annoucement that he had accepted an invitation to visit Communist China won widespread approval from members of Congress in both major parties.

Democrats were nearly unanimous in praising the President's initiative toward closer relations with Peking. Some strongly anti-Communist Republican members warned against changes in the long-standing U.S. policy toward Communist China.

Nixon Administration Initiatives Aimed...

1969

Feb. 18. Secretary of State William P. Rogers implied that the U.S. was prepared to accept a Chinese recommendation that the two countries agree to principles of peaceful coexistence. He indicated that the Nixon Administration intended to extend previous offers for cultural and scientific exchanges. Rogers also said that a U.S. diplomat had been directed to propose the re-establishment of telecommunication links severed Nov. 18, 1968.

July 21. Eased restrictions on American travel to China and permitted tourists to buy Chinese goods up to $100 in value. Scholars, journalists, students, scientists and members of Congress would automatically have their passports validated for travel to Communist China.

July 25. The President—in what was to become known as the Nixon Doctrine—announced the United States would seek to reduce its military presence on the Asian mainland, while providing Asian countries with the economic and military assistance for "self-help."

Aug. 8. Rogers, during his Asian tour, expressed the desire of the U.S. to renew diplomatic talks with Communist China.

November. Suspension of patrol by the Navy's Seventh Fleet in Taiwan Strait.

Dec. 11. U.S. Ambassador to Poland, Walter J. Stoessel Jr., met with Chinese charge d'affaires Lei Yang Chen in Warsaw, paving the way for resumption of U.S.-Chinese bilateral talks—begun in 1955—which had collapsed Jan. 8, 1968.

Dec. 15. U.S. announced that all nuclear weapons on Okinawa would be removed by the end of 1969. They reportedly had been installed as a nuclear deterrent against Communist China.

Dec. 19. Lifted the $100 limit on purchases of Chinese goods and permitted foreign subsidiaries of American companies to trade in nonstrategic goods with China.

1970

Jan. 2. Vice President Agnew, during his Asian tour, said the U.S. should seek "meaningful dialogue" with mainland China. He said he favored "initiatives to develop an atmosphere that will allow us to reduce the amount of military spending...."

Jan. 20. U.S.-Chinese ambassadorial talks resumed in Warsaw after a two-year lapse. A second meeting was held Feb. 20, and a third scheduled for May 20. The Chinese government canceled the May 20 talk due, they said, to the U.S. invasion of Cambodia. No future talks were held.

Feb. 18. Stated in the President's foreign policy report to Congress: "It is certainly to our interest... that we take what steps we can toward improved relations with Peking."

March 16. State Department continued relaxation of travel ban to Communist China.

April 29. The United States authorized the selective licensing of goods for export to the People's Republic.

July 28. U.S. Department of Commerce approved the sale by an Italian company to Communist China of 80 dump trucks containing General Motors engines and parts.

Aut. 26. Restrictions prohibiting American oil companies abroad from permitting foreign ships to use refueling facilities to and from mainland China were lifted.

Oct. 25. White House Press Secretary Ronald L. Ziegler indicated first softening of the U.S. position on UN membership for Communist China. Ziegler said: "The U.S. opposes the admission of the Peking regime into the UN at the expense of the expulsion of the Republic of China." The phrasing hinted at a U.S. "two-China" policy.

1971

Jan. 26. State Department revealed that the United States had been exchanging scientific informa-

United Nations Issue

At the beginning of the 92nd Congress certain resolutions introduced reflected congressional interest in the idea that the 1971 session of the United Nations might open the way for the admission of the People's Republic of China and the simultaneous explusion of the Republic of China. Some members offered a "two China" approach as an alternative to the expulsion of Taiwan.

Presidential Action. President Nixon on July 9, 1970, had directed the 50-member Commission on the Observance of the Twenty-fifth Anniversary of the United Nations to consult official and public opinion regarding United States participation in the UN.

The commission, headed by former U.S. Ambassador to the United Nations Henry Cabot Lodge and including

prominent Americans from many professional fields, held public hearings in six cities before submitting its 100-page report.

On April 26, 1971, it urged that Communist China be admitted to the United Nations. The commission urged that the United States:

• Adopt the position that all firmly established governments should be included in the UN system inasmuch as the benefits to the United States for having such governments within the UN and subject to the international obligations laid down by the charter far outweigh the problems raised by ideological differences between various states; and that no member of the organization living up to its obligations under the charter be expelled;

• "Under no circumstances agree to the expulsion from the UN of the Republic of China on Taiwan but seek agree-

...at Rapprochement with China: 1969-1971

tion with China since before 1949 and had continued to do so.

Feb. 17. The President, during a White House news conference, emphasized that the Laotian operation mounted by the U.S. presented "no threat" to Communist China and "should not be interpreted by Communist Chinese as being a threat against them."

Feb. 25. President Nixon referred, for the first time, to Communist China by its formal name, the People's Republic of China, in his foreign policy report to Congress.

March 15. State Department terminated all restrictions on the use of American passports for travel to China.

April 14. United States terminated 21-year-old embargo on trade with Communist China and announced that a long list of goods eligible for export to China would be released soon. The decision, announced by President Nixon, coincided with a Chinese invitation April 6 to a U.S. table tennis team to visit the mainland and with the team's friendly reception in Peking.

April 19. United Airlines applied to the Civil Aeronautics Board for permission to extend its routing system to include Peking, Shanghai and Canton.

April 21. President Nixon assured the U.S. Table Tennis Association that he "certainly will cooperate" with the association's invitation to the Chinese team to visit the U.S.

April 26. A special presidential commission headed by Henry Cabot Lodge, former chief U.S. delegate to the UN, recommended in a 100-page report that the U.S. try to obtain the admission of Communist China to the UN without the expulsion of Nationalist China. But, the report said, "under no circumstances" should Taiwan be expelled.

April 29. President Nixon expressed the hope that he could visit Communist China "sometime in some capacity."

May 7. U.S.Treasury Secretary John B. Connally announced a general license for the use of dollars in transactions with the People's Republic of China.

June 1. President Nixon announced that "a significant change has taken place among the members of the United Nations on the issue of admission of mainland China," and the U.S. was "analyzing that situation." The Administration, he said, would announce its position at the fall session of the UN.

June 10. A list of 47 categories of items considered exportable to China was released by the U.S.

July 9. President Nixon sent Assistant for National Security Affairs, Dr. Henry Kissinger, to Peking to talk with Premier Chou En-lai, announced July 15.

July 15. President Nixon announced that he will visit Communist China before May, 1972, "to seek normalization of relations between the two countries and also to exchange views on questions of concern to the two sides."

July 17. In view of President Nixon's efforts to improve relations with Peking, the nuclear weapons that were to be removed from Okinawa would not be placed closer to Communist China, U.S. government officials announced.

July 28. The U.S. government suspended American intelligence-gathering missions over Communist China by manned reconnaissance planes and unmanned drones.

Aug. 2. The U.S. ended 20 years of opposition to Communist China's presence in the United Nations by announcing it would "support action...calling for seating the People's Republic of China." The U.S. emphasized its continued resistance to any move to expel Nationalist China from the UN.

Aug. 17. U.S. representative to the UN George Bush, submitted U.S. resolution supporting a "two-China" policy to the UN General Assembly agenda.

Oct. 5. Kissinger announced he would make a second trip to China in late October to prepare Mr. Nixon's visit.

Oct. 25. The UN General Assembly voted to seat Communist China and expel Taiwan.

Oct. 26. Kissinger returned from a six-day visit to China. He said Oct. 27 that Mr. Nixon's trip to China would occur in early 1972.

---

ment as early as practicable whereby the People's Republic of China might accept the principles of the charter and be represented in the organization."

For two decades, the United States steadfastly had opposed the admission of the People's Republic to the General Assembly and to the China seat in the Security Council.

U.S. Acquiescence. The first indication that the United States would switch its stand opposing admission of Communist China to the United Nations came on June 4, 1971. The President at that time announced that "a significant change has taken place among the members of the United Nations on the issue of admission of mainland China," and the United States was "analyzing that situation."

Secretary of State William P. Rogers on Aug. 2, announced that the United States would abandon its firm policy of two decades and support the seating of the People's Republic of China in the United Nations at the fall 1971 UN General Assembly session.

But the Secretary made it clear that the United States would oppose any efforts to "expel the Republic of China or otherwise deprive it of representation in the United Nations."

Avoiding a position on whether the Nationalist Chinese government on Taiwan should retain its seat on the UN Security Council, Rogers said the United States would abide by the views of the majority of UN members.

Chinese Response. Peking responded to the U.S. announcement by accusing Rogers of lying in order to push "the preposterous proposition of two Chinas." Rogers

(Continued on p. 25)

1971 United Nations Roll Calls on China

On Two-Thirds Requirement

Resolution declaring the expulsion of Nationalist China an "important matter" and thus requiring a two-thirds vote rather than a simple majority for passage.

On Seating Peking

Resolution to seat Communist China and expel Nationalist China. *(UN votes on China question 1950-1970, p. 103)*

IN FAVOR—55

Argentina	Ghana	New Zealand
Australia	Greece	Nicaragua
Bahrain	Guatemala	Niger
Barbados	Haiti	Panama
Bolivia	Honduras	Paraguay
Brazil	Indonesia	Philippines
Cambodia	Israel	Portugal
Cent. Afr. Rep.	Ivory Coast	Rwanda
Chad	Jamaica	Saudi Arabia
China	Japan	South Africa
Colombia	Jordan	Spain
Congo (Kinsh.)	Lebanon	Swaziland
Costa Rica	Lesotho	Thailand
Dahomey	Liberia	United States
Dominican Rep.	Luxembourg	Upper Volta
El Salvador	Madagascar	Uruguay
Fiji	Malawi	Venezuela
Gabon	Mauritius	
Gambia	Mexico	

OPPOSED—59

Afghanistan	Ethiopia	Pakistan
Albania	Finland	Peru
Algeria	France	Poland
Bhutan	Guinea	Rumania
Britain	Guyana	Sierra Leone
Bulgaria	Hungary	Singapore
Burma	Iceland	Somalia
Burundi	India	So. Yemen
Byelorussia	Iraq	Soviet Union
Cameroon	Ireland	Sudan
Canada	Kenya	Sweden
Ceylon	Kuwait	Syria
Chile	Libya	Tanzania
Congo (Brazza.)	Malaysia	Trinidad-Tobago
Cuba	Mali	Uganda
Czechoslovakia	Mauritania	Ukraine
Denmark	Mongolia	Yemen
Ecuador	Nepal	Yugoslavia
Egypt	Nigeria	Zambia
Eq. Guinea	Norway	

ABSTENTIONS—15

Austria	Italy	Qatar
Belgium	Laos	Senegal
Botswana	Malta	Togo
Cyprus	Morocco	Tunisia
Iran	Netherlands	Turkey

Absent—Maldives, Oman.

IN FAVOR—76

Afghanistan	Ghana	Peru
Albania	Guinea	Poland
Algeria	Guyana	Portugal
Austria	Hungary	Rumania
Belgium	Iceland	Rwanda
Bhutan	India	Senegal
Botswana	Iran	Sierra Leone
Britain	Iraq	Singapore
Bulgaria	Ireland	Somalia
Burma	Israel	So. Yemen
Burundi	Italy	Soviet Union
Byelorussia	Kenya	Sudan
Cameroon	Kuwait	Sweden
Canada	Laos	Syria
Ceylon	Libya	Tanzania
Chile	Malaysia	Togo
Congo (Brazza.)	Mali	Trinidad-Tobago
Cuba	Mauritania	Tunisia
Czechoslovakia	Mexico	Turkey
Denmark	Mongolia	Uganda
Ecuador	Morocco	Ukraine
Egypt	Nepal	Yemen
Eq. Guinea	Netherlands	Yugoslavia
Ethiopia	Nigeria	Zambia
Finland	Norway	
France	Pakistan	

OPPOSED—35

Australia	Gambia	Nicaragua
Bolivia	Guatemala	Niger
Brazil	Haiti	Paraguay
Cambodia	Honduras	Philippines
Cent. Afr. Rep.	Ivory Coast	Saudi Arabia
Chad	Japan	South Africa
Congo (Kinsh.)	Lesotho	Swaziland
Costa Rica	Liberia	United States
Dahomey	Madagascar	Upper Volta
Dominican Rep.	Malawi	Uruguay
El Salvador	Malta	Venezuela
Gabon	New Zealand	

ABSTENTIONS—17

Argentina	Greece	Mauritius
Bahrain	Indonesia	Panama
Barbados	Jamaica	Qatar
Colombia	Jordan	Spain
Cyprus	Lebanon	Thailand
Fiji	Luxembourg	

Absent—China, Maldives, Oman.

(Continued from p. 23)

confirmed that he had no indication from either Peking or Taipei that they were willing to sit together in the United Nations. Premier Chou En-lai told James Reston, in an interview published in the *New York Times* August 10, that Peking would not join the UN unless Taiwan was excluded.

U.S. Resolutions. Just prior to the opening session Sept. 21 of the UN General Assembly's 26th session in New York, the United States announced Sept. 16 its intention to vote to seat the People's Republic of China in the UN Security Council.

But the Nixon Administration's efforts to prevent the ouster of Nationalist China from the UN encountered a setback Sept. 22 at a meeting of that organization's agenda committee.

The United States submitted two resolutions on the seating of a Chinese delegation in the UN. One text asked the General Assembly to agree that any move to oust Taiwan from its membership be considered an "important question" requiring the approval of two-thirds of the Assembly's members. The other text recommended that Peking be admitted as a Security Council member but noted that Taiwan had a continued right of representation in the General Assembly.

The UN Assembly's General Committee voted Sept. 22 against a U.S. proposal to have the U.S. resolution and a previously submitted Albanian resolution on the seating of a Chinese delegation discussed simultaneously by the General Assembly. The motion was defeated by a vote of 12-9.

The Committee voted 17-2 to put the Albanian resolution on the General Assembly's agenda as item 101. The U.S. resolutions, by a vote of 11-9, were to be placed on the agenda as item 105.

The Albanian resolution submitted July 15 called on the General Assembly to admit Communist China, seat it in the Security Council, and expel Nationalist China from all UN bodies. A similar resolution had been supported by the Assembly in 1970 by a vote of 51-49, but Peking's admission was blocked because the General Assembly had decided the question required a two-thirds majority.

The Albanian resolution was submitted well in advance of the Assembly's Sept. 21 opening date, reportedly to emphasize Peking's insistence on the expulsion of Nationalist China as a condition for its own membership.

Nixon Support. In an unscheduled news conference at the White House Sept. 16 President Nixon declared that the United States would support Peking's seating in the Security Council because such a move "reflects the realities of the situation."

Nixon said "in the event that the People's Republic is admitted to the United Nations, the seat in the Security Council would go to the People's Republic and that, of course, would mean the removal of the Republic of China from the Security Council seat." The President added: "We will vote against the expulsion of the Republic of China (from the UN) and we will work as effectively as we can to accomplish that goal."

On Oct. 4, Secretary of State Rogers warned the United Nations General Assembly that the expulsion of Taiwan might endanger the membership of other nations and weaken the United Nations as a whole. The struggle over Taiwan's continued membership in the UN became the first test of strength between Peking and Washington since Mr. Nixon opened the new dialogue between the two powers in mid-1971.

Kissinger Trip. Presidential assistant Henry A. Kissinger Oct. 20 made a second trip to Peking to make "concrete" plans for President Nixon's China visit. Upon returning, he announced Oct. 27 that Mr. Nixon would visit China after the first of the year.

UN Vote on China. After one week of intense UN debate on the China issue during which the United States was accused of exerting undue pressure for dual representation, the UN General Assembly Oct. 25 voted to admit Peking and to expel the delegates of Taiwan. The vote was 76-35 with 17 abstentions. *(UN votes 1950-1970, p. 103)*

The United States, despite supporting the seating of Communist China, thus lost in its effort to keep Taiwan in the United Nations.

Prior to the vote, the U.S. resolution to declare the expulsion of Taiwan an important question requiring a two-thirds majority was defeated 59-55 with 15 abstentions. The United States had predicted victory on that vote.

The U.S. resolution for dual representation of Peking and Taiwan never came to a vote since the Albanian resolution was considered first and adopted. On the eve of the debate, the Peking government stated that it would accept nothing less than its substitution for the Taiwan regime.

U.S. efforts to retain Taiwan's seat were said to have been badly hurt by the White House's dispatch of Kissinger to Peking in the middle of the China debate and his presence there at the actual time of the vote Oct. 25. Kissinger in fact remained in Peking two days longer than scheduled, returning the day after the UN vote.

Congressional Reaction. Most members of Congress expressed anger at the UN for the expulsion of Nationalist China and many favored slashing U.S. contributions to the peacekeeping organization. Most of the reaction centered around the $3.2-billion fiscal 1972 foreign aid bill which was being debated in the Senate at the time of the UN action and which contained $141-million in outlays to various UN agencies. The bill was rejected Oct. 29 by a 21-47 roll-call vote. *(p. 52, 53)*

Speaking for the Administration, Secretary of State William P. Rogers said the United States "will not support a reduction of funds for the United Nations in retaliation" for the vote. He emphasized that the United States would retain its ties with Nationalist China as before.

The White House had left all statements on the UN vote to Rogers in an apparent effort to keep the President's personal prestige separate from the voting setback and to avoid anything that might give offense in Peking and interfere with the President's 1972 China visit.

But, in what appeared to be a move to divert criticism from himself to the UN, Mr. Nixon, through Press Secretary Ronald L. Ziegler, denounced as "shocking" the "demonstration of undisguised glee shown by some delegates" after the Oct. 25 expulsion of Nationalist China from the UN. Ziegler said that Mr. Nixon supported the UN and wanted to see it succeed, but that action of some delegates "could lead to deterioration of support in Congress and the country" both for the United Nations and for the foreign aid program.

CHIANG REGIME: MAJOR OBSTACLE TO U.S.-PEKING TIES

...we do not wish to create a Formosa irredenta issue about which the Chinese Communists could rally support within China and with which they could divert attention from Soviet actions in the North. We must not place ourselves in the unenviable position of the USSR with regard to the integrity of China and must remain free to take the position that anyone who violates the integrity of China is the enemy of China and is acting contrary to our own interests.

—State Department Reply to Questions contained in House Resolution 452, H Rept 81-1618, Feb. 9, 1950

All that we have to do is to take a look at the map and we can see that if Formosa falls the next frontier is the coast of California.

—Richard M. Nixon, California Senate campaign, Sept. 18, 1950

U.S. commitments to Chiang Kai-shek's Republic of China remain the major stumbling block to President Nixon's efforts to improve relations with the People's Republic of China.

The UN General Assembly vote Oct. 25, 1971, to seat Peking and expel Taipei conveniently removed the issue of China "representation" from the agenda of Mr. Nixon's talks in Peking scheduled for early 1972. But two key issues remained—the U.S. military commitment to Chiang, formalized in the 1954 Mutual Defense Treaty, and Washington's diplomatic relations with Taipei.

Peking regards the defense treaty—Taipei's only military alliance—as a continued intervention in the Chinese civil war, and it views Washington's diplomatic ties with Taipei as a refusal to recognize the People's Republic as the sole legitimate government of China. Neither Peking nor Taipei has ever permitted any government to maintain diplomatic relations with both China's simultaneously.

Mr. Nixon has therefore been understandably reticent when newsmen have brought up the question of diplomatic relations with Peking. He has spoken more generally of normalizing relations with mainland China.

Volatile Issue. The U.S. commitment to 84-year-old Chiang has long been an emotional issue in American politics. The latest demonstration of this came in the week following Taiwan's expulsion from the UN when sharp congressional reaction to the ouster led to the defeat of a Senate effort to repeal the 1955 Formosa Resolution authorizing the President to use armed forces to protect Formosa and contributed to the Senate rejection of the Administration's foreign aid bill. *(p. 46)*

This fact sheet examines the evolution of the U.S. commitment to Taiwan, internal development on Taiwan which may transform that country's political structure when Chiang leaves the scene and Nixon Administration policy regarding Taiwan.

Evolution of the Commitment

The United States government has maintained a military and diplomatic commitment to support the Nationalist Chinese government of Chiang Kai-shek ever since the outbreak of World War II with one six-month exception. The exception came in 1950: President Truman announced Jan. 5 that the United States would "not provide military aid or advice to Chinese forces on Formosa"; six months later following the outbreak of the Korean war, Mr. Truman ordered the U.S. Seventh Fleet to prevent any Communist Chinese attack on Formosa.

During World War II, the United States provided military and economic aid to Chiang. In October 1943, at President Roosevelt's initiative, the United States, Britain and the Soviet Union signed a declaration acknowledging China's status as a great power with the right to participate with the other great powers in prosecuting the war, organizing the peace and setting up postwar international organizations. This paved the way for China's permanent seat on the United Nations Security Council, when the UN Charter was signed in 1945. The Cairo Declaration signed in December 1943 by Roosevelt, Prime Minister Churchill and Chiang called for the restoration of Chinese territories taken by Japan.

Chinese Civil War. In 1946, United States attempts to mediate a solution to longstanding differences between Chinese Nationalists and Communists failed. In the ensuing civil war, the Communists drove the Nationalists from the mainland and established the People's Republic of China Oct. 1, 1949. The Nationalists fled to Formosa.

During the three-year conflict, the United States provided military and economic assistance to the Nationalists. U.S. ships and aircraft were used to transport Nationalist troops. And on several occasions, U.S. Marines became involved in skirmishes with Communist forces and suffered casualties. The Truman Administration, however, refused to send large numbers of troops to China to aid the Nationalists. U.S. aid to the Nationalists from 1946-1949 totaled over $2-billion, according to an estimate by Senator Tom Connally (D Texas).

In the summer of 1949, the U.S. government prepared to write off the Nationalists. A State Department white paper on U.S. policy in China since 1944 said the Nationalist defeat was due more to their own inept leadership than to the insufficiency of U.S. aid. In an accompanying letter Aug. 5 to the President, Secretary of State Dean Acheson said "the only alternative open to the United States was full-scale intervention on behalf of a government which had lost the confidence of its own troops and its own people." Republican critics of the Truman Administration—Senators Styles Bridges (R N.H.), William F. Knowland (R Calif.), Pat McCarran (D Nev.) and Kenneth S. Wherry (R Neb.)—termed the paper "a 1,054-page whitewash of a wishful do-nothing policy which has succeeded only in placing Asia in danger

CHINA

TACHENS

EAST CHINA SEA

MATSU   SENKAKU •

TAIWAN STRAIT

Taipei

QUEMOY

TAIWAN

PESCADORES

PACIFIC OCEAN

SOUTH CHINA SEA

0   50   100
MILES

The Republic of China controls Taiwan, the Pescadores, Quemoy and Matsu. In January 1955, the Nationalists evacuated the Tachens and the Communists took control. Senkaku, where oil was discovered in 1969, is claimed by the Nationalists and the Communists; it reverts to Japan in 1972 under the terms of the U.S.-Japanese treaty returning Okinawa to Japanese administration.

of Soviet conquest." Former Ambassador to China Patrick J. Hurley called the document a "smooth alibi for the pro-Communists in the State Department who had engineered the overthrow of our ally...and aided in the Communist conquest of China." These charges, amplified and elaborated in the 1950s, became the basis of the Republican theme that the Democrats "lost" China. *(China lobbies, p. 31; U.S. elections, p. 54)*

Formosa Written Off. President Truman announced Jan. 5, 1950, that the United States would "not provide military aid or advice to Chinese forces on Formosa." Acheson, elaborating on Truman's statement the same day, said the President's decision was proof that the U.S. would not meddle in the internal affairs of China. In testimony Jan. 10 before the Senate Foreign Relations Committee, Acheson said the first line of U.S. defense in the Pacific would include Japan, Okinawa and the Philippines, but not Formosa.

In the spring of 1950, the Chinese Communists began massing forces to invade Formosa. What apparently saved the Nationalists from an invasion was the Soviet-inspired North Korean attack on South Korea, which occurred June 25. The invasion led to a revision of U.S. Asian defense policy to include Formosa. President Truman stated June 27, that in view of North Korea's action, "the occupation of Formosa by Communist forces would be a direct threat to the security of the Pacific area and to the United States forces." He ordered the U.S. Seventh

Fleet to prevent any Communist attack on Formosa and to see that all Nationalist air and sea operations against the mainland were halted. Truman also rejected Chiang's offer of Nationalist troops to fight in Korea. Although initially favorable to such a scheme as part of a United Nations effort to obtain military forces from as many countries as possible, he was dissuaded by Acheson, who said the use of Nationalist troops could serve as an excuse for the Chinese Communists to enter the war and could weaken Formosa in the event of a Communist attack on the island.*

Large-scale intervention of the Chinese Communist forces in Korea in November 1950 cemented American support of the Nationalist regime. It also brought a resolution in the United Nations General Assembly declaring Peking guilty of aggression. This declaration marked a turning point in the policy of the United States toward admitting Communist China to the United Nations. In the first six months of 1950 prior to the outbreak of the Korean war, U.S. policy on the admission of Communist China to the United Nations had been in flux. Acheson said March 8 that the United States would not vote to seat the Communists in the UN while it recognized the Nationalists, but would also refrain from using the veto and would accept the majority decision of the UN.

"Unleashing" Chiang. President Eisenhower, Feb. 2, 1953, in his first State of the Union address, announced that he was issuing instructions that "the 7th Fleet was no longer employed to shield Communist China." Despite this so-called "unleashing" of Chiang's forces, the President was reported to have privately discouraged offensive actions and to have regarded the announcement as a means of putting pressure on the Chinese Communists to negotiate seriously in the Korean War armistice talks. The Chinese Nationalists followed the President's announcement by heavily fortifying several small islands located a few miles off the mainland and still in their hands—Quemoy, Matsu and the Tachens. A truce ending the Korean fighting was signed July 27, 1953, in Panmunjom, Korea.

Formosa Straits Crises. During the summer of 1954, the Chinese Communists stepped up military pressure on Quemoy, Matsu and the Tachens in retaliation for the negotiation of the U.S.-sponsored Southeast Asia Collective Defense Treaty (SEATO), signed in Manila Sept. 8. Secretary of State John Foster Dulles confirmed Sept. 4 in Manila that the U.S. Seventh Fleet had again been ordered to protect Formosa from a Communist Chinese invasion.

To underscore its support of the Formosa regime, the United States Dec. 2 signed a mutual security pact with the Republic of China. In Peking, Premier Chou En-lai called the treaty a "grave, warlike provocation" and renewed a pledge to "liberate" Formosa.

The dispatch of the Seventh Fleet to the Formosa strait had the effect of "releasing" Chiang. This was formalized in an exchange of notes between Secretary Dulles and Nationalist Foreign Minister George Yeh, which accompanied the treaty. The notes committed Chiang not to attack the mainland. *(Treaty text, p. 28)*

On Jan. 18, 1955, Chinese Communists invaded the offshore island of Ichiang, 210 miles north of Formosa,

_____
* *Truman, Harry S, Memoirs by Harry S Truman, Vol. II, Doubleday & Co., 1956, p. 342 ff.*

and launched a massive bombardment of the Tache islands, eight miles from Ichiang. With a Communist invasion of the Tachens appearing imminent, President Eisenhower, in a special message Jan. 24 to Congress, asked for explicit authority to use American armed forces to protect Formosa, the adjoining Pescadores islands and "related positions and territories."

The President's request received prompt action in Congress. The House Jan. 25 and the Senate Jan. 28 passed by overwhelming majorities H J Res 159 authorizing the President to "employ the armed forces of the United States as he deems necessary" to defend Formosa. The Senate then approved ratification of the U.S.-Nationalist China Mutual Defense Treaty Feb. 9. The Senate acted as the Seventh Fleet helped the Chinese Nationalists to evacuate some 17,000 civilians and 25,000 troops from the Tachen islands. The move was completed without interference from the Communists, who later took over the island. *(Resolution text, next page)*

In August 1958, the Chinese Communists resumed military operations against the Nationalist-held offshore islands, concentrating heavy artillery barrages against Quemoy. As in 1954, tensions mounted rapidly, buoyed by speculation that the Communists were preparing an invasion and that the United States was poised for massive intervention. Through September and October both sides mounted major propaganda campaigns. Soviet Premier Nikita Khrushchev declared Moscow's solidarity with Peking, while President Eisenhower and Secretary Dulles alternated pledges of "no retreat" with pleas for a cease-fire.

Dulles flew to Taiwan Oct. 20 for talks with Chiang. A joint statement by Chiang and Dulles issued Oct. 23 stated that return to the mainland was still Chiang's sacred mission, but the principal means of accomplishing that mission was "not the use of force." The United States and the Nationalists reaffirmed the 1954 treaty and "recognized that under present conditions the defense of the Quemoys together with the Matsus is closely related to the defense of Taiwan and the Pescadores islands." Dulles, in a film interview released by the State Department Oct. 23, said the United States "was not going to attack or tolerate attacks against the Chinese Communists," but that the U.S. government would "stand firm" to resist any Chinese Communist attacks. During Dulles' stay in Taiwan, he reportedly persuaded Chiang to reduce his forces deployed on the offshore islands by one-third. After the Nationalists did cut back their forces on the islands, the Communists soon scaled down their artillery bombardments to an every-other-day affair of no military significance. Since 1959, there has been little tension in the Taiwan strait, and the Communists have ceased bombardment of the offshore islands.

In the 1960s, the U.S. Seventh Fleet presence in the Taiwan strait was reduced to a two-destroyer patrol which was terminated in November 1969.

The end of tension in the Taiwan strait did not diminish the U.S. commitment to Chiang. Under the mutual defense treaty, reinforced by the congressional resolution on Formosa, the United States initiated a massive program of military and economic assistance to Taiwan. In addition, the U.S. military built up its forces on Taiwan, especially with the rise of U.S. involvement in Vietnam. Taiwan became a supply, staging and training area for certain U.S. units used in Vietnam.

Mutual Defense Treaty

The United States and the Republic of China signed a mutual defense treaty Dec. 2, 1954. The Senate approved ratification of the treaty Feb. 9, 1955, by a 65-6 roll-call vote.

In an exchange of notes, signed Dec. 10, 1954, the government of the Republic of China gave a formal undertaking to the United States that its forces would not attack the Chinese mainland without prior consultation with the United States. The Senate Foreign Relations Committee in reporting the treaty Feb. 8, 1955, stated its understanding that the terms of the treaty "apply only in the event of external armed attack, and that military operations by either party from the territories held by the Republic of China shall not be undertaken except by joint agreement."

The following articles contain the treaty provisions regarding the use of armed force:

Art. 2. In order more effectively to achieve the objective of this treaty, the parties separately and jointly, by self-help and mutual aid, will maintain and develop their individual and collective capacity to resist armed attack and Communist subversive activities directed from without against their territorial integrity and political stability.

Art. 5. Each party recognizes that an armed attack in the West Pacific area directed against the territories of either of the parties would be dangerous to its own peace and safety, and declares that it would act to meet the common danger in accordance with its constitutional processes. Any such armed attack, and all measures taken as a result thereof, shall be immediately reported to the UN Security Council. Such measures shall be terminated when the Security Council has taken the measures necessary to restore and maintain international peace and security.

Art. 6. For the purposes of Articles 2 and 5, the terms 'territorial' and 'territories' shall mean, in respect of the Republic of China, Taiwan (Formosa) and the Pescadores; and in respect of the United States, the island territories in the West Pacific under its jurisdiction. The provisions of Articles 2 and 5 will be applicable to such other territories as may be determined by mutual agreement.

U.S. Presence and Aid

The nature and extent of U.S. commitments to Taiwan was the subject of an investigation by the Senate Foreign Relations Subcommittee on U.S. Military Agreements and Commitments Abroad. The subcommittee was chaired by Senator Stuart Symington (D Mo.).

The subcommittee released a 200-page, heavily censored transcript of the Taiwan hearings in July 1970. The document covered four days of testimony by U.S. diplomats and military officials in November 1969 and May 1970.

Information provided by the subcommittee's hearings demonstrated that U.S. policy toward Nationalist China was in a period of transition, marked by several

1955 Formosa Resolution

The joint resolution (H J Res 159, S J Res 28), authorizing the President's use of armed force to defend Formosa and the Pescadores islands, cleared the House Jan. 25, 1955, by a 410-3 roll-call vote and the Senate Jan. 28, 1953, by an 85-3 roll-call vote. The following is the full text:

"Whereas the primary purpose of the United States, in its relations with all other nations, is to develop and sustain a just and enduring peace for all; and

"Whereas certain territories in the West Pacific under the jurisdiction of the Republic of China are now under armed attack, and threats and declarations have been made and are being made by the Chinese Communists that such armed attack is in aid of and in preparation for armed attack on Formosa and the Pescadores; and

"Whereas such armed attack if continued would gravely endanger the peace and security of the West Pacific area and particularly of Formosa and the Pescadores; and

"Whereas the secure possession by friendly governments of the western Pacific island chain, of which Formosa is a part, is essential to the vital interests of the United States and all friendly nations in or bordering upon the Pacific Ocean; and

"Whereas the President of the United States on Jan. 6, 1955, submitted to the Senate for its advice and consent to ratification a mutual defense treaty between the United States of America and the Republic of China, which recognizes that an armed attack in the west Pacific area directed against territories therein described in the region of Formosa and the Pescadores, would be dangerous to the peace and safety of the parties to the treaty: Therefore be it

"Resolved, (etc.,) That the President of the United States be and he hereby is authorized to employ the armed forces of the United States as he deems necessary for the specific purpose of securing and protecting Formosa and the Pescadores against armed attack, this authority to include the securing and protection of such related positions and territories of that area now in friendly hands and the taking of such other measures as he judges to be required or appropriate in assuring the defense of Formosa and the Pescadores.

"This resolution shall expire when the President shall determine that the peace and security of the area is reasonably assured by international conditions, created by action of the United Nations or otherwise, and shall so report to Congress."

apparent inconsistencies. For example, although U.S. military and economic assistance was being phased out, there seemed to be a possibility that the U.S. commitment to Taiwan might be indirectly upgraded by the relocation of U.S. military facilities from other locations in Asia to Taiwan. And although the Nixon Administration had stated its intention of trying to improve relations with Peking, both the United States and Taiwan were simultaneously engaging in activities which could appear provocative to the Communist mainland regime.

Principal Administration witnesses were Walter P. McConaughy, U.S. ambassador to Taiwan (since mid-1966); Vice Adm. John L. Chew, commander, U.S. Taiwan Defense Command; Thomas P. Shoesmith, country director, Republic of China, Department of State; Col. Roy L. Tweedie, vice commander of the 327th Air Division on Taiwan; Peter Knaur, Office of the Assistant Secretary of Defense for International Security Affairs; and Maj. Gen. Richard G. Ciccolella, chief of staff, First U.S. Army, and former chief of the Military Assistance Advisory Group (MAAG), Taiwan.

Activities Questioned. Three activities in particular were subjected to close scrutiny by subcommittee members and staff counsel Roland A. Paul, who conducted much of the questioning. To several members of the subcommittee, these disclosures seemed inconsistent with the Nixon policy of trying to relax tensions with Peking and to avoid new commitments.

● Testimony revealed that the Nationalist government was extending the runways of two airfields to make them capable of handling U.S. B-52s. Administration witnesses indicated that the Nationalists hoped that some U.S. military operations and facilities—including nuclear-armed B-52s—would be shifted from Okinawa to Taiwan, thereby strengthening the U.S. commitment. *(Nixon decision not to relocate nuclear weapons to Taiwan, p. 32)*

However, the runway extension—which began in 1968—had not been discussed among officials of the two governments, nor had American officials sought to question the Nationalist government when the runway expansion was brought to their attention. Although witnesses said they felt it was improper to question the Taiwan government because no U.S. funds were involved, they admitted that the construction activity as well as the hypothetical relocation of B-52s could appear provocative to the Communist Chinese.

Witnesses emphasized that the United States had not encouraged the project, nor was it likely that the B-52s would be transferred from Okinawa to Taiwan. But they offered little explanation as to why the Nationalist government would spend $30 million of its own money on the runway construction.

● The hearings disclosed that the Nationalist Chinese were conducting significantly more small-scale military raids against the mainland than Peking was conducting against Taiwan. These raids were carried out without the prior knowledge of U.S. officials and despite the State Department's view (reiterated during the hearings) that they might provoke an unfortunate Communist Chinese reaction and "really should be avoided."

● Questions were also raised about a joint U.S.-Taiwan military exercise, known as "Forward Thrust," which had been conducted on Taiwan annually for 10 years and involved special forces being airdropped behind "enemy" lines to join "insurgent" forces and link up with the conventional force landing by sea. About 500 U.S. personnel participated, providing advisers and some aircraft. During the hearing, witnesses insisted that the operation was purely defensive, although Paul said that in advance of the hearings he had been informed by U.S. officers in Taiwan that the purpose of "Forward Thrust" was to practice "offensive tactics" against the mainland.

Policymaking Process. The hearings revealed what some subcommittee members considered to be striking problems of policymaking and information flow. For example, the chief of MAAG on Taiwan said he did not know whether nuclear weapons were stationed on the island.

The U.S. ambassador was unable to tell the subcommittee approximately how many persons had been killed or imprisoned on Taiwan for antigovernment activities, nor could he estimate the current number of political prisoners. To this Symington replied:

"I must say it astonishes me that you have no idea of any kind whatever how many political prisoners they have, which is always a good way to know to what extent the general mass of the people support their government. We put out a lot of words when it comes to why we support countries. The right of self-government is a term that recently has cost us many thousand young Americans." (The information on political prisoners was subsequently supplied, but was classified and deleted by the State Department from the published record.)

Treaty Commitment Questioned. Asked during the hearings why national interest required the United States to stand by the mutual defense treaty, McConaughy replied that the considerations of 1954 remained relevant. Taiwan, he said, is an "anchor point in the offshore island chain. If it were in unfriendly hands, I think the security, particularly of the nearest areas, the Philippines to the south and Okinawa and Japan to the north, would be vitally compromised. I also believe that we have an obligation to maintain the liberty of 14 million freedom-loving people there.... I think of the Republic of China as a big plus in a situation where we have a peculiar disequilibrium."

It was later brought out that, while the status of Taiwan might be vital to the security of neighboring countries, the United States was the only country in the world committed to defend Nationalist China. The treaty provides for termination on one year's notice by either party.

U.S. Military Presence. Of the over 9,000 U.S. military personnel stationed in Taiwan in 1969, 6,000 were located at Ching Chuan Kang (CCK) Air Force Base in central Taiwan, providing logistical support for the Vietnam war. Prior to the Tonkin Gulf incident in August 1964, there were 3,700 U.S. military personnel on Taiwan, including 1,127 associated with the Taiwan Defense Command and Military Assistance Advisory Group. During the subcommittee hearing, Col. Tweedie said the post-Vietnam force level on Taiwan was still at the planning stage; however, there were strong indications that the number of U.S. military personnel on Taiwan would be significantly reduced as the U.S. role in Vietnam was scaled down. *(Nixon cutbacks, p. 32)*

The Taiwan Defense Command (TDC) was established in 1955 directly under the U.S. Commander in Chief, Pacific. It has the primary mission of planning the defense of Taiwan, the Pescadores and the offshore islands. All TDC personnel are located in the Taipei area. As of July 1969, 63 officers and 121 enlisted men were part of the TDC. Operating costs in fiscal 1969 were $2 million.

The Military Assistance Advisory Group (MAAG) was established on Taiwan in 1951. MAAG personnel are stationed in 11 locations throughout Taiwan as well as on Quemoy and Matsu. Total MAAG personnel in 1967 numbered 727; in 1969, MAAG strength was reduced to 487. Operating costs were 8.7 million in fiscal 1969.

The major U.S. operating force on Taiwan is the 327th Air Division, which is subordinate to the Thirteenth Air Force, located at Clark Air Base in the Philippines.

CCK is the principal U.S. air base on Taiwan. It was constructed in 1957 and upgraded in 1966 at a cost of $22.7 million to provide additional facilities for Vietnam support units (the new construction was built to last five years). The 314th Tactical Airlift Wing is the primary organization at CCK and is authorized 64 C-130E aircraft. The 4220th Air Refueling Squadron is also located at CCK, with a primary mission of refueling B-52s (the KC-135 tankers to refuel the B-52s arrived in January 1968).

U.S. Withdrawal. There is no restriction on the U.S. right to withdraw personnel from Taiwan, McConaughy said, other than the general treaty statement, which requires consultation regarding the transfer of the resources of either party to which the other had made a contribution. Asked whether the Nationalists would be concerned if the United States withdrew some forces, the ambassador said a substantial withdrawal "would give them some concern."

Concerning the presence of the U.S. Seventh Fleet in the Taiwan straits (which was represented by only a token unit), McConaughy said there was no formal commitment with Taiwan to continue the patrol. "I think they know that in the present situation we do not envisage the withdrawal of the Seventh Fleet from that general area, but we are not committed to keep it where it is."

The ambassador said he thought the Chinese Communists did not feel threatened by the Seventh Fleet. Both Symington and Fulbright questioned this view, the latter quoting from McConaughy's prepared statement: "Any U.S. military presence or military related activity on Taiwan is viewed by the Chinese Communists with especial hostility."

U.S. Assistance. U.S. economic and military assistance to Taiwan has declined substantially in recent years, and both programs were gradually being phased out, said McConaughy. Between 1946 and 1970, Nationalist China received a total of $5.27-billion in U.S. aid. Economic assistance between 1946 and 1970 was $2.36-billion. Taiwan has received no Agency for International Development funds since 1963 but has continued to receive assistance under other programs. In fiscal 1969 Taiwan received a $9.5-million loan from the Export-Import Bank and in 1970 a $72.2-million loan from the bank. Military assistance, including grants, credit sales and excess stocks, totaled $87-million in 1969 and $96-million in 1970.

Taiwan Independence

While it is clear that the future of the U.S. commitment to Nationalist China will depend on such factors as the success of Mr. Nixon's new policy toward Peking, post-Vietnam U.S. military planning and U.S. defense arrangements with other nations in Asia, it is also apparent that U.S.-Nationalist Chinese relations will be influenced by future domestic politics on Taiwan itself. The key question is what kind of government will succeed the one-man rule of 84-year-old Chiang Kai-shek. Of the country's population of 14 million persons, 84 percent are

Formosa's Future

Following are excerpts from an article, "Formosa's Future," by Peng Ming-min published in *The New York Times* Oct. 27, 1971, two days after the UN vote seating Peking and ousting Taipei. Peng, jailed in 1964 for his opposition to Chiang Kai-shek, has been described by Chou En-lai as a leader of the Taiwan Independence Movement. He is now a research scholar at the University of Michigan. *(Box p. 32)*

"...now as world leaders finally admit the absurdities of the Nationalist Chinese fantasies, a new myth emerges: that Formosa has been and must be an integral part of China, and that in order for China to achieve full sovereignty she must annex Formosa.

"...Native Formosans are of Chinese extraction, but have shared centuries of experience unique to them and have developed their own identity.

"Any settlement of the sovereignty over Formosa must come through peaceful negotiations in which the people of Formosa are fully and effectively represented. No one outside may dictate to Formosans to whom they should belong. Neither Peking nor Washington can speak for them. The present regime in Taipei never has spoken legitimately for the majority on Formosa. It cannot do so unless it undergoes a basic structural change and the Formosan majority is represented effectively at every level."

native Taiwanese. Political power, however, has remained vested almost exclusively with the two million mainland followers of Chiang. Increased political participation by native Taiwanese (who do not share the Nationalists' desire to regain the mainland) could have a major influence on Washington-Taipei-Peking relations. An outlawed Taiwanese movement seeks an independent Taiwan.

Background. Following the Japanese surrender in August 1945 in World War II, the Chinese Nationalists under Chiang Kai-shek took control of Taiwan after 50 years of Japanese control and incorporated it as a province into the Republic of China under a constitution adopted in December 1946 in Nanking.

The Taiwanese did not take readily to rule by the mainlanders. In 1947, there was an uprising against the Nationalists by the native Taiwanese. Some 10,000-20,000 Taiwanese were killed in the fighting which ended with the firm establishment of the Nationalist rule.

In 1948-49, as it became clear that the Nationalists were losing the civil war on the mainland to the Communists, the Nationalists withdrew to Taiwan. This brought two million mainland Chinese (including Chiang's 600,000-man army) to Taiwan.

Chiang's Republic of China is based almost entirely on his mainland Chinese followers who fled to Taiwan in 1948-49. Under the Nanking constitution, Taiwan remains a province of the Republic of China. The constitution provides for an all-China National Assembly which was initially elected on the mainland before the 1948-49 emigration. The assembly came to Taiwan in 1948, and in 1949 Taipei was designated as the "temporary capital" of China. This meant that the Republic of China government became superimposed on the provincial Taiwan

government. Mainlanders have been appointed to fill vacancies in the assembly. President Chiang, re-elected by the assembly in March 1966 to his fourth six-year term as president, appoints the provincial governor of Taiwan.

In an April 1971 interview on CBS television, Chiang reiterated his belief that the Nationalists would recover the mainland: "I have full confidence that the Chinese mainland shall and will be recovered. My confidence has never wavered a bit." It has been suggested by the U.S. ambassador to Taiwan that one reason the Nationalists continue to assert that they will return to the mainland is that their claim to rule all of China legitimates their rule over the Taiwanese majority on Taiwan. Ambassador McConaughy told the Senate Foreign Relations Subcommittee in November 1969 that "legitimacy of the perpetuation of the mainlander rule (of Taiwan) is sought by the continued espousal of mainland recovery."

Opposition. During a 10-day visit to the United States in April 1970, Chiang Kai-shek's son and heir apparent, Deputy Premier Chiang Ching-kuo narrowly escaped assassination when he was fired upon in New York April 24 by a Peter Huang, a member of the World United Formosans for Independence. Huang and Tzu-tai Cheng, executive secretary of the organization, were taken into custody and indicted. Trong R. Chai, president of the organization, denied that the group had plotted the shooting but said the attempted assassination would "give great encouragement to all the Taiwanese people." Huang and Tzu-tai were convicted in May 1971 and were scheduled to be sentenced July 9. Released on bail, they did not appear July 9. Their attorney denied knowledge of their whereabouts and suggested that Chinese Nationalist secret police might have abducted and killed them.

Peng Ming-min, described by Chou En-lai as a leading figure in the independence movement, fled Taiwan in January 1970, was granted political asylum in Sweden and then in September 1970 was issued a U.S. visa to teach at the University of Michigan. Peng had been sentenced in 1964 for allegedly attempting to overthrow the government of the Republic of China. He was released 13 months later. *(Box p. 32)*

In an article published Oct. 27 in *The New York Times*, two days after the UN vote expelling the Republic of China, Peng outlined his views for an independent "Formosa"; he did not use the Chinese word "Taiwan" in referring to the island. *(Box this page)*

The Republic of China's expulsion from the UN, according to initial reports from Taipei, may well encourage those forces on the island who oppose the Nationalists and seek a more representative government. In an apparent move to ensure the loyalties of the Taiwanese, the Nationalists' central committee announced Oct. 29 that the "central parliamentary organization should be further strengthened...so as to increase their power to supervise the government as representatives of the people." Nationalist Premier C. K. Yen confirmed that the regime had been studying ways to broaden its popular base.

American Involvement? In March 1971, the Nationalists expelled an American missionary reportedly because of his relations with Taiwanese opposed to the Nationalist government. In May 1971, according to *The New York Times* and other press reports, the U.S. military command in Taiwan transferred five military and civilian aides from Taiwan following Nationalist charges that the aides had assisted the outlawed Taiwan independence movement. According to the press reports, the aides were two Army men, two naval officers and a civilian employee of the U.S. Army Technical Group, a Central Intelligence Agency cover.

Peking Reaction. The Chinese Communists oppose the Taiwan independence movement. They agree with the Nationalists that Taiwan is and should remain a province of China. They are especially concerned that the independence movement might obtain aid from either the United States or Japan. In his interview with *New York Times* columnist James Reston, which appeared in the *Times* August 10, 1971, Premier Chou En-lai said: "Japan has ambitious designs with regard to Taiwan. ...it's even conceivable that they are trying to separate Taiwan from China, and, under the direction of Japan and also possibly with support from some quarters in the United States, to bring about a so-called independent Taiwan." *(Box this page)*

Michigan University Professor Allen S. Whiting, a China expert, told the Joint Economic Committee August 11, 1971, that the Chinese Nationalists and Communists "suspect that the escape of Professor Peng Ming-min in early 1970 was a ploy by U.S. or Japanese intelligence, or both." The Communists, he said, regard Peng and the independence movement "as instruments of a foreign power. Nor are these suspicions incredible. Our (U.S.) military and intelligence investment in Taiwan convinces all observers, whether in Taipei, Peking or Tokyo, that this is seen as an important asset which must be retained by whatever means, whether directly in U.S. hands or through allied control."

Nixon Administration Policy

The Nixon Administration has taken a number of military and diplomatic actions which have diminished the U.S. commitment to the Republic of China.

Military Cutbacks. The Administration has taken four steps to reduce the U.S. military presence on Taiwan:

• In November 1969, the two-destroyer (Seventh Fleet) patrol of the Taiwan strait was quietly terminated. This action which had long been regarded as a necessary "signal" to Peking that Washington sought improved relations led to the resumption of U.S.-Communist Chinese talks in Warsaw in January 1970.

• The number of U.S. forces on Taiwan has been cut from its 1969 high of over 9,000 to a level of about 8,000. Of the remaining 8,000, 6,000 are directly related to the Vietnam war serving in repair and supply functions at the Ching Chuan Kang Air Base. While there has been no change in the number of men at the air base, it is expected that continued reduction of the U.S. role in the Vietnam war would lead to a further cutback at the air base.

• The Administration has decided not to relocate nuclear weapons stationed in Okinawa to Taiwan after Okinawa reverts to Japanese control under the treaty signed June 17, 1971. Although there had been considerable speculation that the atomic weapons would be moved to South Korea, the Philippines or Taiwan, the White House disclosed July 19 that U.S. nuclear weapons removed from Okinawa would not go to any of these three countries. The White House said the decision not to

---

Chou on Taiwan Independence

Premier Chou En-lai made the following statement July 28, 1971, in remarks to a visiting group of American graduate students in Peking:

"We are resolutely opposed to the so-called 'Taiwan Independence Movement' because the people in Taiwan are Chinese.

"...the 'Taiwan Independence Movement' is not a native movement in itself. It is a special movement which has behind it the special manipulation from foreign forces. One of their leaders is Peng Ming-min, who was originally a student at Harvard, who then went back to Taiwan to become a professor and now is also back in the United States. There are also some elements of them in Japan. They are supported by the Japanese government." *(Box p. 31)*

---

move the weapons closer to mainland China was part of its policy of improving relations with Peking. Unstated was another key aspect of the action: a decision not to upgrade the importance of the commitment to Taiwan.

The Okinawa reversion treaty, which Mr. Nixon sent to the Senate in late September 1971, had another aspect of which the Nationalists disapproved. The treaty returned to Japanese administration the Senkaku islands lying about 150 miles northeast of Taiwan. Nationalist China and Communist China claim sovereignty over the islands where oil was discovered in 1969. Nationalist Chinese Foreign Minister Chow Shu-kai called transferring the islands to Japan "absolutely inadmissible." *(Map, p. 27)*

• The Administration announced July 28, 1971, suspension of U.S. air intelligence missions from Taiwan over mainland China by manned SR-71 reconnaissance planes and unmanned drones. U.S. officials in Washington said the decision was aimed at preventing any incident which might mar President Nixon's scheduled trip to China and was in accord with Mr. Nixon's July 15 announcement that neither the United States nor China would "knowingly do something that would undermine the prospects of something that it took so long to prepare and that it took such painful decisions to reach." The officials said that the Chinese Communists had sufficiently good radar to distinguish between an overflight by U.S. aircraft or the kind flown by the Chinese Nationalists.

Congressional Hearings. Two Senators—Jacob K. Javits (R N.Y.) and George McGovern (D S.D.)—called for withdrawal of all U.S. forces from Taiwan in testimony before the Senate Foreign Relations Committee in June 1971. China experts and defense analysts who testified before the committee said that the Nationalists were well-equipped to repulse any Communist attack even if U.S. military support were withdrawn. Whiting testified that mainland China "has never developed the necessary air and sea lift capacity to mount an invasion across the more than one hundred miles of ocean which separate Taiwan from the mainland." It was also unlikely, he said, that the Communists would mount an offensive against Taiwan as long as they were confronted with a Soviet military buildup on their northern frontier.

Treaty Commitment. The Nixon Administration has stated that U.S. defense obligations to defend Taiwan have been unaffected by the new policy towards Peking. In a letter in May 1971 to the Senate Foreign Relations Committee, the State Department said that the U.S defense commitment to Taiwan "was set forth in our Mutual Defense Treaty..." and that U.S. obligations under the treaty were still in force. After Mr. Nixon announced July 15 his invitation to visit mainland China, the Nationalist Chinese government disclosed that Mr. Nixon had written a letter to President Chiang assuring him that U.S. commitments under the treaty remained firm.

Formosa Resolution Repeal. The State Department letter was written in response to a query from Chairman J. W. Fulbright (D Ark.) concerning S J Res 48, a resolution calling for repeal of the 1955 joint resolution authorizing the President's use of U.S. armed forces to defend Formosa. Assistant Secretary David M. Abshire said that the Administration took no position on S J Res 48, since it "believe(d) that the specific crisis situation to which the Formosa Resolution was directed has passed."

The committee Sept. 21 reported S J Res 48 (S Rept 92-363), sponsored by Senators Frank Church (D Idaho) and Charles McC. Mathias (R Md.). The resolution, which would have the force of law, would withdraw authority granted to the President in 1955 to use armed force to protect Formosa and the Pescadores from attack. The committee attached S J Res 48 to the fiscal 1972 foreign aid authorization (HR 9910) when it reported the aid bill Oct. 20 (S Rept 92-404). Debate on the foreign aid bill began Oct. 26, the day after the UN General Assembly had voted to expel Nationalist China and seat the Peking government. The debate took place in an emotional atmosphere charged by the Taiwan expulsion which contributed to general disillusionment with the foreign aid program. The Senate Oct. 29 by a 27-41 roll-call vote killed the foreign aid bill. Earlier in the debate, the Senate voted Oct. 28 by a 43-40 roll-call vote to delete from HR 9910 the provision repealing the 1955 Formosa Resolution.

Aides to Senators Church and Mathias said the Formosa Resolution repealer came up at a poor time immediately after the UN vote. They said the Senators would seek action on S J Res 48 at a later date.

Diplomatic Moves. The Administration has made two major diplomatic initiatives concerning Nationalist China:

• It supported the seating of Communist China in the United Nations, thereby reversing 20 years of opposition to representation of the Peking regime.

• It has sought to normalize relations with Peking in a series of moves which will be climaxed by President Nixon's forthcoming trip to mainland China. Both these actions drew sharp criticism from Taipei. On July 15, 1971, when President Nixon announced his invitation to visit China, Nationalist Chinese Premier C. K. Yen said that the United States had been "deceived by the Chinese Communists." Yen said that improved U.S. relations with Communist China "could lead to a tragedy far more serious than that involved in the fall of the Chinese mainland" in 1949. Taipei, said Yen, remained firm in its "faith and determination to recover the Chinese mainland and to resist any external adverse tide."

On August 2, when Secretary of State William P. Rogers announced that the United States favored admission of Communist China to the United Nations but would oppose efforts to expel Nationalist China, Taipei criticized the statement. The Nationalist foreign ministry asked UN member states to uphold its "unquestionable" right to membership in the UN. The ministry warned that the UN "would surely be confronted with the ever-increasing danger of infiltration, subversion and eventual destruction."

The Administration's efforts to retain UN membership for the Republic of China failed Oct. 25 as the UN General Assembly adopted the Albanian resolution to seat Peking and expel Taipei. Many observers said the presence in Peking of presidential assistant Henry A. Kissinger during the UN debate on the China question contributed to the defeat of U.S. effort to keep Taiwan in the world body.

In Taipei, Chiang denounced the UN vote as an "illegal action." "The government of the Republic of China," he declared, "is the true representative of the 700 million Chinese on the mainland."

A major concern in Taipei is that the UN expulsion followed by Mr. Nixon's trip to mainland China will induce a number of countries to cut diplomatic relations with Taiwan and open diplomatic relations with mainland China. Eleven countries have cut relations with Taipei and exchanged ambassadors with Peking in 1971. Sixty-one nations recognize the Peoples Republic of China and 58 recognize the Republic of China. No country has ever maintained diplomatic relations with both China's simultaneously.

Nixon Objectives. The Administration has stopped short of saying it seeks diplomatic ties with Peking. Mr. Nixon has formulated his objectives in more general terms. In announcing July 15 his planned trip to China, he said the "meeting between the leaders of China and the United States is to seek the normalization of relations between the two countries...." In an allusion to the U.S. commitment to the Republic of China, he said: "Our action in seeking a new relationship with the People's Republic of China will not be at the expense of old friends."

It is too early to say whether Mr. Nixon will be able to achieve normalization without diplomatic relations and without further weakening the U.S. tie to the Republic of China. Premier Chou En-lai said July 19 that if diplomatic relations are to be established between Washington and Peking, the government of the People's Republic must be recognized as "the sole legitimate government representing the Chinese people." In addition, Chou insisted that Taiwan be recognized as "an inalienable part of China's territory."

The China analysts who testified before the Senate Foreign Relations Committee in June generally agreed that a further improvement of U.S. relations with the People's Republic of China could only occur at the expense of the Republic of China. Jerome Alan Cohen, Harvard University, said Peking would only negotiate seriously with Washington "if we are prepared to negotiate withdrawal of recognition from Taipei and its conferral upon Peking." Whiting said the "Chinese are unlikely to feel an improvement of relations (with the United States) is so urgently necessary as to abandon... their claim to Taiwan."

U.S. ALLIES ADJUST TO NIXON DOCTRINE, CHINA POLICY

On July 25, 1969, in Guam, the first step on a four-country Asian trip, President Nixon provided the press with a background briefing describing what was to become America's new foreign policy for Asia: money and arms, not men, to help Asian nations become militarily self-sufficient.

The information was amplified at each stop as the President spoke with leaders in the Philippines, Indonesia, Thailand and South Vietnam, and stressed a new stance of self-reliance for the 1970s. It become known as the Nixon Doctrine.

Asian Reappraisal. The doctrine paralleled the Administration's efforts to improve relations with mainland China. The Chinese leaders had long insisted that any improvement of relations with the United States required a reduced American military presence in Asia. And American Presidents since Harry S Truman had insisted that a large U.S. presence in Asia was required to contain an aggressive mainland China. It was perhaps inevitable, therefore, that when President Nixon made the decision to reduce the U.S. presence in Asia, he also began to describe the Chinese in markedly less belligerent terms and sought to normalize relations with Peking.

The new policy from Washington has caused policy readjustments in every nation lying on the fringe of China. South Korea, Japan, Taiwan, the Philippines, South Vietnam and Thailand had based their foreign policies for two decades (1950-1970) on the assumption that the United States and mainland China would be hostile opponents. They are all tied by extensive defense arrangements to the United States. Each of these countries, therefore, has been required to reappraise its foreign policy in the context of Mr. Nixon's approach to Peking.

Nixon Doctrine

The President said in Guam that Communism no longer offered the same appeal to developing nations as it did even 10 years earlier and that a tremendous growth of nationalism and regional pride had signaled a period in which Asia must be for the Asians. He said the United States could not dictate policies for Asian development or defense.

But, the President did say that Communist China, North Vietnam and North Korea maintained aggressive and belligerent attitudes that threatened the peace of the world. And, the greatest threat to world peace, he said, would come from the Pacific.

The policies contained in the Nixon Doctrine became key points in the President's message Feb. 18, 1970, on U.S. foreign policy for the coming era and again on Feb. 25, 1971, in his second foreign policy report to Congress.

The new formula for peace was presented by the Administration as a milestone in American foreign policy —a new approach to foreign policy to match a new era of international relations. The President announced in 1970 its elements as:

"First, the United States will keep all of its treaty commitments.

"Second, we shall provide a shield if a nuclear power threatens the freedom of a nation allied with us or of a nation whose survival we consider vital to our security.

"Third, in cases involving other types of aggression we shall furnish military and economic assistance when requested in accordance with our treaty commitments. But we shall look to the nation directly threatened to assume the primary responsibility of providing the manpower for its defense."

The President stressed that the Nixon Doctrine sought to reflect the need for continuity as well as the mandate for change.

On June 26, 1970, Dr. Henry A. Kissinger, assistant to the President for national security affairs, said that the United States could no longer physically or psychologically define or resist aggression at every point in the world.

The tangible expression of the new partnership, the President said, was to be greater material contributions by other countries.

The Doctrine and East Asia

In his second foreign policy report to Congress on Feb. 25, 1970, Mr. Nixon detailed his plans for U.S. relations with East Asia and the Pacific and said the area was "at the heart of the task of creating a stable structure of world peace."

He said the United States would strive to establish a structure composed of the renewed vigor of smaller Asian states, the expanding role of Japan, and the changing interests of the Soviet Union and the Peoples Republic of China.

Japan. The Nixon Doctrine's goal in U.S. policy toward Japan was to maintain the spirit of cooperation and good will had existed since World War II.

China. The U.S. policy would be to establish a dialogue with Peking—but not at the expense of Asian allies nor U.S. treaty commitments in the area.

Indochina. The Nixon Doctrine would "seek the opportunity for the South Vietnamese people to determine their own political future without outside interference..." and support the continued withdrawal of American troops.

A negotiated settlement for all Indochina remained the Administration's highest priority—but, the President said, if that were not possible, then the United States would follow the alternate route to peace—phasing out

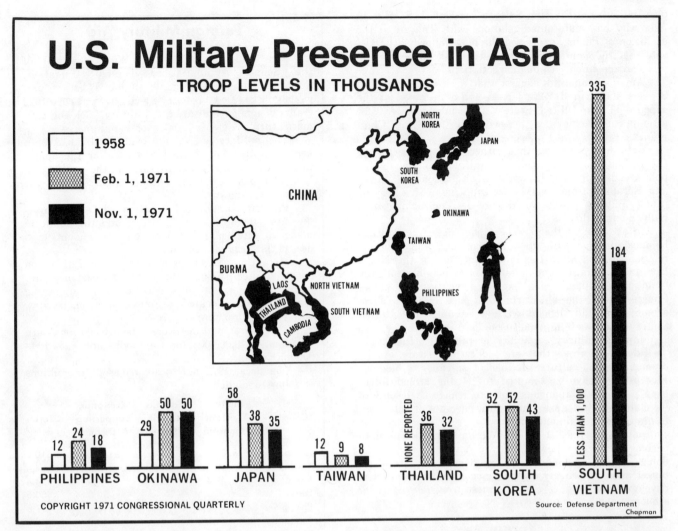

U.S. Military Presence in Asia
TROOP LEVELS IN THOUSANDS

1958

Feb. 1, 1971

Nov. 1, 1971

PHILIPPINES	OKINAWA	JAPAN	TAIWAN	THAILAND	SOUTH KOREA	SOUTH VIETNAM
12 24 18	29 50 50	58 38 35	12 9 8	NONE REPORTED 36 32	52 52 43	LESS THAN 1,000 335 184

COPYRIGHT 1971 CONGRESSIONAL QUARTERLY

Source: Defense Department
Chapman

U.S. involvement while giving the region's friendly countries the time and the means to defend themselves.

Repercussions. The U.S.-China rapprochement and the curtailing of U.S. military presence in Southeast Asia produced enormous repercussions. It created:

• The necessity for nations in Southeast Asia to individually work out their own accommodations with Communist China.

• An atmosphere in which the existing relationships between the United States and Asian countries could be redefined and reworked.

• A receptive atmosphere in the United Nations for admission of the Peoples Republic of China. China was admitted Oct. 25, 1971.

Asian Reaction. Although Asian leaders have begun to accept the Nixon Doctrine as the emerging reality of U.S. foreign policy in that part of the world, their reception has been diverse and questioning. In every case, however, they have been required to re-examine their China policies.

Japan

Yasuhiro Nakasone, director general of the Japanese Defense Agency, recorded his impression of the Nixon Doctrine during a visit to Washington in September 1970.

"Maybe it is a proper doctrine for the United States," he said, "but from the Asian viewpoint this doctrine, what it tries to achieve is quite clear. But as to the application, we in Asia hope that you would proceed...so that certain severe shocks from the Asian nations can be avoided."

Japanese pride in its growing economic role (now having the third-highest GNP in the world) apparently has been matched by its own wariness regarding how large a military role it will have to assume should the United States seek more thorough disengagement. Although the Japanese government is moving slowly toward rearmament for national security and toward more flexible relations with the People's Republic of China, Japanese officials continue to reiterate the need for a power balance in Asia that would include a sizeable U.S. presence.

Addressing the opening of the Diet's 65th session, Japanese Premier Eisaku Sato Jan. 22, 1971, reiterated his government's desire to improve relations with the People's Republic of China. It was the first time that Sato had referred to the Communist government by its official name. And on Aug. 25, Chinese officials visited Japan for the first time in seven years.

Improved U.S. relations with China and China's entry into the United Nations will have a serious impact on Japan. Premier Sato, a staunch U.S. ally in Asia who has maintained relations with Taiwan to the exclusion of Peking, expressed the hope following the UN vote that the Communist and Nationalist Chinese would reach an agreement "through negotiations."

American analysts suggest that a closer relationship between Japan and Peking need not be attained at the expense of the United States, but could parallel U.S. attempts to achieve a reconciliation with the Communists.

Sato has predicted that rather than China joining the United States and the Soviet Union to provide tri-polar leadership to the world, such nations as Japan and European Common Market countries with economic if not military power would join decision-making in a multi-polar world.

In addition to the serious impact upon the political balance inside Japan, upon its economy, and upon its relations with China, the implementation of the Nixon Doctrine has raised the question of a possible military buildup in Japan. Asian experts have testified before Congress that the objectives and pace of Japan's re-armament would depend on how abruptly the United States withdraws from Asia. *(p. 66-68)*

Japan's military capability at present is limited to "self-defense forces" that are modest in nature. As its economic and cultural influence spreads throughout East Asia, Tokyo is tempted to let the armed forces keep pace. And Japan has come to realize that some of its claims in the East China Sea may put it into con-frontation with mainland China.

Sato said Aug. 31, 1971: "We have the potential to become a military power. But we have no intention of doing do, and the money we would otherwise spend on bigger military budgets will go for economic aid to under-developed nations." *(For Japanese reaction to U.S. economic policy, see p. 59-63)*

Korea

The Koreans have been concerned about the proposed departure of American troops from South Korea. In 1969, Korean President Park Chung Hee was informed of the prospects of removing 20,000 U.S. troops by June 1971 and, perhaps, all American troops by 1975 when the Republic of Korea armed forces had been modernized. A total of 9,000 troops were removed be-tween Feb. 1 and Nov. 1, 1971, leaving 43,000 troops in the country.

Korean leaders have said that the U.S. troop cut-back could augur total military withdrawal and might tempt North Koreans to move southward. A request by Korea for alteration of the Nixon Doctrine, in Seoul's case, was rejected in July 1971.

The United States in fiscal 1970 funneled $150-mil-lion in additional military assistance grants and trans-fers of military equipment amounting to about $120-mil-lion to the South Koreans to help them modernize their army.

Despite the concern of South Koreans, effects of im-proved U.S.-China relations have been felt. Apparently acting under Peking's guidance, the North Koreans have recently switched to a softer line—even to the extent of opening talks with anti-Communist South Korea on the reunion of families separated in 1950-53. Specialists

Foreign Military Aid

Sen. William Proxmire (D Wis.), chairman of the Senate Appropriations Foreign Operations Subcommittee, July 9 made public a list of pre-viously classified country-by-country fiscal 1972 grants of foreign military aid, military sales and esti-mated surplus defense articles for 43 nations.

The military aid figures traditionally had been kept classified for at least a year after the appro-priation was made, Proxmire said, on the ground that U.S. relations with other nations might suffer if the figures were known.

Proxmire described his action as "a long over-due first step in helping Congress and the public to make an intelligent judgment on the amounts and uses of this year's foreign aid."

More than $1.3-billion of the total $2.1-billion to be granted through the military assistance pro-gram, foreign credit sales and economic supporting assistance was allocated to Southeast Asian nations, according to Proxmire's figures.

The largest portions were $565,000,000 for South Vietnam, $310,000,000 for Cambodia and $254,400,-000 for Korea.

The fiscal 1972 aid totals released (in millions of dollars) included:

Country	Military Assistance Program	Foreign Credit Sales	Economic Supporting Assistance	Totals
Cambodia	$200.0	--	$110.0	$310.0
Taiwan	19.5	45.0	--	64.5
Korea	239.4	15.0	--	254.4
Laos	--	--	50.0	50.5
Philippines	17.0	--	10.8	17.8
Thailand	--	--	40.0	40.0
Vietnam	--	--	565.0	565.0

in the United States believe that Peking may be willing to enter into negotiations aimed at winning the with-drawal of the 43,000 U.S. troops stationed in South Korea. This new position could also have an effect on at-tempts to lessen tensions in the Korean peninsula, which has been divided since the end of World War II.

Taiwan

The most important impact of the changes in U.S. foreign policy will occur on Taiwan, the island redoubt of Chiang Kai-shek's Chinese Nationalists, who still claim to represent all China. Their expulsion from the UN is likely to have significant consequences. Chiang's loss of status may inspire elements within his regime to seek to work out some kind of deal with the Communists. American writer Edgar Snow, who spent six months in China in 1971, has reported that Communist and Na-tionalist officials have been secretly in contact for some time. *(Taiwan chapter, p. 26)*

Philippines. Philippine President Ferdinand E. Marcos, who expressed skepticism at renewing relations with Communist China, said on July 19: "I am certain that this alteration and change in the policy of the

United States will mean that every Asian nation and leader must now review the basis for all the agreements between the United States and their respective countries." In 1969, Marcos had said that his government accepted "the urgent need to strive toward a modus vivendi" with Communist China.

Thailand. Foreign Minister Thanat Khoman of Thailand disclosed on May 14, 1971, that Thailand was seeking to improve relations with Communist China through the mediation of an unnamed third country.

Austrailia. Prime Minister William McMahon May 13, 1971, announced a relaxation of restrictions on nonstrategic trade with Communist China as a first step toward establishing normal relations with Peking. One month prior to McMahon's announcement, China had canceled its annual wheat order for political reasons. The order had amounted to 32 percent of all wheat exported by Australia since 1960. The Chinese had decided to buy wheat instead from Canada which recognized the Peking government.

New Zealand. Prime Minister Sir Keith Holyoake said May 13, 1971, that his government would welcome talks with China to improve relations. In June, Holyoake expressed a desire to send a trade and goodwill mission to Peking.

Nixon Doctrine in Congress

It is clear that the Nixon Doctrine and the Administration's new China policy have caused readjustments in the foreign policy of the Asian states lying on the perimeter of China and in some cases have led to misunderstandings in those countries.

It is equally clear that the doctrine—which requires a substantial outlay in foreign aid by the U.S. taxpayer—has led to some readjustments in congressional thinking on foreign assistance. Differences about just what the Nixon Doctrine means about "lowering our overseas presence and direct military involvement" abroad were imbedded in the revolt against foreign aid in the Senate Oct. 29, 1971, when it defeated the foreign aid bill for fiscal 1972.

The Administration fears that the Senate's action could have a profoundly adverse effect on U.S. policy, although in early November it seemed probable that some form of foreign aid bill would clear Congress in 1971.

Critics of the level and structure of the foreign aid proposal say that what the United States needs most is a re-examination of its objectives in the world to bring these goals in line with its resources.

The Nixon Administration insists that that is exactly what it is in the process of doing, through the Nixon Doctrine. The Administration has charged critics of the aid levels with frustrating chances for negotiations and impeding the withdrawal of U.S. troops.

"We would not like to be in a position where we would have to leave overseas men we had intended to bring home," a Defense Department spokesman said in response to the Senate's assault on Administration plans. "We think the substitution of money for U.S. manpower is a policy worth pursuing."

The critics are demanding further clarification of the Nixon Doctrine. But Secretary of State William P. Rogers maintains, in effect, that there is no need for further clarification. Rogers repeated Nov. 2 that the Senate action "will be a damaging blow to the Nixon Doctrine," because:

"The Nixon Doctrine, as you know, provides that we will gradually reduce our troop strength in some of the Asian countries and, at the same time, support them financially and in military ways so they can take up the slack."

Administration officials maintain that the $341-million in military and economic aid for Cambodia, a major part of the controversy resulting in defeat of the foreign aid bill, is a prime example of the operation of the Nixon Doctrine.

If that is what the Nixon Doctrine means, the critics counter—citing an increase in U.S. funds for Cambodia from an original $8.9-million in 1970 to more than $500-million of accumulated costs projected through 1972—they disapprove it.

Questioning the doctrine, Sen. Mark O. Hatfield (R Ore.) said: "I trust that the 'Nixon Doctrine' means something other than supplying the American arms and money, rather than the American lives for the regimes we want to survive."

President Nixon Aug. 31 had invoked executive privilege to avert a suspension of foreign military aid threatened by the Senate Foreign Relations Committee. The committee July 28 voted to cut off military aid funds unless the Administration turned over a five-year plan for military assistance. On Aug. 6 Secretary of Defense Melvin R. Laird said the Pentagon could not comply with the request because "we have no document... which constitute(s) a current five-year plan...." But in a memorandum made public by Laird Aug. 31, the President said that "it would not be in the public interest to provide the Congress the basic planning data on military assistance" requested by the committee.

Criticism

Townsend Hoopes told the Joint Economic Committee in January 1971 that the Nixon Doctrine had become "an instrument for carrying on the cold war by other means" and seemed to be furthering "a policy in which insubstantial fringe states are expected to become the principal agents of containment."

Hoopes, Deputy Assistant Secretary of Defense for military assistance under the Johnson Administration said:

"This approach leads to proposed military assistance programs that are larger than necessary, if a continuing American commitment is assumed. It leads to programs that are absurdly small if it is assumed that the American commitment is in doubt and that the U.S. government will at the same time frown on any effort by the recipient to reach a genuine understanding with Communist China."

Sen. Charles McC. Mathias Jr. (R Md.) an outspoken critic of the Indochina war, said in November 1970 "the best way to contain China is to leave Southeast Asia and thus create conditions under which a new arrangement must endure. The states of the region must be constrained to devise their own collective security ties, responding to the real power conditions in the region," he continued. "When these countries do adjust, the political situation may well be more favorable to our interests after we leave than it is now while we try to manipulate events."

CHINA POLICY: HEAVY LOBBYING ON BOTH SIDES OF ISSUE

President Nixon's 1971 reversal of the longstanding U.S. opposition to seating of Communist China in the United Nations, coupled with U.S. moves pointing toward recognition of Peking, rekindled an old and bitter controversy.

The U.S. government's series of actions was preceded and followed by vigorous activity, much of it behind the scenes, from what some used to call the China Lobby. In 1971 as in the past, however, that term was oversimplified.

The many groups and agents, both domestic and foreign, who worked to influence U.S. policy comprised not one China lobby but several.

Changed Circumstances

What stance should the United States take toward the Communist capture of China, with as much as 20 percent of the world's population and a budding nuclear capability?

That question faced the U.S. government again in 1971. Some version of the question has divided Americans and their leaders for a quarter-century or more.

The lineup of organized interests on competing sides reflected this division in 1971, as previously. Many veterans of past engagements were on the scene. This time, however, there were changed factors which affected the alignments and could be expected to influence the nature of the battle over U.S. China policy.

A split along the lines commonly called liberal and conservative was observable, as in past confrontations over China. Both of those camps, however, were in turn divided by other considerations including those centered on economic grounds, attitudes toward Communism and war, international organization and nationalistic loyalties.

Among factors which influenced the alignments of forces in the 1971 China campaign were the following:

• The new moves toward closer relations with the People's Republic of China came, for the first time, from a Republican President with a reputation for opposing Communism dating back to the Alger Hiss case. This factor promised to subdue a renewal of the harsh domestic battles over alleged Communist subversion which dominated earlier phases of China policy controversy.

• The Communist government had been in command of mainland China for more than two decades, since December 1949. No longer was there debate over helping Chiang Kai-shek's Nationalists to regain the China mainland by force. Taiwan—and continued U.S. guarantees of her independence—had become the central issue.

• The leaders of the two big communist powers, China and the Soviet Union, had been feuding. Some saw an opportunity to try to widen a wedge between them.

• Major U.S. business interests sought to open trade and other business dealings with mainland China. They called her an untapped market—a view opponents discounted.

• Many former foes of accepting Communist control of China had vanished from U.S. power circles. Age, death and elections had taken their toll.

No longer was there in the Senate William F. Knowland (R Calif. 1945-59), Senate Republican leader who told his party's national convention in 1956 he would oppose Red Chinese membership in the UN "as long as I have a voice and a vote" in the Senate.

Nor was there a Gen. Douglas MacArthur who commanded UN troops in Korea against the Chinese Communists, nor an Alfred Kohlberg, whose letter-writing earned him a nickname he took to his grave: "The China Lobby Man."

Among the missing, though some of his old associates were on hand, was the defunct Institute of Pacific Relations' Prof. Owen Lattimore, who called Knowland part of "the China Lobby" and the "Senator from Formosa." Lattimore was described by the Senate Judiciary Committee as "a conscious articulate instrument of the Soviet conspiracy" in a 1952 report based on hearings by the Internal Security Subcommittee. Lattimore denied the charge.

• A decade of discussion, much of it in groups of a dozen or so persons, had taken place in U.S. academic and policy-shaping circles. During that period, the question of lowering the bars to the Peking government lost its stigma and became an openly debated possibility.

Meanwhile, some former opponents of a thaw switched their positions with time. One was Sen. Jacob K. Javits (R N.Y.), who said he later helped change U.S. policy on China while a member of the U.S. delegation to the United Nations.

Even as the struggle to influence public opinion in the United States and in the United Nations raged, opponents of seating the Peking government conceded the outlook was dark from their standpoint. Though they continued to fight, they manned a second line of defense pegged to an effort to prevent Taiwan's expulsion from the United Nations, accompanied by U.S. withdrawal of its protection.

General Alignments

The various elements who make up the 1971 China lobby represented many interests for and against UN membership to Peking. A few were registered under the Federal Regulation of Lobbying Act or the Foreign Agents Registration Act; others were not, though many of their activities were aimed at influencing American policy.

One group, the **Committee of One Million**—Against the Admission of Communist China to the United Nations, was a veteran of U.S. China policy struggle. Among those siding with it in general policy, with varying degrees of activity, were a former Senator's public relations firm representing the Republic of China (Taiwan); the AFL-CIO; the American Legion; the Veterans of Foreign Wars; the American Security Council and several organizations which regarded themselves as conservative or anti-Communist.

An active leader in the fight for Peking admission, the **Committee for New China Policy,** was active in Congress, the executive branch and the United Nations. Its main figure was the son of a former Far East missionary; the Committee of One Million's central figure was a former China medical missionary.

Other organizations actively favoring Mainland China's admission included the National Committee on United States-China Relations, supported by at least two major foundations; the Citizens to Change United States China Policy, which included three former State Department officials who worked to change U.S. policy toward China in the Kennedy Administration; several national church organizations, and several photo and publications registrants for the People's Republic of China under the Foreign Agents Registration Act.

Others involved in the policy struggle included numerous business and scholarly interests which have promoted discussion of opening relations with Communist China or giving her China's seat in the United Nations. The American Farm Bureau Federation and leaders of an organization of multinational corporations were among those supporting the Nixon Administration's moves toward opening of trade relations with the China mainland.

In addition, other foreign governments have sought to influence U.S. policy, just as American officials sought to influence them. Japan, Britain and Australia were among those, in addition to the two Chinas, with much at stake on U.S. action in the Far East.

As expected, the Nixon Administration's moves toward opening the door to Peking brought much favorable response from pressure groups on that side of the fence.

Varied reaction came from the other side, however. For example, the **American Legion**—a longtime proponent of aiding Nationalist China—after hearing Secretary of State William P. Rogers urge confidence in President Nixon, passed two resolutions on Sept. 2, 1971. One endorsed Mr. Nixon's planned visit to Peking but suggested he make no concessions that could facilitate Communist subversion. The other reiterated the organization's opposition to opening diplomatic relations or granting a UN seat to the Communist government.

The executive council of the **AFL-CIO,** another longtime foe of the Peking regime, voted 24-4 on Aug. 10, 1971, to urge Mr. Nixon to reexamine his new China policies. President George Meany told newsmen: "We are just as positive as ever that Red China is a dictator nation which denies freedom to its people and is not eligible for United Nations membership."

And the **American Security Council** in its Aug. 9, 1971, "Washington Report" carried an article by Frank J. Johnson, its foreign editor, which said Mr. Nixon and his foreign affairs adviser, Henry A. Kissinger, apparently "understand that power—military power—and the

evident will to use it" is sometimes necessary to preserve peace. Hence, he said, announcement of Mr. Nixon's planned Peking trip "is a cause for somewhat less alarm" than it otherwise would be. Still others, including the **American Conservative Union** and its allies, suspended support of Mr. Nixon, partly because of his China policy.

Commercial Interests

James C. H. Shen, Ambassador of the Republic of China, told the National Press Club on June 24, 1971, that "much of today's pressure for a thaw with Peiping comes from hopeful business interests seeking profitable mainland markets." Their argument, he added, is "shot full of holes."

A considerable number of business interests have shown for some time a desire to open commercial dealings with Communist China. They included some leading U.S. companies, as well as some which have become multinational in nature. They possessed prestige and connections.

Many sources agreed, nevertheless, that the prospects for favorable trade were uncertain even if Chinese officials responded to the 1970-71 American initiatives.

As early as 1964, David Rockefeller, president of the **Chase Manhattan Bank** and then a vice president of the **Council on Foreign Relations,** indicated he would favor limited commercial contacts if they could be arranged without yielding on principles.

In Hong Kong to open a new branch bank, Rockefeller called the question of commercial relations with Communist China "one of the most difficult, complex and perplexing problems" faced by U.S. business.

Business interests which had showed during the 1971 "thaw" period they would like to do business with the Chinese mainland included:

General Motors: Called Communist China a "tremendous and potentially big market."

Monsanto: Had for years traded with Mainland China through third countries such as Italy, Japan and France, according to *Business Abroad*.

Xerox Corporation: President C. Peter McColough told stockholders on May 20, 1971, that a London subsidiary had missions in Peking exploring market chances.

Pan American World Airways: President Najeeb E. Halaby told shareholders on May 4, 1971, that Pan Am had been quietly seeking approval from Peking for three years to resume service on the China route Pan Am served in 1947-49. He said he saw "a real possibility" of doing so. Halaby has said he feels China is a big untapped market for commercial aircraft. He is a director of the Council on Foreign Relations.

Trans World Airlines: President Forwood C. Wiser said in Hong Kong on May 8, 1971, that TWA would operate charter flights to Communist China if the Peking government granted permission.

United Air Lines: Applied for flight authority.

Boeing Company: Listed among industry spokesmen who met with Gov. Daniel J. Evans (R) of Washington before Evans wired Chou En-lai, Peking premier, in May 1971 expressing a desire to arrange "exploratory talks of significance" on possible trade with Communist China.

Lawrence Fairhall reported from Hong Kong in *Business Abroad* (June 1971) that a majority of American businessmen in Hong Kong and elsewhere in Asia "are keen to do business with mainland China," though many had doubts about the results. *(Far East trade, p. 59)*

After the new series of U.S. moves got under way in the Nixon Administration, Donald M. Kendall, chairman of the **Emergency Committee for American Trade (ECAT),** said in April 1971 the lifting of the direct trade ban with mainland China was "very good news." But he said he did not expect "any great, short-term impact on our trade."

Kendall, president and chief executive officer of PepsiCo Inc., was a client of President Nixon's former law firm. ECAT is the leading organization to advance the interests of multinational corporations in the United States.

Kendall was not alone in his conservative estimates on possible results. James T. Lynn, Under Secretary of Commerce, said in May 1971: "At this point, no one knows how much trade might be expected." While he saw "limited new opportunities" for more trade, he added:

"But too much should not be expected too soon."

A study for the **National Committee for United States China Relations,** a leading advocate of opening the door to mainland China, also projected minor impact from trade. Prof. Robert F. Dernberger of the University of Michigan estimated in 1971 that the maximum sales to mainland China would reach no more than 1 percent to 2 percent of American exports in the next few years.

Under favorable conditions, Dernberger said, China might by 1980 buy up the $650 million in U.S. minerals, industrial equipment and machinery. Chinese sales to the United States, he said, might reach $250 million in raw and processed agricultural products and other items.

Nationalist Ambassador Shen noted that mainland China's total two-way foreign trade in 1970 was $4.2 billion. Taiwan, with 14.7 million persons, had trade of nearly $3.1 billion in the corresponding period. He figured the trade at $192.50 per capita for Taiwan, $5.50 for mainland China.

The **American Farm Bureau Federation** urged the government to authorize the sale of U.S. grains and other farm products to Communist China. Federation President William J. Kuhfuss wrote President Nixon that the Farm Bureau's directors on June 8, 1971, urged the removal "of cargo preference and part-cargo restrictions on sales to Communist countries."

Mr. Nixon on June 10 announced that farm products and fertilizer would be included among commodities for which export sales could be made to Communist China under general license. He announced elimination of cargo preference restrictions on sales to all Communist nations with which trade was then permitted.

Active China Lobbies

Committee of One Million, 1735 DeSales St. NW, Washington, D.C.

Chairman: Walter H. Judd (U.S. Rep., R Minn., 1943-63). Secretary: Lee Edwards. Steering Committee: Rep. John M. Ashbrook (R Ohio), ranking Republican, Internal Security Committee; Rep. Thomas E. Morgan

Foreign Aid Lobbying

The two ranking members of the Senate Foreign Relations Committee criticized lobbying on foreign aid in 1969, singling out a proposal to supply the Nationalist government on Taiwan with jet fighter planes. They differed, however, on who did the lobbying.

The dispute over addition of $54.5-million for a squadron of Phantom F-4D jets contributed to a seven month delay in enactment of the fiscal 1970 foreign aid appropriations bill. The measure (PL 91-194) was signed Feb. 9, 1970.

Sen. J.W. Fulbright (D Ark.), chairman of the Foreign Relations Committee, mentioned the Taiwan item among others when he hit at lobbying on Dec. 11, 1969.

"I fear we have come to the point where some lobbyists for foreign governments are more effective in promoting their special projects than members of this body are in promoting projects for their own states and districts," Fulbright said.

Lobbying on the Taiwan planes item also was criticized by Sen. George D. Aiken (R Vt.), ranking Republican on the committee. However, he said he was satisfied it was airplane manufacturers who got the Taiwan item inserted in the House, rather than foreign interests. "I feel quite sure it was American industrial concerns that did that," Aiken said.

The Taiwan plane item eventually was dropped.

Among those who opposed the Nationalist China military aid was Rep. Donald M. Fraser (D Minn.), who on June 4, 1970, obtained deletion from the fiscal 1971 foreign aid appropriations bill of a congressional policy statement opposing seating of Communist China in the United Nations. The statement, carried for 14 years, was knocked out by a chair ruling that it was a policy statement in an appropriations measure and contrary to House rules.

Fraser, then head of the Democratic Study Group, was among Representatives who joined in recommendations by the U.S.-China committee of the Members of Congress for Peace Through Law. That committee in 1971 urged seating of Mainland China in the United Nations. Fraser is a national vice chairman of Americans for Democratic Action, a longtime advocate of similar action on China.

Fulbright has frequently criticized lobbying by foreign interests. His committee was chiefly responsible for 1966 enactment of changes which narrowed the scope of the 1938 Foreign Agents Registration Act and increased the government's burden of proof in certain respects.

The changes were described as tightening the Act and were for the most part supported by the Justice Department under former Attorney General Nicholas deB. Katzenbach. Former Assistant Attorney General J. Walter Yeagley, in charge of internal security said that some of the changes had nevertheless had "a hampering effect" on enforcement.

(D Pa.), chairman, Foreign Affairs Committee; Rep. Clement J. Zablocki (D Wis.), second-ranking Democrat,

Foreign Affairs Committee; Sen. Peter H. Dominick (R Colo.), and Sen. Hugh Scott (R Pa.), minority leader.

The Committee of One Million—Against the Admission of Communist China to the United Nations was founded in 1953 as what its leaders described as "an authentic people's movement." Its formation stemmed from a petition to President Eisenhower opposing admission of Communist China to the UN and initiated by former President Hoover; Charles Edison, former Secretary of the Navy and Governor of New Jersey; Joseph C. Grew, former Ambassador to Japan; Judd, a former medical missionary in China; Rep. John W. McCormack (D Mass. 1928-71); Sen. John Sparkman (D Ala.), and Sen. H. Alexander Smith (R N.J. 1944-59), Sen. Dominick's uncle.

Since 1953, Edwards said, the group "has led the fight against the various Red China lobbies which abound in America. The major reason for the committee's success is that anti-Communist conservatives and liberals work and win together."

Opponents have in recent years questioned the strength and effectiveness of the committee, whose public list of prominent supporters had dwindled substantially by 1971. The **Ripon Society,** an advocate of closer relations with Communist China, spoke of the "puff adder menace" of the committee.

When Edwards testified at Senate hearings July 20, 1971, Chairman J. W. Fulbright (D Ark.) of the Foreign Relations Committee asked: "Do you really have one million members?" Edwards replied, "Yes, sir." Fulbright asked if all were dues-paying members. "Unfortunately not all of them are," Edwards said. Asked how many were, he said: "I would say about 5 percent."

Supporters said the committee's position reflected majority opinion in the United States. Among recent evidence they cited was a poll by the Opinion Research Corporation of Princeton, N.J., commissioned by the committee in July 1971. Taken in six states—California, Illinois, Florida, New Jersey, Ohio and Texas—the poll showed that while 40 percent favored admission of Mainland China to the United Nations (with 42 percent opposed), 66 percent of those favoring said they would oppose admission if it meant elimination of the Republic of China from the UN (compared with 10 percent favoring).

Edwards emphasized that the committee "is not totally and irrevocably opposed to the admission of Communist China to the United Nations." Rather, he said, it supports the recommendation of the Lodge commission. He said that "what the commission recommends is exactly the longstanding position of the Committee of One Million." The Lodge group favored admission of all governments which accept the principles of the UN Charter.

After a period of dormancy in the 1960s, the committee in October 1970 announced "a nation-wide information program and petition drive." It said this was prompted partly by disclosure that "powerful, well-financed groups (like the recently announced Committee for a New China Policy)" were pressing for recognition of the Peking regime and its admission to the United Nations.

The Committee of One Million was a primary source of information for its allies, upon occasion distributing Nationalist China material and supplying data to members of Congress. Some of its material was used in a

House floor discussion June 9, 1971, by 26 Representatives against relaxing bars against Mainland China under existing conditions. Its "China Report" in July 1971 after announcement that the United States would cosponsor a resolution to admit the People's Republic of China to the United Nations urged readers:

"Write-write-write—The situation is serious but defeat is not inevitable. With your help we will 'Stop Red China.' "

Since August 1969, the committee has been headquartered at the office of Edwards & Associates, a public relations firm opened in 1965. Edwards was press assistant to Sen. John Marshall Butler (R Md. 1951-63), 1961-62. During the presidential campaign of 1964, Edwards was successively news director for the National Draft Goldwater Committee, director of information for the National Goldwater for President Committee and deputy director of public relations for the Republican National Committee. He became secretary of the Committee of One Million in 1968. His father is Willard Edwards, Washington columnist for the *Chicago Tribune.*

In a 1968 book, *YOU Can Make the Difference,* Lee Edwards and his wife Anne detailed ways for conservatives to make their influence effective. They said "conservatives must learn to work with people who may differ with them on one or even a dozen philosophical points— as long as there is agreement on the goal of the project in question."

Edwards also was active in public relations for the Friends of the FBI, the Dirksen Republican Forum and Young Americans for Freedom, among others. In August 1971, he headed a new group named "Americans for Agnew." It sent telegrams to an undisclosed number of selected persons inviting them to sponsor an effort in the next year "to ensure that Agnew will be on the ticket in 1972."

The **American Conservative Union, Young Americans for Freedom (YAF),** *Human Events* and *National Review* in 1971 joined in supporting a resolution opposing appeasement of Communist China. Ashbrook, national chairman of the American Conservative Union, was succeeded in 1971 by M. Stanton Evans of *The Indianapolis News.*

The YAF, which in the spring of 1971 sponsored a speaking tour by Judd in Illinois, Indiana, Ohio and Minnesota, was founded in 1960 at the home of William F. Buckley Jr., editor of *National Review.* With more than 60 members of Congress on its advisory board, the YAF in 1971 described itself as "the largest anti-Communist youth organization" with 60,000 members and more than 800 chapters.

Republic of China. On June 3, 1971, a firm named GM Washington Consultants Inc. registered with the Justice Department as public relations consultants for the Republic of China. Former Sen. George L. Murphy (R Calif. 1965-70), company president, said he would "personally direct and supervise the public relations program" for the Taiwan government.

Under political action, Murphy said, the firm would "attempt to bring to public and governmental notice the long, friendly, mutually beneficial relationship which has existed between the United States of America and the Republic of China for over 20 years through use of news media, speeches, meetings and other conventional public relations methods."

The contract called for a fee from the Nationalist China government of $80,000 from May 12, 1971, to Dec. 31, 1971, plus $20,000 a month expenses. Murphy was to receive $35,000 annual salary on a part-time basis. Defeated in his 1970 bid for re-election, Murphy formerly was president of the Screen Actors Guild and had directed public relations for Metro-Goldwyn-Mayer Studios, Desilu Productions and the motion picture industry.

The firm was formed Nov. 4, 1968, as GM International Inc. by Robert K. Gray, Lawrence C. Merthan and Dewey Hutchins of Hill & Knowlton, a public relations firm. Gray, senior vice president of Hill & Knowlton, served as the original president. The name was changed on May 11, 1971, and Murphy reported owning 44 percent of the authorized voting shares. Mrs. Duane Miller of Bloomfield, Mich., owned 51 percent of the authorized shares. Murphy told the Justice Department there were no other shareholders.

Other persons who later registered to work for GM Consultants on the Republic of China account were Jack E. Buttram, formerly with Sen. Paul J. Fannin (R Ariz.) and Hill & Knowlton, as public relations counsel; Hugh C. Newton, whose other employers included the National Right to Work Committee, Committee of One Million, United Virginia Bank and the Air Transport Association, to do special writing and research part-time; De Witt S. Copp as part-time writer-researcher; Roy Perrin McNair as writer and research analyst, and Malcolm M. Burleson as consultant for radio-television work.

The firm said it would deal with Ambassador Shen.

The Chiang Kai-shek government had had no public relations counsel in the United States, according to a spokesman, since discontinuing the services of the Hamilton Wright Organization. Shen, formerly in the Chinese information ministry, took part in that decision, which followed adverse publicity during and after Senate Foreign Relations Committee hearings in 1963 on activities of nondiplomatic representatives of foreign principals in the United States.

Hamilton Wright Jr., executive vice president of the company, was temporarily suspended by the Public Relations Society of America for alleged violations of ethics. The society, on the basis of the information brought out in the hearings, said Wright failed to disclose the origin of news articles and film shorts projecting the Nationalist China viewpoint. Wright denied engaging in unethical practices and challenged fairness of the hearings.

A spokesman for GM Consultants said the firm was "bending over backward" to avoid any actions that might be considered questionable.

Murphy and Buttram also registered July 9, 1971, under the Federal Regulation of Lobbying Act.

National Committee on United States-China Relations Inc., 777 United Nations Plaza, New York City.

Chairman: Alexander Eckstein, professor of economics, University of Michigan. He was economist for the UN Food and Agriculture Organization, 1946-49 and 1950-51; senior economist, State Department, 1951-53; author of *The National Income of Communist China,* 1962, and *Communist China's Economic Development and Foreign Trade,* published in 1966 by the Council on Foreign

Relations. Eckstein testified at 1966 Senate hearings in support of closer U.S. relations with the China mainland, on a gradual basis.

The committee was founded in June 1966 and described itself as an independent, nonpartisan educational organization which receives most of its financial support from the Ford Foundation and the Rockefeller Brothers Fund. It works with educators on the teaching of China affairs in U.S. schools and sponsors seminars and international scholarly meetings on China.

Among the founders was Robert A. Scalapino, chairman of the political science department at the University of California, Berkeley. He has been a consultant to the Rockefeller and Ford Foundations and was a principal debater in a national teach-in against the U.S. role in the Vietnam war in May 1965. He supported U.S. policy.

A spokesman said the committee devoted major attention in 1971 to the prospects for actual relations with the People's Republic of China. The committee sought to design programs for groups that might have early contact with Mainland China. It was handling arrangements for a visit to the United States of the Chinese table tennis team, in cooperation with the U.S. Table Tennis Association.

Activities included a two-day conference of more than 2,500 people in New York City in 1969 chaired by Prof. Edwin O. Reischauer of Harvard University, former ambassador to Japan, and A. Doak Barnett of Brookings Institution. Speakers included Senators Edward M. Kennedy (D Mass.), who advocated withdrawal of U.S. forces from Taiwan and establishment of consular missions in Communist China, and Jacob K. Javits (R N.Y.), who urged a "psychology readjustment" to prepare for a thaw in U.S.-China relations.

During the conference the **Chinese Consolidated Benevolent Associations,** which said they represented all Chinese-American organizations in New York, Washington, Boston, Philadelphia, Baltimore and Pittsburgh, advertised in *The New York Times* (March 20, 1969) saying:

"Ostensibly, the committee does not advocate any policy proposal because it is supported principally by the Ford Foundation and the Rockefeller Brothers Fund. However, those in control...have been giving prominence only to those points of view contrary to official American policy and to the majority of American public opinion."

Citizens to Change United States China Policy, 110 Maryland Ave. NE, Methodist Bldg., Washington, D.C.

Chairman: Prof. Allen S. Whiting, University of Michigan. He was director of research and analysis, Far East, State Department, 1962-66, and deputy U.S. consul general, Hong Kong, 1966-68; with Rand Corporation, 1957-61.

Executive secretary: Robert A. Burton, who was director of the Eastern Civilization Program at the University of Kansas, 1962-71. Burton was with the U.S. Consulate General, Hong Kong, 1951-54, and with American Universities field staff, Hong Kong, 1958-62.

Treasurer: Board member Donald Wilson, a United Presbyterian Church official at the Interchurch Center, New York City.

The group was formed by Whiting following a split-off from the Committee for New China Policy. Thomas B. Manton, founder of the CNCP, said Whiting and his backers walked out in disagreement primarily with the CNCP advocacy of an abrupt end to U.S. support of Nationalist China; Whiting favored gradualism.

Whiting said he had never been in CNCP but that a group split off from CNCP and asked him to head it. *(See Committee for New China Policy, this page)*

Both the organization and Burton registered as lobbyists June 15, 1971. Policy objectives included ending all trade embargoes against mainland China; withdrawal of U.S. military from Taiwan; recognition of mainland China as the sole UN representative of China, and establishment of economic, social, cultural and diplomatic relations with Communist China "on the basis of the principles of equality, mutual respect, and nonintervention in each other's affairs."

Board members included two other former State Department officials with responsibility for Far Eastern affairs—Roger Hilsman and James C. Thomson Jr. Hilsman was Assistant Secretary of State for Far Eastern Affairs, 1963-64, and Thomson held posts as special assistant in the Bureau of Far Eastern Affairs and later as a National Security Council staff member, 1964-66.

Hilsman wrote in *To Move a Nation*, 1967, that when he was in charge of Far Eastern policy Whiting and Thomson were among those who helped him draft a 1963 speech outlining a basic policy change from former Secretary of State John Foster Dulles' policy.

The Dulles policy assumed that the Chinese Communist regime was a "passing and not a perpetual phase." The Hilsman speech, delivered after President Kennedy's death, projected U.S. policy on the public acknowledgement that the communist regime was apparently there to stay.

Other board members included former Representatives George E. Brown Jr. (D Calif. 1963-71) and Charles O. Porter (D Ore. 1957-61); David Hunter, deputy general secretary, National Council of Churches; Edward Snyder, Friends Committee on National Legislation; Hans Morgenthau, City University of New York professor, and Jeremy J. Stone, executive director, Federation of American Scientists.

Committee for New China Policy, P. O. Box 493, Newton Center, Mass.

Cochairmen: Daniel Tretiak, W. Richard Dell and Robert E. Gomperts. Tretiak was formerly connected with the Westinghouse Advanced Study Group, was a former resident of and writer in Hong Kong and now teaches at York University, Toronto, Canada. Dell was director of international publications, Encyclopedia Britannica, in Chicago. Gomperts, president of a California import-export firm, ran unsuccessfully as the 1970 Democratic candidate for Congress against Rep. Paul N. McCloskey Jr. (R Calif.).

Thomas B. Manton, Burma-born son of an American missionary, founded the committee in April 1969 and was its first general secretary. "We are the only American group with fairly consistent contact with the Chinese in that period," he said.

While director of international affairs for the United Church of Christ in 1970, Manton served as a part-time consultant to the U.S.-China committee of the Members of Congress for Peace Through Law. He sent members of Congress a statement in mid-1971 by the foreign ministry of the Peking government which he said had not appeared in the American press. Manton said such mailings go only to members of Congress.

In 1971, Manton headed the United Nations committee of the Committee for New China Policy and traveled for several months in Europe urging prime ministers and foreign ministers to support admission of Communist China to the United Nations as the only China representative.

"We are the only group with a strict one-China policy," Manton said. Until 1971, he said, his organization had maintained "a low profile" which it was gradually abandoning for a more public stance.

Manton said members of his group have been advising Henry A. Kissinger, President Nixon's foreign policy adviser, and Senators Edward M. Kennedy (D Mass.) and Edmund S. Muskie (D Maine). He has been advising Sen. George McGovern (D S.D.), he said.

Manton in 1971 also was director of country councils with The Asia Society, which he said is a nonprofit educational group. The society, which includes cultural exchanges in its activities, was set up in 1959 by John D. Rockefeller III, chairman of the board in 1971.

Board members listed by the Committee for New China Policy include Union Seminary President John C. Bennett, D.F. Fleming, Stanley Lubman, Hans J. Morgenthau, Charles O. Porter and Howard Zinn. Lubman, of the University of California, like Porter, was also with Citizens to Change United States China Policy. He testified at Senate hearings June 29, 1971. *(p. 86)*

The group's policy statement was largely similar to that of Citizens to Change United States China Policy.

Members of Congress for Peace Through Law. Rep. Patsy T. Mink (D Hawaii), chairman of the U.S.-China committee of Members of Congress for Peace Through Law, testified at Senate hearings June 24, 1971, advocating seating of the People's Republic of China in the United Nations. She recommended U.S. diplomatic relations with Peking as soon as feasible.

"We should recognize what is inevitable—that the China seat in the UN will be occupied by representatives of the People's Republic of China," she said. Twenty-one Representatives and Senators Mark O. Hatfield (R Ore.), McGovern and Harold E. Hughes (D Iowa) associated themselves with her statement.

Mrs. Mink, who headed the full organization in the 91st Congress and was succeeded by Hatfield for the 92nd, said the China committee for two years had held luncheon meetings for members of Congress at which specialists on China spoke.

Other Influences

Mrs. Mink in her 1971 testimony referred to the change in recent years concerning public discussion of what she called "the once-forbidden subject of China relations."

Forces which played a role in bringing about that change of attitude were an important factor in the China policy struggle. They included some who might commonly be regarded as lobbyists, but the most influential included others infrequently considered in that light.

The Council on Foreign Relations was prominent among educational organizations that have had a hand through the years in shaping U.S. China policy. It is now headed by David Rockefeller.

EVOLUTION OF CONGRESSIONAL CHINA POLICY 1946-1971

The principal thrust of congressional interest in Chinese and Far Eastern affairs has changed significantly in the 22 years since Mao Tse-tung's Communist forces routed Chiang Kai-shek's Nationalists and proclaimed the People's Republic of China in late 1949.

In the 1940s, the most vocal congressional critics of U.S. Asian policy urged greater U.S. support of the Nationalist government in the civil war against the Communists. By 1966, critics of U.S. China policy, although in a minority, suggested a softer stance toward China involving resumption of trade, diplomatic recognition and Peking's admission into the United Nations.

Throughout the post-World War II period, a majority had prevailed on Capitol Hill which supported President Truman's hands-off policy in the Chinese civil war (1946-1949), his defense of Taiwan after June 1950, President Eisenhower's defense of Taiwan and the offshore islands, opposed recognition and UN membership for mainland China and, in an intimately related issue, supported and financed the U.S. military effort in Indochina under Presidents Kennedy, Johnson and Nixon.

Congressional support for the "China Lobby" point of view in the 1940s came mostly from Republicans; pressure for a "containment without isolation" policy toward China in the 1960s emanated for the most part from the Democrats, with the Senate Foreign Relations Committee as a base.

By 1971, conservatives on the China question in Congress found themselves in retreat. A Republican President had eased trade and travel restrictions with China, reversed the traditional U.S. policy on UN membership and planned to make a personal visit to Peking.

For the first time in two decades, Congress in 1971 failed to go on record against Peking's admission to the UN. Instead, most members of the House and Senate confined themselves to support of the Administration's effort to save Taiwan's seat in the world organization.

Civil War 1946-1949

During the late 1940s, the Truman Administration maintained a hands-off policy toward the Chinese civil war despite pressure from a vocal minority of Senators and Representatives for the increased involvement of the United States on behalf of Generalissimo Chiang Kai-shek and his Nationalist forces. The only significant concession to this minority was the China Aid Act which cleared Congress in 1948.

On Feb. 18, 1948, President Truman sent a special message to Congress recommending a $570-million aid program for China. The Administration program made no provision for military aid to the Nationalist government in its struggle against the Communists, who were then making rapid progress in Manchuria. The message said, however, that the proposed shipments of food, raw mate-

rials and fertilizers from the United States would permit the Nationalist government "to devote its (own) limited dollar resources to the most urgent of its other needs." On April 2, 1948, Congress passed the bill. The economic aid appropriation had been reduced to $338-million, but $125-million had been added for the Chinese government to use as it saw necessary, which presumably meant for military aid. The total amount was $463-million. On April 3, President Truman signed the bill into law.

On Feb. 25, 1949, Sen. Pat McCarran (D Nev.) introduced a bill to provide a $1.5-billion loan to Nationalist China for military and economic purposes. Asked for comment by the Senate Foreign Relations Committee, Secretary of State Dean Acheson wrote April 14, 1949, that there was "no evidence" that such aid would "alter the pattern of current developments in China," to which the United States had given $2-billion since 1945 without stemming Communist forces. Sen. Styles Bridges (R N.H.) called for an investigation of China policy, accusing Acheson of what "might be called sabotage of the valiant" Nationalists. Senators McCarran and Knowland supported Bridges. Senators Tom Connally (D Texas) and J. W. Fulbright (D Ark.) defended Acheson. No action was taken on McCarran's bill.

But on April 14, 1949, Congress extended the 1948 China Aid Act by authorizing the President to use unobligated funds as he determined necessary for aid to those areas of China that remained free of Chinese Communist control. The funds were made available until Feb. 15, 1950.

In June, 1949, when it was rumored that the State Department was studying the possibility of recognizing a Chinese Communist regime, 21 Senators (16 Republicans and five Democrats) sent a letter to President Truman expressing bitter opposition to any such move and calling for increased aid to the Nationalists. Sen. Arthur H. Vandenburg (R Mich.) declared in a Senate speech that the U.S. policy toward China had been a "tragic failure." But Sen. Connally replied: "Would you send your own sons to fight in the Chinese civil war?"

China White Paper. On Aug. 6, 1949, the State Department released a White Paper on China, pointing out that the Nationalists were on the verge of collapse because of the military, economic and political shortcomings of the Chiang regime, and that no amount of additional aid would have prevented their defeat at the hands of Communist forces. The document set off a new burst of criticism from Republicans.

Rep. Mike Mansfield (D Mont.) Aug. 25 called for an investigation of lobbying on behalf of the Nationalists. He suggested that money provided earlier "to help China, but siphoned off for private use, is being used to finance attacks on our Secretary of State and other officials charged with conducting our relations with China." Among groups supporting Chiang and denouncing the White Paper were the China Emergency Committee, headed by Frederick C. McKee, and the American China

Policy Committee, headed by Alfred Kohlberg. Talk of a pro-Chiang "China Lobby" persisted for many years, but the issue was never fully clarified.

The Senate Sept. 22 passed the Mutual Defense Assistance Act, adding to the funds requested by the President $75-million for use in the "general area" of China. The House accepted the item, for which Sen. Knowland was chiefly responsible, and it was retained in the final law.

Disunity Over Asia Policy. Early in 1950, bipartisan cooperation on questions of foreign policy was strained by the charges of Sen. Joseph McCarthy (R Wis.) that American policies in the Far East had been influenced by Communist sympathizers in the State Department (*box*); by Republican demands that the President "fire Acheson"; by Mr. Truman's statements that Sen. Bridges and other minority Senators were "trying to sabotage the foreign policy of the United States"; and by continuing complaints from GOP leaders that they were "never consulted" on Far Eastern policy.

A warning that congressional dissatisfaction with American policy in the Far East went deeper than the Administration apparently had supposed was given early in the 1950 session of Congress when the House Jan. 19 defeated, 191 to 192, a bill to appropriate $60-million for additional economic aid to the Republic of Korea during the period Feb. 15 to June 30. The President had requested $150-million. The appropriation of $60-million was later approved, 240 to 134, but only after an authorization for continued assistance to the Chinese Nationalists on Formosa had been added to it.

Korean War

Less than five years after V-J Day, the United States in mid-1950 found itself locked in a full-scale war in a little-expected quarter—Korea. Political disunity receded after President Truman's June 27 action in ordering American forces to South Korea and in reversing previous policy by ordering the 7th Fleet to "prevent any attack on Formosa." Subsequent American setbacks in the conflict brought all but unanimous support for the President's Korean policies and the legislation needed to implement them.

After Communist China's entry into the Korean war and her rejection of two UN appeals for a cease-fire in the conflict, the United States called on the General Assembly to label the Peking regime as an aggressor. Underscoring congressional support for this move, the House and Senate quickly passed resolutions to the same effect. H Res 77, introduced by House Majority Leader John McCormack (D Mass.), called on the UN to "immediately act and declare the Chinese Communist authorities an aggressor in Korea." The House approved the resolution by voice vote on Jan. 19, 1951. The Senate Jan. 23, 1951, adopted a similar resolution (S Res 35), introduced by Sen. John L. McClellan (D Ark.), also by voice vote.

Following Senate action on S Res 35, McClellan called up two other resolutions. S Res 36 declared that Communist China should not be admitted to the UN. Sen. Brien McMahon (D Conn.) said that, although he agreed, the matter should be studied because the United States might want to change its position if a split developed between Moscow and Peking. Sen. Spessard Holland (D

McCarthy and China Policy

A speech by Sen. Joseph R. McCarthy (R Wis.) Feb. 9, 1950, to the Ohio County Women's Republican Club in Wheeling, W. Va., led to one of the most bitterly controversial investigations in the history of Congress. A special subcommittee of the Senate Foreign Relations Committee was set up to investigate McCarthy's charges that Communists were knowingly employed by the State Department and were directing its policies, especially in the Far East.

The subcommittee held 31 days of hearings between March 8 and June 28, 1950. During the course of the hearings, McCarthy charged ten individuals by name with varying degrees of Communist activities.

Among those named was Prof. Owen J. Lattimore, Johns Hopkins University. On the case of Lattimore, McCarthy said he would "stand or fall." In executive hearings, McCarthy March 20 said Lattimore was "the top of the ring of which (Alger) Hiss was a part." Asked if he was sure Lattimore was the biggest Russian spy, McCarthy said: "By far and away. I think he is the top Russian spy."

Lattimore spent three days on the stand, April 6 and May 2 and 3. He denied charges that he was a Communist, challenged McCarthy to repeat his charges off the Senate floor "so he can be held accountable in a court of law."

Report. In the final report (S Rept 2108), filed July 20, 1950, the Democratic majority found "no evidence to support the charge that Owen Lattimore is the 'top Russian spy,' or for that matter, any sort of spy." Each of the other nine primary "cases" submitted by McCarthy was also found to be without substantiation or was rejected because the person involved had never been an employee of the government.

Aftermath. Although he soon lost interest in the Far East, McCarthy and his repeated accusations of Communist influence throughout the government remained a key domestic issue. The main result of his accusations on U.S. Asian policy was to make officials favoring improved relations with Communist China reluctant to speak out.

Taking over the chairmanship of the Senate Government Operations Committee and the Permanent Investigations Committee in 1953, McCarthy investigated the State Department, Voice of America, Department of the Army and other agencies. An opinion-stifling "climate of fear" in many government agencies was said to be one of the results of his probes. The Army-McCarthy hearings, televised in the spring of 1954, were the climax of McCarthy's career, and led finally to his censure by the Senate Dec. 2, 1954. He died May 2, 1957.

Fla.) said this would leave the Administration in doubt as to the Senate's views. S Res 36 was adopted, 91-0. (A similar amendment opposing China's UN membership passed every Congress until 1971. *Box p. 53*)

The third resolution (S Res 37), calling for "the complete interruption of economic relations" between UN members and Communist China, was referred by voice vote to the Senate Foreign Relations Committee on the motion of Majority Leader Ernest W. McFarland (D Ariz.). No further action was taken on S Res 37.

The House May 15, 1951, passed a resolution identical to S Res 36 after Secretary of Defense George C. Marshall had declared that the United States should use its veto in the Security Council, if necessary, to keep Communist China out of the UN. The Secretary had also said that Formosa "must never be allowed to come under control of a Communist government or a government under Soviet domination."

Also on May 15, both the House and Senate unanimously adopted a resolution (S Con Res 31) which urged the UN General Assembly to "take action leading to... an embargo on the shipment to Communist China of arms, ammunition, and all other materials which might add to the war-making potential of Communist China."

MacArthur. However, the unity that President Truman successfully had maintained in Congress was eroded with the President's removal of Gen. Douglas MacArthur April 11, 1951, from his Asian commands. Most Republicans and a few Democrats, dissatisfied with a situation that seemed to promise nothing better than a stalemate in Korea, bitterly attacked the President for his action. Some Republicans, such as Sen. William E. Jenner (Ind.), talked openly of impeachment. Sen. McCarthy said it was the "greatest victory the Communists have ever won."

In the midst of the political storm, MacArthur returned to Washington. In an address before a joint session of Congress April 19, and in subsequent testimony before the joint Senate Foreign Relations-Armed Services Committees, MacArthur recommended that Communist China be blockaded, that restrictions on "air reconnaissance" of China's coastal areas and Manchuria be removed, and that the restrictions on the forces of the Republic of China on Formosa also be removed, with "logistical support" of their operations against Communist China supplied by the United States. MacArthur said that such actions would quickly bring Communist China to its knees.

Hearings. The joint Senate committee hearings on Far Eastern policy, conducted in May and June of 1951, put on record a large number of secret documents, including the Wedemeyer report on Korea of September 1947 (part of a report on China which had already been released).

On June 1, over the protest of Secretary of State Dean Acheson, the committees voted 15-9 to make public a State Department memorandum of Dec. 23, 1949, which said that Formosa had "no special military significance" and that its loss to the Communists was expected.

Although the hearings were closed, transcripts of the testimony were made public after material directly relating to future war plans had been deleted. A Republican move to hold the hearings in the open was blocked in the Senate, 41 to 37, after all 70 Senators who were not members of the Foreign Relations or Armed Services Committees had been invited to attend by the two committees.

A skillful defense of Administration policies during eight days of testimony and cross-examination apparently restored Secretary Acheson's prestige somewhat. In the House, a Republican amendment to the State Department's fiscal 1952 appropriation (HR 4740) which would have had the effect of removing the Secretary from the federal pay roll was defeated on July 26, 1951, by a standing vote of 171 to 81.

On Aug. 17, the joint committee voted 20-3 to file no formal report on the investigation. Richard B. Russell (D Ga.) said the group wished to avoid "renewal of bitter controversy" at a time when Korean truce negotiations were in progress. The hearings, he said, had "forced a definite policy in the Far East when we did not have one," had been partly responsible for a change in attitude toward the Nationalist Chinese island of Formosa and had led to an economic blockade of Communist China.

An Aug. 19 statement issued by the eight Republican members of the joint committee condemned the manner of Gen. MacArthur's dismissal, described the Administration's Far Eastern policy as a "catastrophic failure," asserted that the constitutional authority of the Congress to declare war had been bypassed in Korea, and warned against any peace of "appeasement" with the Chinese Communists. Sen. Wayne Morse (then R Ore.) issued his own statement Sept. 5 praising the President for his actions.

Formosa—1955

As the eight years of fighting in Indochina between the French and the Viet Minh ended, and as the Southeast Asia Treaty Organization became a reality, Communist China increased military operations against the offshore islands of Quemoy, Matsu and the Tachens. To underscore its support of the Formosa regime, the United States Dec. 2, 1954, signed a mutual security pact with the Republic of China. Meanwhile, Sen. Knowland (R Calif.) was calling for a blockade of the mainland to force the release of 13 Americans captured in Korea and sentenced Nov. 22, 1954, as spies by the Chinese Communists. Tensions were mounting as the Democratic-controlled 84th Congress convened Jan. 5, 1955, and President Eisenhower asked the Senate for prompt approval of the U.S.-Nationalist security pact. (See p. 27-28)

On Jan. 18, 1955, Communist forces seized the offshore island of Ichiang, 210 miles north of Formosa, and seemed prepared to invade the nearby Tachen islands. The situation led the President to ask Congress, in a special message Jan. 24, for explicit authority to use American armed forces to protect Formosa, the adjoining Pescadores islands, and "related positions and territories." Despite some misgivings concerning aspects of the bill which they considered vague (such as the President's or Secretary Dulles' intent regarding Quemoy, Matsu and the offshore islands), the Democratic leaders in Congress hastened to comply with the President's request.

H J Res 159, authorizing him to "employ the armed forces of the United States as he deems necessary" in the defense of Formosa, was reported by the House Foreign Affairs Committee the same day, unanimously and without amendment. The House passed it Jan. 25, on a 410-3 roll-call vote, after hearing Speaker Sam Rayburn (D Texas) state his belief that the resolution added nothing to the constitutional powers of the President and should not be taken as a precedent that would bind him in the future.

On Jan. 26, the Senate Foreign Relations and Armed Services Committees, sitting jointly, voted 27-2 to report the resolution without change, after rejecting amendments to restrict the President's authority. In floor debate

Jan. 26-28, Senators Morse (D Ore.) and Flanders (R Vt.) warned of a "preventative war," while Senators Kefauver (D Tenn.), Humphrey (D Minn.), and Lehman (D N.Y.) attacked the resolution's ambiguity regarding the offshore islands. But the Senate Jan. 28, by lopsided margins, rejected three restrictive amendments and passed H J Res 159 on an 85-3 roll call. Voting "nay" were Morse, Langer and Lehman.

SEATO Treaty. Senate action on the Southeast Asia Collective Defense Treaty, submitted by the President Nov. 10, 1954, was postponed until the Formosa resolution was approved. The Foreign Relations Committee cleared the treaty Jan. 21, 1955, and the Senate approved ratification Feb. 1, 1955, by an 82-1 roll-call vote.

China Treaty. On Feb. 8, the Senate Foreign Relations Committee voted 11-2 to approve the mutual security treaty signed with the Republic of China in December 1954. The committee, however, stated its understanding that its terms "apply only in the event of external armed attack, and that military operations by either party from the territories held by the Republic of China shall not be undertaken except by joint agreement." Two other "understandings" were expressed, to the effect that any extension of the treaty area would require the concurrence of a two-thirds majority in the Senate, and that nothing in the treaty "shall be construed as affecting or modifying the legal status or sovereignty" of Formosa and the Pescadores.

Sen. Morse, nevertheless, proposed adding this last point to the text of the treaty. The Senate rejected the move, 11-57, as it did a second Morse amendment to strike out a reference to defense of "such other territories as may be determined by mutual agreement," 10-60. Ratification of the treaty was then approved Feb. 9, 1955, by a vote of 65-6. Opposed were Senators Morse (D Ore.), Langer (R N.D.), Lehman, (D N.Y.), Chavez (D N.M.), Gore (D Tenn.) and Kefauver (D Tenn.).

New Policy Proposals

In 1957, a handful of Senators advocated revising U.S. China policy, with no substantial results. The most important recommendation was made by Sen. Theodore F. Green (D R.I.), chairman of the Senate Foreign Relations Committee. On Feb. 18, Green said the U.S. "should recognize Red China sooner or later. We don't like their form of government, but the country is a great country and organized, and I do not myself see why we should recognize these other Communist countries and withhold recognition of China unless we are going to apply that to other Communist countries." Secretary of State Dulles told a news conference Feb. 19 that it would be "premature, to say the least," to discuss recognizing Communist China, but he added that "none of us are talking here in terms of eternity."

On June 16, 1957, Sen. J. W. Fulbright (D Ark.), second-ranking majority member of the Senate Foreign Relations Committee, suggested during a television interview that recognition of Communist China by the United States was inevitable in course of time; the only question was "when and how you do it." Fulbright favored negotiations on recognition and on modification of the embargo in return for such concessions as a Peking pledge to stay out of Formosa.

On July 18, 1957, after pressure was exerted by some members of Congress and the press, a crack in the American policy of trying to hold Communist China virtually in quarantine showed up for the first time when Secretary Dulles offered to validate the passports of a limited number of American newsmen for travel in China for a limited period. The Chinese Communists later refused to allow the newsmen into the country on grounds that the decision had not been reciprocal.

Formosa—1958

But the rising tide of congressional sentiment for a revision in U.S. policy toward China was quickly quelled in the fall of 1958 as Communist China resumed military operations against the Nationalist-held offshore islands. As President Eisenhower and Secretary Dulles alternated pledges of "no retreat" with pleas for a cease-fire, Senate Democrats voiced their concern. On Sept. 13, Sen. John F. Kennedy (D Mass.) commented that in Formosa, "the weight of military, diplomatic, political, and historical judgment would dictate a contrary policy." Kennedy was joined by Sen. Ralph W. Yarborough (D Texas), who asserted that Mr. Eisenhower was getting "bayonet-happy." Sen. Green expressed "profound concern" Sept. 12 over the President's policy of employing armed forces "in a way which might risk deeper military involvement." The President, Green said, "has a duty to request policy guidance from Congress."

On Oct. 4, 10 Democratic House members sent a telegram to President Eisenhower making a new demand for a special congressional session on the Far East. They said they had found "the great majority" of their constituents were "deeply disturbed with the Administration's Quemoy policy," and they believed "we should disentangle ourselves from Chiang Kai-shek's aspirations on Quemoy, and should endeavor to bring the mantle of the UN over Formosa...." *(Additional detail on 1958 crisis, p. 28)*

Policy Studies

On Nov. 1, 1959, the Senate Foreign Relations Committee released a study prepared by a private research firm, Conlon Associates, Ltd., of San Francisco, Calif., on U.S. foreign policy in Asia. The study recommended that the U.S. gradually shift its policy, leading to recognition of Communist China, U.S. support for seating Peking in the UN, recognition of Taiwan as a new republic and its seating in the UN General Assembly. Committee Chairman J.W. Fulbright said the study was "very provocative," and that "while I do not believe that the U.S. should recognize Communist China at the present time... I do not believe it is wise to continue to ignore over 600 million people ...in the naive belief that they will somehow go away."

On Jan. 3, 1960, Sen. Henry M. Jackson, chairman of a Senate Government Operations subcommittee, issued a report entitled "National Policy Machinery in Communist China," noting that "the Chinese Communist party has attained a degree of unity and stability at its higher levels which is unequaled by other major Communist parties." The report concluded that the Communist leadership in China had uplifted the country "from a prostrate colossus to a giant on the march, in ten short years."

Kennedy Administration

Despite reports to the contrary, the Kennedy Administration offered no immediate plans for basic changes in the U.S.China policy. On May 3, 1961, Senate Minority Leader Everett M. Dirksen (R Ill.) introduced a resolution restating congressional opposition to the seating of Communist China in the UN. An identical measure was introduced the same day in the House by Rep. Clement J. Zablocki (D Wis.) and 55 other members.

Dirksen submitted the resolution, which was also endorsed by Senate Majority Leader Mike Mansfield, following conferences initiated after Senate debate April 14 over the President's reaffirmation of long-standing U.S. policy on the question of Chinese representation in the UN. Asked if the resolution had been approved by Secretary of State Dean Rusk, Dirksen said "that is my definite understanding."

The resolution declared it "the sense of Congress that it supports the President in his affirmation that the United States shall continue to meet its commitments to the people and Government of the Republic of China and shall continue to support the Government as the representative of China in the United Nations (and) further, the United States shall continue to oppose the seating of the Chinese Communist regime in the United Nations so long as that regime persists in defying the principles of the United Nations Charter. Further, it is the sense of the Congress that the United States supports the President in not according diplomatic recognition to the Chinese Communist regime."

The Senate July 28 adopted S Con Res 34 by a 76-0 roll-call vote and sent it to the House. The Senate accepted two amendments offered by Sen. Thomas J. Dodd (D Conn.) which, he said, were designed to justify to the world this country's "determination to keep Red China out of the United Nations." The amendments restated that Communist China should not be seated because it had "flagrantly violated basic human rights," had imposed a brutal regime on the Chinese people, had derived its authority from usurpation and tyranny and had become the "major source of the international illicit narcotics traffic."

On Aug. 31, 1961, the House unanimously passed the resolution. During debate, several members argued that the language of the resolution was too restrained. Only two members—Representatives Thomas L. Ashley (D Ohio) and William Fitts Ryan (D N.Y.)—spoke against it. Both answered "present" on the roll call.

Indochina

The 1954 Geneva Agreements on Indochina failed to resolve the political conflicts of the area, and by 1961, the Communist regime of North Vietnam was giving support to guerrilla operations against the U.S.-backed governments of Premier Boun Oum in Laos and President Ngo Dinh Diem in South Vietnam. In 1962, the scale of American aid increased rapidly as more than 10,000 U.S. military personnel undertook to train the expanded forces of President Diem and assist them in countering the highly effective guerrilla techniques of the Communist Viet Cong.

Vietnam Report. On Feb. 24, 1963, a special report was submitted to the Senate Foreign Relations Committee by a four-man panel headed by Senate Majority Leader Mansfield. In an investigation of U.S. aid to Southeast Asia, the report concluded that "there is no interest of the United States in Vietnam which would justify, in present circumstances, the conversion of the war...primarily into an American war to be fought primarily with American lives." The report recommended that the United States conduct a thorough reassessment of its "over-all security requirement on the Southeast Asia mainland" aimed at consideration of a reduction in the U.S. aid programs, although "extreme caution" should be used, "for if the attempt is made to alter the programs via a congressional meat axe cut...it runs the risk of not merely removing the fat but of leaving a gap which will lay open the region to massive chaos and, hence, jeopardize the present Pacific structure of our national security."

On Sept. 12, 1963, Sen. Frank Church (D Idaho) proposed a resolution calling for U.S. withdrawal from South Vietnam if "cruel repressions" of the Buddhists by the government continued. Church charged that the situation in Vietnam had "worsened" while the U.S. effort had increased.

Fulbright Criticism. On March 25, 1964, Sen. J. W. Fulbright (D Ark.), chairman of the Senate Foreign Relations Committee, began to criticize the Johnson Administration's Far East policies. In a speech entitled "Old Myths and New Realities," a general criticism of American foreign policy, the Senator called for a re-evaluation of U.S. Far Eastern policies and added that "whatever the outcome of a re-thinking of policy might be, we have been unwilling to take it because of the fear of many government officials, undoubtedly well-founded, that even the suggestion of new policies toward China or Vietnam would provoke a vehement outcry."

Fulbright asserted that the United States should "introduce an element of flexibility, or, more precisely, of the capacity to be flexible, into our relations with Communist China." He added that the foremost of the new realities about China "is that there are not really 'two Chinas' but only one, mainland China, and that is ruled by Communists and likely to remain so for the indefinite future." The Johnson Administration's reaction to Fulbright's speech was cool.

Tonkin Resolution. The conflict in Vietnam went badly for the United States in the mid-1960's. The South Vietnamese government seemed unable to rally its people in the war against the Communists, while the U.S. commitment, both in men and money, was significantly increased. As congressional concern mounted, President Johnson May 18, 1964, requested $125-million additional economic and military aid for South Vietnam. The request for $70-million in additional economic aid and $55-million in additional military aid for Vietnam was quickly approved May 20 by the House Foreign Affairs Committee.

On Aug. 2 and 4, U.S. destroyers patrolling the Gulf of Tonkin off the coast of North Vietnam reported torpedo attacks by Communist PT boats and President Johnson ordered an air strike at their bases resulting in the destruction of 25 boats. On Aug. 5, the President asked Congress to enact a resolution to "give convincing evidence to the aggressive Communist nations, and to the world as a whole, that our policy in Southeast Asia will be carried forward, and that the peace and security of the area will be preserved."

Republicans as well as Democrats endorsed the President's actions. Only Senators Morse (D Ore.) and Ernest Gruening (D Alaska) objected that, in Morse's words, "continuation of the U.S. unilateral military action in Southeast Asia, which has now taken on the aspects of open aggressive fighting, endangers the peace of the world." On Aug. 7, 1964, the Senate voted 88-2 and the House 414-0 to pass a resolution (S J Res 189, H J Res 1145) declaring support for "the determination of the President as Commander-in-Chief, to take all necessary measures to repel any armed attack against the forces of the United States and to prevent further aggression." The resolution also affirmed U.S. intentions to aid any member or protocol state of the SEATO pact "requesting assistance in the defense of its freedom" (PL 88-408).

Rising Costs. The escalating military situation in South Vietnam also meant a steep rise in costs. During 1965, the House May 5 and the Senate May 6, by nearly unanimous roll-call votes, passed and sent to the President a bill (H J Res 447) making fiscal 1965 supplemental appropriations of $700-million to meet mounting military requirements in Vietnam. The actions came less than 53 hours after President Johnson had appealed to Congress to "provide our forces with the best and most modern supplies and equipment" and to show "prompt support of our basic course: resistance to aggression, moderation in the use of power; and a constant search for peace." The President signed the bill May 7 (PL 89-18).

Vietnam Report. As congressional debate over Vietnam increased, the Senate Foreign Relations Committee, on Jan. 7, 1966, released a report on Vietnam by Senate Majority Leader Mansfield. The new report, entitled "The Vietnam Conflict: The Substance and the Shadow," concluded that "the situation, as it now appears, offers only the very slim prospect of a just settlement by negotiations or the alternative prospect of a continuance of the conflict in the direction of a general war on the Asian mainland." Militarily, the report said that the large-scale introduction of U.S. forces "has blunted but not turned back the drive of the Viet Cong."

Vietnam Hearings. The Mansfield report and President Johnson's decision to end a 38-day pause in the bombing of North Vietnam touched off an even more heated congressional debate, especially in the Senate.

On Feb. 4, 1966, the Senate Foreign Relations Committee began hearings on an Administration bill (S 2793) authorizing $415-million in supplemental fiscal 1966 foreign economic aid, of which $275-million was earmarked for emergency aid to South Vietnam. The hearings were televised nationally and were used by the Committee as a springboard to conduct a public inquiry into the Administration's "general policy" in Vietnam. Witnesses included David E. Bell, administrator of the Agency for International Development; Gen. James M. Gavin (ret.); George F. Kennan, former ambassador to the Soviet Union; Gen. Maxwell D. Taylor (ret.), special consultant to President Johnson; Secretary of State Dean Rusk; and Vice President Hubert H. Humphrey, who met informally with the Committee after his return from South Vietnam.

Authorization. On March 1, 1966, Congress moved nearer to action on supplemental appropriations for U.S.

activities in Southeast Asia as it passed several authorizing bills. Passage of the measures came in contrasting atmospheres in the two chambers as Senators continued lengthy and at times acrimonious debate of President Johnson's Vietnam policies while the House acted quickly and with only limited outright criticism of the increased U.S. commitment to the war. However, 78 Democrats signed a statement which said that their vote for a defense supplemental appropriations authorization did not mean they supported an enlargement of the military effort.

China Hearings. On March 8, 1966, the Senate Foreign Relations Committee began hearings on U.S. policy toward Communist China, an outgrowth of the Vietnam hearings. Describing the hearings as "educational," Chairman Fulright said: "At this stage, perhaps the most effective contribution the Committee can make is to provide a forum for recognized experts and scholars in the field of China."

The main theme to emerge from the next three weeks of testimony was that U.S. policy had not only contained China, but also had attempted to isolate her, which had been both unwise and unsuccessful. Dr. John K. Fairbank of Harvard's East Asian Research Center typified the theme when he concluded: "Containment alone is a blind alley unless we add policies of constructive competition and international contact.... Peking's rulers shout aggressively out of manifold frustrations.... Isolation intensifies their ailment and makes it self-perpetuating, and we need to encourage international contact with China on many fronts."

The majority of witnesses proposed three basic changes in U.S. policy: official diplomatic recognition of Communist China, an expansion of trade relations, and admission of Communist China into the United Nations. These changes were opposed by a minority of witnesses, one of whom was former Rep. Walter H. Judd (R Minn. 1943-63). Judd said that "our choice—with Red China just as it was with Japan and Hitler—is not between checking and not checking, it is whether to check early, while we can, and with allies—or try to check the aggression later, when it is stronger, closer and we have fewer and weaker friends and allies."

On May 19, 1966, the House Foreign Affairs Committee on the Far East and Pacific released a report on its open hearings, held between Jan. 25 and March 10, on U.S. policy towards Asia. The report recommended that the United States, despite rebuffs, should continue to seek peaceful contacts with China while at the same time preventing her from any aggressive expansion. To do this, it continued, would require both increased assistance and cooperation from Western European allies and increased U.S. efforts to build up the strength of "the independent countries of the continent—from India and Pakistan to Japan and Korea."

Vietnam Preoccupation

From 1966 through 1968, the Vietnam conflict emerged as the dominant issue in Congress, overshadowing civil rights, the war on poverty and the other programs of Lyndon Johnson's Great Society. Its cost alone soared to more than $2-billion a month. By early 1968, more than 500,000 U.S. troops were committed to South Vietnam and casualty figures had risen above the 100,000 mark.

As the war and the American commitment intensified, so did congressional debate. But appropriations to carry out the Administration's war policy were approved by large margins since most dissenters found it awkward to vote against supplies or in favor of restrictions on the grounds that they did not wish to expose men already committed to battle to unneeded risks.

During consideration of President Johnson's request for supplemental 1967 defense funds for the further prosecution of the war, several restrictive amendments were proposed in the House and Senate. All were rejected except for a policy declaration of support for efforts to prevent expansion of the war, to bring the war to an honorable conclusion and to provide necessary support for servicemen in Vietnam.

Senate Foreign Relations Committee. A major font of criticism of Administration aims in the war was the Senate Foreign Relations Committee under Chairman Fulbright. By 1968, Secretary of State Dean Rusk repeatedly had refused to testify in public hearings conducted by the committee.

In 1967, the Committee held three sets of hearings on subjects relating to the war:

• In January and February on the "responsibilities of the United States as a great power."

• In August on a resolution (S Res 151) asserting that U.S. commitments to a foreign power required legislative approval. The committee Nov. 20 reported an amended resolution (S Res 187) but no floor action was taken on the measure.

• In October and November on two resolutions (S Con Res 44, S Res 180) urging that a solution to the war be sought through the United Nations. The committee Nov. 21 reported S Res 180 and the Senate Nov. 30 unanimously adopted the measure. No action was taken by the House.

House Action. Although there was less anti-war activity in the House than the Senate, 52 House members (48 Republicans and four Democrats) on Sept. 25, 1967, introduced resolutions (H Con Res 508, 509, 510) calling for a congressional review of U.S. war policy. Sponsors claimed that "a great uneasiness" among members and the public had emerged since the passage of the Gulf of Tonkin resolution of 1964. They also pointed out that 123 House members had not been members of Congress when the Tonkin Gulf resolution passed. The resolutions were referred to the Rules Committee, which took no action.

Three weeks later, a bipartisan group of 30 House members sent a letter to President Johnson asking him to halt the bombing of North Vietnam. Sixty-seven House Democrats had written Mr. Johnson June 23 asking him to renew efforts to have the UN Security Council consider the Vietnam conflict.

1968. In 1968, there was not a single significant roll call taken on the Vietnam issue, although there were more hearings in the Senate. Instead, debate on the war shifted from Congress to the presidential campaign. The muting of congressional opposition was attributable in large measure to President Johnson's March 31 announcement that he had ordered an immediate bombing halt over most of North Vietnam and that he was withdrawing from the race for the Presidency.

Nixon Administration—1969-70

Indochina. U.S. involvement in Indochina and the nation's global defense commitment provided the focus of congressional concern in foreign affairs during the 91st Congress (1969-70). U.S. activities in Asia, more than any other region, planted the seeds of congressional anxiety about the nature and repercussions of American commitments abroad.

In February 1970, President Nixon formally outlined what had become known as the "Nixon Doctrine," which had as its goal avoiding direct U.S. military involvement in remote corners of the globe. Mr. Nixon said the central thesis of his policy was "that the United States will participate in the defense and development of allies and friends, but that America cannot—and will not—conceive all the plans, design all the programs, execute all the decisions and undertake all the defense of the free nations of the world."

But in 1969 and 1970, the apparent extension of the Vietnam conflict into neighboring Laos and Cambodia—at the same time the Administration was attempting to "Vietnamize" the war in South Vietnam—gave rise to the fear that the United States was still bogged down in what Sen. Fulbright termed the "second Indochina war."

Congressional developments concerning Indochina during the 91st Congress included:

1969:

• Senate approval Dec. 16 of an amendment to prohibit a commitment of U.S. ground troops to Laos and Thailand. The prohibition was added to the defense appropriations bill (HR 15090) on a 73-17 roll call and retained in the House-Senate conference report.

• Introduction of scores of resolutions in both the House and Senate, mostly by doves, urging immediate or more rapid troop withdrawals. Administrations supporters countered with resolutions supporting the President's policies.

1970:

• A seven-week Senate debate—from May 13 to June 30—on Cambodia following U.S. military action in Cambodia beginning April 30 and ending June 30.

• Senate adoption June 30 of an amendment barring retention of U.S. forces in Cambodia. The House rejected the amendment July 9, but a revised version cleared Congress Dec. 22.

• Congressional repeal of the 1964 Gulf of Tonkin resolution, often cited by the Johnson Administration as congressional authorization for increased U.S. involvement in Southeast Asia.

• Congressional approval of an Administration request for supplementary military and economic aid for Cambodia.

• Senate rejection Sept. 1 of an amendment to cut off all funds for the war in Vietnam.

China Issue Renewed. The Nixon Administration's Vietnamization and troop withdrawal policy in Indochina combined with its goal objective of a reduced U.S. military presence in Asia prompted many members of Congress to call for a re-evaluation of U.S. policy toward China. There was stepped up activity in Congress concerning China in 1969 through 1971 in the form of policy declarations by leading members and House and Senate hearings on China policy.

In March 1969, Sen. Edward M. Kennedy (D Mass.) urged the United States to discard the "passions of the past," terminate restrictions on trade and travel to the China mainland, establish consular relations as a step toward full diplomatic recognition and reverse opposition to Peking's membership in the UN. Kennedy said these steps should be taken without jeopardizing U.S. ties with Taiwan.

Kennedy was joined by Senators Mark O. Hatfield (R Ore.), Jacob K. Javits (R N.Y.) and Symington and Rep. Paul Findley (R Ill.). On March 10, Senate Majority Leader Mansfield called for an end to special travel restrictions and said trade in non-strategic goods should be put on the same basis as U.S. trade with other Communist nations.

On Sept. 25, by a 77-3 roll-call vote, the Senate passed a resolution (S Res 205) declaring the sense of the Senate that U.S. recognition of a foreign government did not "of itself imply that the United States approves of the form, ideology or policy of that foreign government." Secretary Dulles had argued against recognizing Peking because doing so would imply U.S. approval.

Although Alan Cranston (D Calif.), the author of the resolution, argued that it should not be construed primarily as laying the groundwork for recognition of Peking, Thomas J. Dodd (D Conn.), who voted against passage, said, "if the resolution is not intended to clear the way for the recognition of Communist China...then it is difficult to understand the motivation behind it...."

A similar interpretation of the resolution was contained in a Nov. 21, 1969, letter to the President signed by a bipartisan group of 39 Representatives and 8 Senators expressing "full support and agreement with your Administration's policy of seeking ways to normalize relations with Peking." This endorsement, they wrote, was evidenced by passage of S Res 205.

But while those members seeking changes in U.S. Far East policy made most of these speeches, there was powerful opposition. In 1969 and 1970, Congress reaffirmed in routine resolutions its opposition to the seating of Communist China in the United Nations.

And during debate on a foreign aid bill (HR 15149) Dec. 9, 1969, the House adopted, 83-54, an amendment by H. R. Gross (R Iowa) prohibiting U.S. assistance to countries that aided or traded with Peking. But the amendment subsequently was dropped from the final bill.

Finally, a group of powerful Representatives attempted unsuccessfully in 1969-70 to give an additional $54.5-million in military assistance to Taiwan. Principal sponsors of the addition were Otto E. Passman (D La.), Robert L. F. Sikes (D Fla.), House Minority Leader Gerald R. Ford (R Mich.) and Armed Services Chairman L. Mendel Rivers (D S.C.). Argued Sikes: "Taiwan is a... needed brake on Red Chinese aggression."

And in reaction against early moves by the Nixon Administration to relax tensions with the Peking regime, some Republicans criticized the President. In a Senate speech late in 1970, Sen. Barry Goldwater (R Ariz.) stated: "Nothing can be gained but a great deal can be lost by admission of Red China to the United Nations or its diplomatic recognition by the United States."

Hearings. In November 1969 and May 1970, the Senate Foreign Relations Subcommittee on U.S. Commitments Abroad held hearings in executive session on U.S. commitments to Nationalist China. The hearings, containing testimony by Administration witnesses, published in July 1970, disclosed that U.S. policy toward Taiwan was in a period of transition as U.S. economic and military assistance to Taiwan was being phased out. *(Details on hearings p. 21-24)*

In the fall of 1970 the House Foreign Affairs Subcommittee on Asian and Pacific Affairs held its first hearings on China policy since 1966. Most of the experts on China and the Soviet Union who testified before the Subcommittee urged a normalization of relations with mainland China. Many of the same witnesses testified in June 1971 before the Senate Foreign Relations Committee again recommending improved relations with Peking. *(Excerpts from House China hearings, p. 57; Senate hearings p. 77)*

Nixon Administration—1971

By mid-summer of 1971 the Nixon Administration already had revealed two of its three major alterations in U.S. policy toward Communist China: the end of the trade embargo (June 10) and the President's planned trip to Peking (July 15).

The third stage came Aug. 2, when Secretary of State William P. Rogers announced that the United States would support the seating of Communist China in the United Nations. The Secretary said the United States would oppose any efforts to "expel the Republic of China or otherwise deprive it of representation" in the UN. He avoided the question of which China would serve on the Security Council, saying only that the United States would abide by the views of the majority of UN members on the question. *(For late 1971 Nixon policy and UN vote p. 16-25)*

Involvement. White House congressional liaison chief Clark MacGregor said the State Department had briefed key members of Congress "well in advance" of Rogers' announcement. The Secretary and other department officials had made 20 to 30 phone calls to House and Senate leaders, members of the Senate Foreign Relations and House Foreign Affairs Committees and other members who had expressed particular interest in China policy, MacGregor said.

UN Commission. Eight members of Congress served on President Nixon's special commission on the United Nations which recommended April 26 that the People's Republic be admitted to the UN.

The commission reported that it had found growing public support in the United States for the involvement of the Chinese Communists in the work of the UN as well as "a deep American commitment to the continued representation of the Republic of China on Taiwan."

The eight members of Congress serving on the commission were: Senate Foreign Relations Committee Chairman J. W. Fulbright (D Ark.), House Foreign Affairs Committee Chairman Thomas E. Morgan (D Pa.), Sen. George D. Aiken (R Vt.), Sen. John Sherman Cooper (R Ky.), Sen. John Sparkman (D Ala.), Sen. Robert Taft Jr. (R Ohio), Rep. Cornelius E Gallagher (D N.J.) and Rep. Sherman P. Lloyd (R Utah).

The 50-member commission, headed by Ambassador Henry Cabot Lodge and including prominent Americans

Change in Positions

The change in opinion among many members of Congress during 1971 on the issue of seating Communist China in the United Nations was exemplified by the actions of three of the five congressional members of the Committee of One Million Against the Admission of Communist China to the United Nations.

Listed as members of the organization's steering committee were: Representatives John M. Ashbrook (R Ohio), ranking Republican, Internal Security Committee; Thomas E. Morgan (D Pa.), chairman, Foreign Affairs Committee, and Clement J. Zablocki (D Wis.), second-ranking Democrat, Foreign Affairs Committee, and Senators Hugh Scott (R Pa.), minority leader, and Peter H. Dominick (R Colo.).

Sen. Scott was cosponsor of the resolution (S Con Res 38) praising President Nixon for his planned journey to Peking. He also lauded the administration's shift in policy regarding the UN China seat.

Rep. Morgan was one of eight members of Congress included on the special commission that recommended to Mr. Nixon that Peking be admitted to the UN.

Rep. Zablocki told Congressional Quarterly Feb. 17 that his views had changed and the he would support the admission of the People's Republic to the UN under the theory of universality, which calls for the admission of all nations. But he said he would not favor expulsion of Taiwan as a condition of Peking's membership.

Lee Edwards, secretary of the Committee of One Million, told Congressional Quarterly Sept. 28 that he had recently talked to Zablocki and had been reassured that Zablocki still opposed the admission of Communist China to the UN.

But Ivo Spalatin, the congressman's administrative assistant, disagreed. After checking with Zablocki, Spalatin reported that the February report was correct, that Zablocki had altered his views and supported a two-China policy as long as Taiwan was able to retain its seat in the UN.

from many professional fields, held public hearings in six cities before submitting its 100-page report.

Conservative Positions. On Sept. 28, 21 senators and 33 house members of both parties joined in issuing a statement declaring that if the Republic of China were expelled from the United Nations, "we would feel compelled to recommend a complete reassessment of U.S. financial and moral support of the UN."

The statement was drafted by Senators James L. Buckley (Cons-R N.Y.) and Bill Brock (R Tenn.). At a news conference the same day, Buckley said each member who signed the statement would have a different interpretation of the word "reassessment."

When the assembled members were asked why Congress had failed to go on record—for the first time in 20 years—as opposing Peking's admission into the UN, Sen. Strom Thurmond (R S.C.) stated that although he continued to support such a policy, "I'm not sure the

majority of Congress would oppose the seating of Communist China in the United Nations this year." Thurmond added that he supported President Nixon's planned journey to Peking.

Walkout. But the news conference quickly broke up when two of Congress' staunchest conservatives—Representatives John G. Schmitz (R Calif.) and John R. Rarick (D La.)—disassociated themselves from the statement and walked out.

Schmitz, a member of the John Birch Society, referred to the Peking regime as a "bandit government" run by a "bunch of butchers." He explained that he and Rarick could not accept any statement that would acquiesce in the admission of Communist China into the UN.

Congressional Warning. On Oct. 11, Sen. Buckley visited the United Nations personally, met with U.S. Ambassador to the UN George Bush and then warned that, as the representative of 21 senators, he would "immediately introduce legislation calling for the dramatic reduction" of U.S. contributions" to the UN if Taiwan were expelled. Buckley said his views reflected "the views of Congress."

On Oct. 13, President Nixon received a petition signed by 336 of the 430 members of the House (there were five vacancies) opposing "strongly and unalterably" the expulsion of Taiwan from the UN. According to the White House, the President thanked the members who presented him with the petition—most of them among the more conservative members of the House—for their "support of the Administration on this issue."

Reaction to UN Vote

The expulsion of Nationalist China from the United Nations Oct. 25 produced immediate response—mostly angry and accompanied by threats of retaliation—from members of Congress. Action, statements and floor speeches Oct. 26 included:

• A move by senators from both parties for a reduction in U.S. financial support of the United Nations, and specifically in the $141-million authorization for UN funds in the $3.2-billion foreign aid authorization bill on which debate began Oct. 26.

• A demand by Sen. Barry Goldwater (R Ariz.) that the United States withdraw from UN membership.

• Announcement by James L. Buckley (Cons-R N.Y.) the night of the vote that he was drafting legislation calling for a major reduction in U.S. financial contributions to UN activities.

• A move to delete a provision in the foreign aid authorization bill repealing the Formosa Resolution of 1955. The resolution authorized the President to use armed force to protect Nationalist China against armed attack. (p. 53)

• A promise by John J. Rooney (D N.Y.), chairman of the State-Justice-Commerce Appropriations Subcommittee, to reduce UN funds in the bill when it comes up again in 1972. They totaled $107.9-million in the fiscal 1972 bill which was signed into law Aug. 10.

• A move to base UN contributions from each country on population. Under the proposal, made by Philip M. Crane (R Ill.), U.S. contributions to the UN would equal the same percentage as U.S. total population is to total population of all UN member nations, or 7.6 percent. If

Congress and the UN Issue

From 1950 to 1970, Congress expressed its opposition to the seating of Communist China in the United Nations at least 30 times.

Every year, statements expressing this opposition have been attached to appropriations bills and enacted into law.

Every year, that is, until 1971.

The last time Congress went on record opposing admission of the People's Republic of China into the UN was in 1970, when it cleared a bill signed by President Nixon Oct. 21 (PL 91-472) providing appropriations for the Departments of State, Justice and Commerce. That routine bill, along with the annual foreign aid appropriations measure, had been used in past years as the vehicle for the China resolution.

In 1970, the section on China stated: "It is the sense of Congress that the Communist Chinese Government should not be admitted to membership in the United Nations as the representative of China."

A more extensive policy statement on the China question had been included in the foreign aid bill since 1956. But it was stricken for the first time in 1970 as one of several deletions granted by point of order. In the past, the appropriations bill had been submitted to the House under a rule waiving points of order.

The deleted provision was similar to that included in the fiscal 1970 foreign aid appropriations bill (PL 91-194), signed by the President on Feb. 9, 1970. That bill included the traditional statement as Section 105:

"The Congress hereby reiterates its opposition to the seating in the United Nations of the Communist China regime as the representative of China, and it is hereby declared to be the continuing sense of Congress that the Communist regime in China has not demonstrated its willingness to fulfill the obligations contained in the Charter of the United Nations and should not be recognized to represent China in the United Nations."

That provision, which was rendered obsolete by omission from the later (fiscal 1971) bill, asked the President to inform Congress of the implications for U.S. foreign policy in the event the Peking regime was seated in the UN.

1971 Deletion. On June 24, 1971, as the House was considering the State, Justice, Commerce appropriations bill for fiscal 1972 (HR 9272—PL 92-77), Rep. Sidney R. Yates (D Ill.) made a point of order against the China resolution "as being legislation on an appropriation bill."

In reply, the floor manager of the bill, Rep. John J. Rooney (D N.Y.), stated: "This provision has been in this bill for many, many years. It goes back to the time that the late Senator from Nevada, Pat McCarran (D 1933-54), was chairman of Senate appropriations for this bill. However, I am constrained to have to concede that the point of order has merit."

The point of order was sustained and the resolution was deleted from the bill.

applied to total contributions, this would cut the U.S. outlay from $318-million to approximately $80-million for 1972.

House Speaker Carl Albert (D Okla.), in answer to the proposals for retaliation against the UN and those countries which supported the ouster of Nationalist China, said, "I...feel it would be heaping one irresponsibility on another to diminish our support of the United Nations because of our displeasure with this vote." He was joined by Foreign Aid Appropriations Subcommittee Chairman Otto E. Passman (D La.).

Formosa Resolution Repeal. The Senate Foreign Relations Committee held hearings in June 1971 on five resolutions calling for changes in U.S. China policy. *(Hearing excerpts and summary of resolutions, p. 77)*

The Committee Sept. 21 reported S J Res 48 (S Rept 92-363), sponsored by Senators Frank Church (D Idaho) and Charles McC. Mathias (R Md.). The resolution, which would have the force of law, would withdraw authority granted to the President in 1955 to use armed force to protect Formosa and the Pescadores from attack. *(Text, 1955 congressional action p. 29, 30, 46)*

The Committee attached S J Res 48 to the fiscal 1972 foreign aid authorization (HR 9910) when it reported the aid bill Oct. 20 (S Rept 92-404). Debate on the foreign aid bill began Oct. 26, the day after the UN General Assembly had voted to expel Nationalist China and seat the Peking government. The debate took place in an emotional atmosphere charged by the Taiwan expulsion which contributed to general disillusionment with the foreign aid program. The Senate Oct. 29 by a 27-41 roll-call vote killed the foreign aid bill.

Earlier in the debate, the Senate voted Oct. 28 by a 43-40 roll-call vote to delete from HR 9910 the provision repealing the 1955 Formosa Resolution.

The amendment deleting the provision was sponsored by Bill Brock (R Tenn.) and James L. Buckley (Cons-R N.Y.). Deputy Secretary of Defense David Packard, testifying Oct. 28 on the treaty to return Okinawa to Japan, told the Foreign Relations Committee he opposed the provision in HR 9910 repealing the resolution.

In debate Oct. 27, the Senate adopted an amendment by Ted Stevens (R Alaska) making repeal of the Formosa Resolution effective April 15, 1972. As reported, HR 9910 repealed the 1955 resolution effective as of adjournment of the first session of the 92nd Congress. Stevens described his amendment a "matter of timing" to make it "certain" that repeal of the 1955 resolution would not appear to express a congressional intent to abandon Taiwan in the wake of its expulsion from the UN.

Gordon Allott (R Colo.) said repeal of the 1955 resolution would be "an invitation to the Red Chinese to attack Taiwan," and Peter H. Dominick (R Colo.) said it would be "adding insult to the Republic of China." Church said that "nothing in the repeal of the Formosa Resolution would impair the formal obligation to come to the defense of Taiwan (under the 1954 treaty)."

In debate Oct. 28 on the Brock amendment deleting the Formosa Resolution repealer, Brock said repeal of the resolution soon after the UN vote "would be interpreted around the world as total abdication of an old and valued friend and ally, Nationalist China." Minority Leader Hugh Scott (R Pa.) said repeal "would be at the very least misinterpreted by the Asian press. It is really unnecessary to go to the extent of repealing it."

CHINA POLICY: INFLUENCE ON U.S. ELECTIONS SINCE 1948

China wouldn't have gone Communist—if the Truman Administration had had backbone.

—Richard M. Nixon, vice presidential candidate,
Oct. 10, 1952

Richard M. Nixon capitalized on his new China policy during the 1972 presidential campaign, leaving Democratic party opponent George McGovern issue-less on the China question. Nixon's trip to Communist China early in the election year was a reversal of the hard-line U.S. policy toward China of two decades.

Paradoxically, reaffirmation of that uncompromising policy had been spelled out tersely in his own party's platform four years earlier. The Democratic platform in 1968 had stressed coexistence and cooperation with the Peking regime and had spoken of "freeing that nation and her people from their narrow isolation."

By adopting, in effect, the Democratic party's previous China position for his 1972 campaign, Nixon defused the issue. In fact, he used his China trip as a campaign talking point, citing the diplomatic initiative as part of his search for a generation of world peace.

1972 Party Platforms

The Democratic platform adopted at the convention in Miami Beach in July 1972 commented only briefly on the China question, and the Democrats' discomfiture was evident. "The beginning of a new U.S.-China relationship is welcome and important," the platform stated. "However, so far, little of substance has changed, and the exaggerated secrecy and rhetoric of the Nixon administration have produced unnecessary complications in our relationship with our allies and friends in Asia and with the U.S.S.R.

"What is needed now is serious negotiation on trade, travel exchanges and progress on more basic issues. The U.S. should take the steps necessary to establish regular diplomatic relations with China."

The Republican platform, adopted at the national convention in Miami Beach a few weeks later, took credit for ending the isolation of China and for starting "constructive new relationships with the Soviet Union and the People's Republic of China."

"Before this administration," the GOP platform declared, "a presidential visit to Peking would have been unthinkable. Yet our President has gone there to open a candid airing of differences so that they will not lead some day to war. All over the world tensions have eased as...the strongest of the nations and the most populous of nations have started discoursing again.... While profound differences remain between the United States and China, at least a generation of hostility has been replaced by frank discussions. In February 1972 rules of international conduct were agreed upon which should make the Pacific region a more peaceful area now and in the future."

1948

On Nov. 2, 1948, in the midst of some of the most severe fighting of the Chinese civil war, Harry S Truman surprised most political observers by winning a full term as President. Democrats not only won the White House over highly favored New York Gov. Thomas E. Dewey (R) but also regained control of the House and Senate.

Almost three months before the election—on Aug. 13—Secretary of State George C. Marshall had advised the staff of the U.S. embassy in Nanking (the Nationalist regime's capital) that it was "not likely that the situation will make it possible for us at this juncture to formulate any rigid plans for our future policy in China."

Up to that point, support for much of the Truman Administration's foreign policy had been bipartisan, due mostly to the efforts of Sen. Arthur H. Vandenburg Jr. (R Mich. 1928-51), chairman of the Senate Foreign Relations Committee and a converted isolationist.

But on Oct. 3—one month before the presidential election—the House Foreign Affairs Subcommittee on World Communism, chaired by Rep. Frances P. Bolton (R Ohio 1940-69), issued a report calling China the "active theater" in the cold war. The report said the Communists were using China as the testing ground for tactics they might employ in an attempt to take over the world. The subcommittee recommended that the United States give Chiang Kai-shek's Nationalist government a "guarantee of territorial and political integrity."

And in the Senate, Republicans H. Styles Bridges (N.H. 1937-61), Homer E. Capehart (Ind. 1945-63), William F. Knowland (Calif. 1945-59), William Langer (N.D. 1941-59) and Kenneth S. Wherry (Neb. 1943-51) urged the Administration to provide more military and economic aid to Chiang Kai-shek.

During the campaign, Gov. Dewey, flanked by the brothers Dulles—John Foster (later to become Secretary of State) and Allen W. (later director of the Central Intelligence Agency)—as foreign policy advisers, charged that the Truman Administration had done far too little to protect China from the Communists.

The Republican platform for 1948 stated: "We will foster and cherish our historic policy of friendship with China and assert our deep interest in the maintenance of its integrity and friendship." The Democratic 1948 platform, in contrast, cited only the Truman Administration's achievement in providing China with "vital aid."

Two days after the election, President Truman told Congress that "many difficulties" were involved in making aid to China effective and that U.S. officials constantly had to oversee how funds were expended.

1952

By 1952, the Chinese Communists successfully had routed the Nationalist forces, sent Chiang Kai-shek and his allies in flight to Formosa, proclaimed the People's Republic and signed a 30-year treaty with the Soviet Union. The Communist North Koreans had launched their Soviet-inspired attack on South Korea (June 25, 1950), and a successful U.S. military drive to the Yalu River in North Korea had brought masses of Chinese "volunteers" into the conflict (October 1950). The United Nations' "police action" had become a bloody and frustrating war, the conduct of which became a prime issue in the 1952 campaign.

Since Chiang's fall, the Truman Administration had attempted to maintain a "hands off Formosa" policy despite strong Republican objections. But the invasion of Korea prompted the President on June 27, 1950, to station the U.S. 7th Fleet in the Formosa Straits both to protect the island from the Communists and to prevent any further Nationalist attacks on the mainland.

McCarthyism. The four years between presidential elections also had seen the advent of McCarthyism, as Sen. Joseph R. McCarthy (R Wis. 1947-57) repeatedly charged that many State Department officials, especially those responsible for U.S. Far Eastern policy, were either Communists, sympathizers or dupes. Although he subsequently lost interest in China, McCarthy and his accusations remained a key campaign issue.

Political rhetoric concerning the Far East was as bitter, emotional and often vicious in the months leading up to and during the 1952 election campaign as at any time during the postwar period. Republicans openly blamed the Democrats for the fall of Chiang and the invasion of South Korea. Many agreed with McCarthy that there had been Communist influence on policy-making in the Far East and called for investigations.

As McCarthy and his allies increased their attacks, naming specific officials in the department, President Truman personally replied. On May 2, 1952, Mr. Truman condemned what he called "political gangsters" who "are motivated by such a lust for power that they are willing to wreck the lives and careers of innocent public servants" by creating "an atmosphere in which a charge is a conviction in the public mind despite the lack of evidence." He added: "I think they are worse than Communists, and I think they are partners with them."

As the election approached, the rhetoric sharpened. Campaigning for the GOP presidential nomination, Sen. Robert A. Taft (Ohio 1939-53) advocated arming the Nationalist Chinese for a full-scale attack on the mainland. On Jan. 12, 1952, he said the State Department's "pro-Communist policies...fully justified" Sen. McCarthy's demands that the department be investigated.

Another presidential contender, former Minnesota Gov. Harold E. Stassen (R), charged the "blinding, blundering, bewildering" Far East policy of the "spy-riddled" Truman Administration was directly responsible for U.S. casualties in Korea.

GOP Convention. On July 7, 1952, Gen. Douglas MacArthur, whom Mr. Truman had dismissed as commander of U.S. and UN forces in the Far East because of the general's repeated public statements urging expansion of the conflict into Communist China, made the keynote speech of the Republican National Convention in Chicago.

MacArthur charged that the Administration had "condemned" the people of China to "Communist tyranny" and contended that when the Chinese entered the Korean conflict, "our leaders lacked the courage to fight to a military decision, even though victory was readily within our grasp—a victory which...might well have saved continental Asia from Red domination."

John Foster Dulles wrote a strongly worded plank in the Republican 1952 platform charging that the Administration had "squandered the unprecedented power and prestige" the United States had enjoyed since the end of World War II, had scuttled the Nationalist Chinese regime, had caused the Korean war through ambiguous policy statements and then "produced stalemates and ignominious bartering" after war broke out.

On July 11, the convention chose Dwight D. Eisenhower and Sen. Richard M. Nixon (Calif. 1950-53) as its presidential and vice presidential candidates. Nixon had won his Senate seat in 1950 in a hard-fought race against Rep. Helen Gahagan Douglas, a liberal Democrat (1945-51). Mr. Nixon's charges that Mrs. Douglas frequently voted with Rep. Vito Marcantonio (American Labor Party, N.Y. 1935-37; 1939-51), whose voting record often had been described as pro-Communist, established Mr. Nixon's reputation, to some, as an unscrupulous campaigner.

Democrats. The Democrats, also meeting in Chicago, July 26 chose Illinois Gov. Adlai E. Stevenson and Sen. John Sparkman (Ala.) as their candidates and adopted a platform pledging "a continued effort, by every honorable means, to bring about a fair and effective peace settlement in Korea in accordance with the principles of the United Nations' charter.... We reject the ridiculous notions that would have the United States face the aggressors alone. That would be the most expensive—and the most dangerous—method of seeking security."

It added: "Our military and economic assistance to the Nationalist Government of China on Formosa has strengthened that vital outpost of the free world and will be continued."

Campaign. During the campaign, Mr. Eisenhower endorsed the Truman Administration's decision to enter the Korean conflict but accused the President of allowing the nation to become militarily weak and of announcing "to all the world that it had written off most of the Far East as beyond our direct concern." Secretary of State Dean Acheson's 1950 definition of the U.S. "Asian defense perimeter" so as to exclude Korea had directly invited Communist aggression, Mr. Eisenhower charged.

Stevenson defended the Administration's conduct of the war, and on Oct. 18, President Truman charged in Providence, R.I., that Mr. Eisenhower "held out a false hope to the mothers of America in an effort to pick up a few votes" by calling for a withdrawal of U.S. troops from the front lines. Mr. Truman pointed out that 50 percent more South Koreans were fighting in the conflict than were Americans.

But on Oct. 24, Mr. Eisenhower found what many observers felt was a paydirt issue in a nation deeply disturbed by the war, its mounting casualties and the stalemate in truce negotiations. He told an audience in Detroit, Mich., that he would "forego the diversion of politics" after the election and "concentrate on the job of ending the Korean War." The former general pledged: "I shall go to Korea" in an effort to end the conflict. Stevenson quickly denounced the proposed trip as a "slick idea that gets votes by playing upon our hopes for a quick end to the war." President Truman charged that Gen. Eisenhower was attempting a "superman" approach to the problem and that "anybody who poses and talks like a superman is a fraud."

On Nov. 4, Gen. Eisenhower and Mr. Nixon were elected by a wide majority. The Republicans also gained control of both houses of Congress by narrow margins.

1956

From 1952 through 1956, French power in Southeast Asia collapsed and the United States, although not signing the Geneva accord ending the seven-and-one-half-year war in Indochina, acceded to the partition of Vietnam while bolstering its campaign to thwart Communist China's designs on Formosa and Southeast Asia.

1955 Formosa Crisis. On Jan. 18, Communist forces seized the offshore island of Ichiang, 210 miles north of Formosa and seemed prepared to invade the nearby Tachen islands. The situation led President Eisenhower to ask Congress, in a special message Jan. 24, for explicit authority to use U.S. armed forces to protect Formosa, the adjoining Pescadores islands and "related positions and territories." It was essential to U.S. security that Formosa "should remain in friendly hands," Mr. Eisenhower said.

What remained unclear was the Administration's intent regarding Quemoy, Matsu and the other offshore islands. To many Democrats, these islands—unlike Formosa—clearly belonged to Mainland China, and the question of their disposition was an internal matter outside the scope of legitimate U.S. security interests. They feared that the Nationalists, in their efforts to regain the mainland, would use this "fatal ambiguity" over the offshore islands to maneuver the United States into a war with Communist China.

Congress Jan. 28 passed a resolution granting the President the authority he had requested. On Feb. 9, the Senate ratified a mutual defense treaty with Nationalist China (signed by Secretary of State Dulles on Dec. 2, 1954) whereby both countries agreed to meet an armed attack against U.S. or Nationalist territories, including Formosa, the Pescadores islands and "such other territories as may be determined by mutual agreement."

The Nationalist government Feb. 5 requested U.S. protection of a withdrawal operation from the Tachen islands. Fighting continued for some weeks in the Quemoy and Matsu area, then abated, although a formal cease-fire never was concluded.

Stevenson Statement. On an April 11 national radio program, Adlai Stevenson (who was to announce his candidacy for the 1956 Democratic presidential nomination seven months later) proposed that the United States should seek an international declaration "condemning the use of force in the Formosa Strait" and an agreement by free nations "to stand with us in the defense of Formosa against any aggression, pending some final settlement of its status."

He stated: "The possibility of war just now seems to hinge upon Quemoy and Matsu, small islands that lie almost as close to the coast of China as Staten Island does to New York." He asked: "Are the offshore islands essential to the security of the United States? Are they, indeed, even essential to the defense of Formosa—which all Americans have agreed upon since President Truman sent the 7th Fleet there five years ago?"

Stevenson concluded: "Should we be plunged into another great war, the maintenance of our allies and the respect and the good will of the uncommitted nations of Asia will be far more important to us than the possession of these offshore islands by Chiang Kai-shek ever could be."

Secretary Dulles replied the next day that Stevenson "suggests, as original ideas, the very approaches which the government has been and is actively exploring."

Chinese Offer. The State Department June 12, 1956, revealed it had rejected a Chinese proposal (made on May 12) that Secretary of State Dulles and Chinese Foreign Minister Chou En-lai meet to discuss Taiwan and other problems. The department said the proposed talks would be held on too short notice and pointed out that 13 Americans were still being held by the Communists.

Conventions. On Aug. 16-17, 1956, Adlai Stevenson and Sen. Estes E. Kefauver (Tenn. 1949-63) were nominated at the Democratic convention in Chicago.

The party's 1956 platform pledged "determined opposition to the admission of Communist China into the UN," and urged "a continuing effort to effect the release of all Americans detained by Communist China." It charged that Secretary Dulles "brags of 'brink of war' " rather than making "our peaceful purpose clear beyond dispute...."

On Aug. 22, President Eisenhower and Vice President Nixon were renominated at the Republican convention. In a convention speech, Senate Minority Leader William F. Knowland (Calif.) pledged to fight Chinese Communist membership in the UN "as long as I have a voice and a vote" in the Senate. (He was defeated two years later in the California gubernatorial election.)

The GOP platform pledged "to oppose the seating of China in the UN" and denounced "any trade with the Communist world that would threaten the security of the United States and our allies."

Campaign. War in the Middle East and uprisings in Hungary and Poland dominated the news during the last weeks of the 1956 campaign, eclipsing domestic issues and changing the emphasis in international policy debates. China rarely was mentioned.

In a Sept. 5 news conference, President Eisenhower defended his Far East policy, stating that when he took office the French "were involved in a hopelessly losing war in Indochina" and could have lost "the whole peninsula." The Geneva settlement, the President said, "at least gave the free world a firm foothold and under stronger leadership." The Korean conflict was still going on, he said, "under conditions where it was impossible to win. (We were) suffering losses merely to hold the line we then had. It was settled and we still hold that line."

Gen. Eisenhower was re-elected Nov. 6 with the largest popular vote in history and a plurality matched only three times in the last century. But the Democrats retained control of the House and Senate.

1960

In 1957, the Administration restated its determination to keep Communist China out of the UN and its opposition to the establishment of diplomatic relations with Peking. But Secretary Dulles expressed some flexibility on the question of trade and, on Aug. 22, the State Department announced that restrictions on travel to China by some newsmen were being lifted. Three days later, the Chinese accused the United States of "insufferable arrogance" in agreeing to "send its correspondents to China just on the basis of its own unilateral decision" and "refusing reciprocal visas to Chinese correspondents."

Formosa Again. While the United States was preoccupied with events in the Middle East, Communist China resumed military operations against the Nationalist-held offshore islands in August 1958, concentrating heavy artillery barrages against Quemoy. As in 1954-55, tensions mounted rapidly, buoyed by speculation that the Communists were preparing an invasion and that the United States was poised for massive intervention.

Through September and October, both sides mounted massive propaganda campaigns. Soviet Premier Khrushchev declared Moscow's solidarity with Peking, while President Eisenhower and Secretary Dulles alternated pledges of "no retreat" with pleas for a cease-fire. Dulles flew to Formosa Oct. 20, reportedly to persuade Chiang Kai-shek to reduce the size of his forces deployed on the offshore islands, and the Communists soon scaled down the bombardment of Quemoy to an every-other-day affair of no military significance.

In the midst of the crisis, a number of Democrats in Congress expressed concern that the Administration was overly anxious to get militarily involved in a situation that did not warrant such involvement.

One of them, Sen. John F. Kennedy (D Mass. 1953-60), stated Sept. 13 that "the weight of military, diplomatic, political and historical judgment would dictate a contrary policy concerning Formosa." His statement came one week after Vice President Nixon's observation that the United States "could make no greater mistake than by appearing to be a paper tiger" in the Far East, because "in dealing with dictatorships you do not maintain peace by appearing to be weak but only by maintaining strength militarily and diplomatically."

During the 1958 congressional election campaign, Mr. Nixon Oct. 13 rebutted a statement issued by the Democratic Advisory Council charging that the Republicans were leading "us to the brink of having to fight a nuclear war" and urging that the United States refer the dispute over Quemoy and Matsu to the United Nations. Mr. Nixon said the council had "the same defensive, defeatist, fuzzy-headed thinking which contributed to the loss of China and led to the Korean war."

Conventions. On July 13-14, 1960, the Democrats nominated Sen. Kennedy and Senate Majority Leader Lyndon B. Johnson (Texas 1949-61) as their presidential and vice presidential candidates. The Democratic platform reaffirmed "our pledge of determined opposition to the present admission of Communist China" to the UN and "likewise to defending Formosa." It added: "Although normal diplomatic relations between our governments are impossible under present conditions, we shall welcome any evidence that the Chinese Communist government is genuinely prepared to create a new relationship based on respect for international obligations, including the release of American prisoners."

The Republicans July 27 chose Richard Nixon as their candidate, with U.S. Ambassador to the UN Henry Cabot Lodge as his running mate. The GOP platform only stated that opposition to Communist China's entry into the UN and the establishment of diplomatic relations with Peking would continue.

Campaign. The only debate on China policy between Kennedy and Nixon during the campaign concerned the importance of defending Quemoy and Matsu.

In two televised debates on Oct. 7 and 13, the candidates expressed differing opinions. Mr. Kennedy criticized the ambiguity of the nation's commitment to defend the two offshore islands, saying it was "unwise to take the chance of being dragged into a war which may lead to a world war over two islands which are not strategically defensible," and that "our line should be drawn in the sea" between Formosa and the mainland.

Mr. Nixon countered that "these two islands are in the area of freedom (and) we should not force our Nationalist allies to get off of them and give them to the Communists." The issue blossomed as Mr. Kennedy called Nixon "trigger-happy" while Mr. Nixon said Mr. Kennedy was advocating a course of "surrender."

On Nov. 8, Kennedy defeated Nixon in the closest presidential election of the 20th century.

1964

The next four years witnessed the evolution of the Sino-Soviet split, the deterioration of the Chinese Communist economic program (the "Great Leap Forward"), the Chinese-Indian border dispute, the Cuban missile crisis and the assassination of President Kennedy.

Vietnam. But most important to U.S.-Chinese relations was America's growing involvement in Indochina. By the time of his death, President Kennedy's Administration had supplied South Vietnam with 16,000 U.S. military advisers and large amounts of economic and military aid.

After Mr. Kennedy's death, the Johnson Administration quickly moved to shore up what political stability there was in South Vietnam with increased military aid, including more troops.

Gulf of Tonkin. On Aug. 2 and 4, 1964, U.S. destroyers patrolling the Gulf of Tonkin off the coast of North Vietnam reported torpedo attacks by Communist PT boats and President Johnson ordered a retaliatory air strike at their bases. Congress Aug. 7 overwhelmingly passed the Gulf of Tonkin resolution authorizing the President "to take all necessary measures to repel any armed attack against the forces of the United States and to prevent further aggression."

Campaign. The Republicans July 15 had nominated Sen. Barry Goldwater (Ariz.) as their presidential candidate and adopted a platform stating: "We are opposed to the recognition of Red China. We oppose its admission into the United Nations. We steadfastly support free China." On Vietnam, the platform charged that the Democrats had "encouraged an increase of aggression in South Vietnam by appearing to set limits on America's willingness to act."

The Democrats Aug. 26 chose President Johnson as their candidate for President, with Sen. Hubert H. Humphrey (Minn.) as his running mate. The Democratic platform did not make the usual mention of Communist China, but said only: "We will support our friends in and around the rim of the Pacific and encourage a growing understanding of peoples, expansion of cultural exchanges and strengthening of ties."

U.S. policy in Vietnam became a double-edged campaign issue as Sen. Goldwater found in it evidence of the Administration's "no-win" policy against Communism while Mr. Johnson linked his actions in the Gulf of Tonkin to those of the United States in the Cuban missile crisis as examples of the successful application of force with restraint.

On Sept. 28, the President told a Manchester, N.H., audience that he was opposed to getting involved in "a war with 700 million Chinese." He also pledged that the United States was "not going north (in Vietnam) and drop bombs at this stage."

Mr. Johnson's overwhelming victory at the polls Nov. 3 supplied no answer to the increasingly pressing question in Vietnam—whether to step up the degree and scope of U.S. involvement in the war or encourage efforts to seek a negotiated settlement of the conflict.

1968

That question was answered in the next four years by Lyndon Johnson, who ordered the bombing of North Vietnam only three months after the 1964 election. From that point on, the U.S. commitment in the Vietnam struggle grew precipitously. It often overshadowed serious domestic problems, distorted the U.S. economy and loomed over U.S. foreign policy. Its costs soared to more than $2-billion a month; reflecting the expense of the war, the federal budget by fiscal 1969 was at a record $186-billion, with $80-billion of that for defense. The U.S. troop commitment by late 1968 was 535,000, and in the wake of the enemy's Tet offensive, U.S. casualties were running high.

The burden of the conflict was brought home to the American people by regular television coverage, anti-war demonstrations, inflationary pressures and the 1968 tax surcharge, and by the presidential campaign bids of three Democrats strongly opposed to the war— Senators Eugene J. McCarthy (Minn. 1959-71), Robert F. Kennedy (N.Y. 1965-68) and George McGovern (S.D.).

The first indication of U.S. readiness to de-escalate the conflict came March 31, 1968, when President Johnson—in the same speech in which he announced he would not run for re-election—said he had ordered a limited bombing halt of North Vietnam. On Oct. 31, only days before the election, Mr. Johnson extended the bombing freeze to all of North Vietnam.

Conventions. The Republicans, meeting in Miami Aug. 5-8, chose Richard Nixon once again as their presidential candidate, with Gov. Spiro T. Agnew (Md.) as his running mate.

The GOP platform's section on China stated: "Under existing conditions, we cannot favor recognition of Communist China or its admission to the United Nations."

The Vietnam plank was surprisingly dovish, calling for decreased U.S. involvement and for vigorous pursuit of negotiations. The section was widely interpreted as an eclectic effort, reflecting the thinking of Gov. Nelson A. Rockefeller (N.Y.) and Mr. Nixon, with few concessions to the more conservative views of Gov. Ronald Reagan (Calif.). The plank was drafted primarily by Rep. Peter H. B. Frelinghuysen (N.J.), a Rockefeller supporter, and it replaced a negatively worded plank in the original draft which warned that any negotiated settlement would be "unacceptable" unless it assured Vietnamese self-determination.

While violence erupted in the city streets and thousands of police and guards imposed security precautions unprecedented in the annals of American political conventions, the Democrats met in Chicago Aug. 26-29 and nominated Hubert H. Humphrey (Minn.) for President and Sen. Edmund S. Muskie (Maine) for Vice President.

The Democratic platform did not mention the issue of recognizing Communist China or allowing her into the United Nations. Instead, it stated: "The immediate prospects that China will emerge from its self-imposed isolation are dim. But both Asians and Americans will have to coexist with the 750 million Chinese on the mainland. We shall continue to make it clear that we are prepared to cooperate with China whenever it is ready to become a responsible member of the international community. We would actively encourage economic, social and cultural exchange with Mainland China as a means of freeing that nation and her people from their narrow isolation."

The platform met the demands of the party's liberals word for word in almost every section except that which dealt with U.S. policy in Vietnam.

Unlike the GOP platform, which urged decreased U.S. involvement in Vietnam, Democrats called for a continued strong American war effort. While the Democrats agreed with Republicans that the South Vietnamese eventually should take over their nation's defense, they gave no indication that an expanded Vietnamese role could lead to U.S. troop reductions in the near future.

Campaign. The Vietnam war had dominated pre-convention activity, especially among the Democrats. It loomed over the general election as the single most important issue. Both candidates knew that, but each had to play it differently. The burden of the issue was on Humphrey and the Democrats.

Nixon avoided most discussion of Vietnam policy because he said he did not want to jeopardize the peace negotiations under way in Paris.

But Humphrey, plagued by heckling by anti-war elements virtually everywhere he sought to speak, had to make a break and establish some measure of independence from the unpopular war program of the Johnson Administration. His significant step to win some of the anti-war Democrats to his side came in a Sept. 30 nationally televised address from Salt Lake City, Utah, when he said he would stop the bombing of North Vietnam "as an acceptable risk for peace."

President Johnson actually took that step one month later. Humphrey appeared satisfied. The combination of his own softened stand and the President's decision won him, at least for the moment, the support of many of the Democrats who had been most disaffected at Chicago.

But in a close election, Mr. Nixon weathered Humphrey's strong comeback and won by a half-million vote margin.

TRADE WITH CHINA AND JAPAN: PROSPECTS AND PROBLEMS

Warmer commercial and political relations with Communist China—a prospect fostered by President Nixon's invitation to visit Peking and his earlier termination of the 21-year embargo on dealing with the mainland Chinese—somewhat overshadowed other aspects of American trade with the Far East in 1971.

But the Chinese market is not likely to play a major role in U.S. foreign trade in the near future. America's major Far Eastern trade prospects—and problems—are with Japan.

Japan's burgeoning exports to the United States, resulting in a growing U.S. deficit in trade with Japan, probably were the primary influence behind the international part of President Nixon's new economic policy. Mr. Nixon on Aug. 15 imposed a temporary 10-percent surcharge on most imports and suspended the exchange to gold of surplus dollars held by foreign governments and central banks.

Japan is, second only to Canada, both the largest market for U.S. goods and the largest source of U.S. imports. It is America's fastest-growing market and the greatest importer of U.S. farm products.

Balance of Trade. But Japanese exports to the United States have outdistanced the flow of U.S. goods to Japan, giving this country a deficit in its trade relations with Japan since 1965. Trade experts in the Commerce Department estimated in mid-1971 that the deficit for the year would exceed $2.5-billion.

The deficit with the Japanese has produced a deficit in U.S. trade with the Far East, which was a major factor in Commerce Secretary Maurice H. Stans' forecast July 27 that the United States faced the probability of an over-all world trade deficit in 1971—the nation's first for a full year since 1893. The U.S. world trade balance has declined from steady surpluses of $5-billion to $7-billion in the early 1960s to the level of $1-billion to $2-billion since 1967.

Trade surpluses during the 1960s offset much of the imbalance in the U.S. international payments position caused by the Vietnam war, other military spending abroad, foreign travel by Americans, foreign aid and American investment abroad. The dwindling trade balance contributed to the $3-billion deficit in 1970's basic balance of payments position (excluding short-term influences), according to the Treasury Department.

The pressure of imported Japanese goods—chiefly textiles but also including radios, tape recorders, cameras, bicycles, motorcycles, automobiles and many other manufactured items—was the leading justification for legislation in 1970 which, if enacted, would have imposed severe quota limitations on many imports. Enactment of the Trade Act of 1970 was averted by a filibuster in the Senate during the closing days of the 91st Congress.

U.S. Trade with Far East

(in billions of dollars)

	Exports	Imports	U.S. Balance
Japan			
1972	$ 5.0	$ 9.1	$—4.1
1971	4.1	7.3	—3.2
1970	4.7	5.9	—1.2
1969	3.5	4.9	—1.4
East and South Asia			
1972	4.4	5.2	—0.8
1971	4.0	3.9	+0.1
1970	4.0	3.4	+0.6
1969	3.5	3.0	+0.5
Oceania			
1972	1.4	1.1	+0.3
1971	1.2	0.9	+0.3
1970	1.2	0.9	+0.3
1969	1.0	0.8	+0.2
Total Far East			
1972	10.8	15.4	$—4.6
1971	9.3	12.1	—2.8
1970	9.9	10.2	—0.3
1969	8.0	8.7	—0.7

Note: Not all totals add exactly, due to rounding.
East Asia includes Burma, Thailand and Malaysia to South Korea, Indonesia, the Philippines and Taiwan.
South Asia includes from Afghanistan to East Pakistan.
Oceania includes principally Australia and New Zealand.

SOURCE: U.S. Commerce Department

Japan is the dominant Far East trader. It accounted for more than half the $10.2-billion total of U.S. imports from the Far East in 1970 and imported nearly half of America's Far East exports, which came to $9.9-billion. At a total of $10.6-billion, U.S.-Japanese trade was the second-largest bilateral trading relationship in the world. *(Table of exports, imports and U.S. balance in Far East trade, above)*

Further, Japan is the largest supplier of goods to Asia. It is in the process of becoming the largest market for the exports of Asian nations. Since the Chinese-Soviet rift became pronounced in 1963, Japan has replaced the Soviet Union as mainland China's foremost supplier. The Japanese trade with China exceeded that of any other developed nation during the decade of the 1960s, both in total value and in growth.

China Trade

In sharp contrast to the vigorous if unbalanced Japanese trade, U.S. trade with mainland China has lain

Trade with Mainland China

Non-Communist Countries

(In millions of dollars)

Year	Exports	Imports
1952	$ 272	$ 368
1953	287	433
1954	293	380
1955	317	487
1956	434	641
1957	528	624
1958	767	756
1959	651	698
1960	637	767
1961	647	644
1962	589	693
1963	732	849
1964	964	1,157
1965	1,252	1,409
1966	1,422	1,804
1967	1,410	1,656
1968	1,286	1,603
1969	1,366	1,656
1970	1,665	1,670
1971	1,529	1,842

SOURCE: U.S. Commerce Department

moribund under an embargo imposed by former President Harry S Truman in December 1950, after China attacked American forces in the Korean War. But President Nixon's progressive relaxation of cold war prohibitions against U.S. contact with China has demonstrated his belief that the most populous nation on the earth has important political and economic roles to play in the world.

Mr. Nixon said as much in a speech July 6, three days before his assistant for national security affairs, Henry A. Kissinger, began secret meetings with Premier Chou En-Lai in Peking which resulted in the invitation to the President to visit the Chinese capital. China is potentially "one of the five great economic superpowers," Mr. Nixon said, which will determine the course of great events in the remainder of the 20th century. An end to two decades of Chinese isolation, he said, would remove a threat to world peace but would mean "an immense escalation of their economic challenge." *(Nixon Administration China Policy, p. 16)*

The President had begun in July 1969 to ease travel and trade restrictions with China. On June 10, 1971, he lifted restrictions on export of a wide variety of non-strategic goods to China and on commercial imports from the mainland.

Limited Prospects. Trade prospects for the near future are limited, even if Mr. Nixon's Chinese trip is entirely successful. China's total foreign trade has been estimated at approximately $4.3-billion a year, divided about equally between imports and exports. In contrast, U.S. exports totaled $43.2-billion in 1970; imports came to $40-billion.

Just over $3-billion of the Chinese total was with non-communist nations in 1969, according to the Commerce Department. China's exports totaled almost $1.7-billion; her imports were slightly less then $1.4-billion. Both totals were below those for 1966, the peak year. This was also the last year of peak consumption of Australian and Canadian wheat which began with a period of Chinese crop failures from 1959 to 1961. *(Table of Chinese trade trends, this page)*

Under favorable conditions, it has been estimated, U.S. exports to China might rise as high as $900-million by 1980. Metals, mainly steel, and wheat topped Chinese imports in 1969, according to the Commerce Department, and demand was strong for crude rubber, fertilizers and textile fibers. China provided a good market for various types of machinery in the mid-1960s, but this demand had fallen off sharply by 1969. The Chinese are known to want certain manufactured items, such as airplanes, transportation and earth-moving equipment and measuring and controlling instruments. Most items in these categories were not freed by Mr. Nixon's order on June 10, although export licensing for them remained possible on an individual-case basis.

Competition. To the extent that the United States might compete for the Chinese market, it would have to compete not only with communist countries but also with friends, allies and current competitors. Japan has replaced the Soviet Union as the leading exporter to mainland China, meeting the largest share of the steel and fertilizer demand. Among others with substantial Chinese trade in 1969 were West Germany, Britain, Australia and Canada. *(Table of major non-communist traders with China, p. 61)*

The leading Chinese exports in 1969, according to the Commerce Department, were food (mainly to Hong Kong), manufacturered textiles (already the subject of friction between the United States and Japan and other Asian manufacturing nations) and crude materials. Although China has not attempted to maintain an individual balance of trade with each of its trading partners to the extent that Eastern European countries have, the limited market for Chinese exports was expected to have a bearing on Chinese acceptance of imports from the United States.

Obstacles. China has in past years placed substantial obstacles in the path of Western European traders who wanted to sell to the mainland. The excesses of the "cultural revolution," during which some western traders were detained and mistreated, have not been encountered recently, and indications are that western traders are welcomed. But ordinarily they are allowed to enter the country only to attend the semi-annual trade fairs at Canton, at which the Chinese have become accustomed to concluding most of their foreign trading transactions.

As in most trade with the Soviet Union and Eastern Europe, westerners deal with "middleman" representatives of trading corporations. Dealings with the actual users or suppliers of products are rare. Further, Chinese practices prolong negotiations and make sales of new products difficult.

Professor Stanley Lubman of the University of California (Berkeley) Center for Chinese Studies described the result in testimony before the Senate Foreign Relations Committee June 29:

"Purchases of western products are most likely approved long before the fair by the end-user and the ministry to which it is responsible; in addition, purchases depend on prior allocations of scarce foreign exchange. As a result, Chinese negotiators come to Canton with a 'shopping list' from which departures on short notice are extremely difficult. Westerners have to bombard the Chinese trading corporations with technical literature and samples and wait for expressions of interest which may come only after many months, if at all."

According to Lubman, Chinese contract clauses vary from those of western contracts, and performance demands and determinations are rigid. The lack of informal contacts between partners in a deal results in complicated and protracted negotiation of disputes. These and other difficulties are intensified by Chinese distrust of westerners—a condition only gradually being ameliorated by individual contacts. Concern to avoid disclosing economic intelligence has sometimes led the Chinese to provide less than full specifications for a product; this, in turn, has resulted in Chinese claims based on alleged defects in purchased products. *(Lubman testimony, p. 86)*

International politics may influence the choice and treatment of customers, according to Lubman. But in general he found the Chinese record good on adherence to specifications and timely payment and political interference with contracts very rare.

Trade with Japan

American textile manufacturers, under strong pressure from Japanese and other Asian imports, were nearly successful in their efforts to enact rigid category-by-category import quotas in the Trade Act of 1970. The textile industry enjoyed significant political influence with the Nixon Administration. Together with the footwear industry, which faced severe competition from European shoes, textile manufacturers organized imposing support in Congress. Other U.S. industries which were meeting import competition and for which protective legislative machinery was established in the bill joined in urging Congress to limit the access of foreign exporters to the American market.

Japanese Restrictions. Certain restrictive practices of the Japanese, as well as other nations, gave weight to the protectionist argument.

In 1963 Japan had restrictions in force limiting import quantities of 217 industrial and agricultural items. By June 1971 the total had been reduced to 60. Much of the reduction was attributable to American pressure.

Japan's restrictive practices were contrary to the General Agreement on Tariffs and Trade, the 1947 basic multilateral trade agreement to which most nations have subscribed. Japan's resort to protectionist policies was accepted originally because of its devastation in World War II.

Secretary of State William P. Rogers, in a speech June 30, assessed the current situation simply:

"Japan no longer needs the panoply of economic protection that seemed appropriate only a decade ago.... Japan has become a major power, both politically and economically....Japan must act with the sense of responsibility appropriate to its new position. Its economic policies, for example, must be subject to the same criteria as those of the other major developed countries. In our bilateral economic relationships, Japan cannot expect privileges in the United States which it is not itself prepared to extend."

Growth. Japan's gross national product (total economic output) is now third in the world, coming after only the United States and the Soviet Union. Japanese GNP tripled in the last decade; its exports quadrupled, and its foreign exchange reserves tripled. In the same period, U.S. exports to Japan rose three times as fast as those to the rest of the world.

The Japanese enjoy certain advantages over the United States: higher rates of productivity in many Japanese industries, the effect of inflation on American ability to compete and the Japanese retention of import restrictions.

The U.S. consumer benefits from low-cost imports from Japan, Rogers conceded in his June 30 speech. "Nevertheless, when Japanese imports increase at a rapid rate over a short period of time—as they have in a number of fields—they can raise difficulties for particular American firms, workers and communities."

Meanwhile, he said, the U.S. competitive position has been weakened by Japanese restrictions. He cited quotas on computers and integrated electric circuits and limitations on American capital investment in Japan.

"While Japan is making efforts," he said, "the fact is that the rate of progress toward their removal has not been sufficient to affect the balance of trade....The pace of Japan's economic achievements abroad has continued to outstrip the effect of its liberalization programs in opening its markets at home, and the imbalance of trade, instead of lessening, is continuing to grow."

U.S. Trade Deficit. Rogers' statements were borne out by U.S. trade-balance figures. In the first six months of 1971, the United States imported $1.4-billion more from Japan than it exported. The deficit in the first half of 1970 was approximately $500-million. The deficit

Major Traders with China

All Non-Communist Countries

(in millions of dollars)

Countries	Exports			Imports		
	1960	1965	1971	1960	1965	1971
Asia:						
Japan	$ 3	$ 245	$ 579	$ 21	$ 225	$ 323
Hong Kong	2	3	3	208	406	558
Singapore			15			132
	28	7		57	106	
Malaysia			17			44
Ceylon	25	36	26*	28	24	19*
Australia	23	164	27	10	26	41
Canada	9	98	202	6	13	23
Europe:						
West Germany	95	79	139	69	73	95
United Kingdom	90	72	69	69	83	77
Italy	40	56	59	24	38	64
France	53	60	113	23	44	71
Total	$637	$1,252	$1,249	$767	$1,409	$1,447

SOURCE: U.S. Commerce Department   *Jan.-Aug.

for the first half of 1971 was equal to the previous full-year record deficit, which occurred in 1969.

Part of the growing 1971 U.S. trade deficit with Japan was attributed to special factors. The oncoming dock strike and threatened steel strike led many American buyers to stock heavily in steel and other products earlier in the year. A modest recession in Japan led the Japanese to push exports in order to move inventories and maintain production.

Liberalization Program. Further, a number of factors mitigated the case against Japan's trade practices. Among these was an apparent acceleration in lifting restrictions. The Japanese government announced an eight-point liberalization program early in June.

Direct foreign investment in Japanese business had been severely limited in the past. Investment in an established business generally had been limited to about 30 percent; many new businesses had been required to accept joint arrangements under which 50-percent Japanese ownership was retained. The Japanese automobile industry had been shielded from foreign investment.

But in June, the government approved the Chrysler Corporation's acquisition of 35 percent of the Mitsubishi Motors Company, a major Japanese producer. Similar acquisitions by the Ford Motor Company and the General Motors Corporation were under consideration. The Japanese government also approved in June the proposal of Data General Corporation to license manufacture of mini-computers in Japan.

Complaints about past Japanese policies on foreign investment in Japanese business have ignored the fact that Japanese overseas investment has been limited. The greater part of Japan's investments in foreign countries have been concentrated in Southeast Asia in raw material production.

Japan's overseas investment was less than $2-billion at the end of 1970, and only about one-third of it was direct investment. The remainder was in loan guarantees and long-term production contracts. While limited, U.S. investment in Japan is more than five times greater than Japanese investment in the United States.

Japanese investors showed interest in the Alaskan North Slope oilfield, although they were not among the successful bidders in late 1969 for a North Slope lease. Japanese firms won contracts to supply pipe for the planned pipeline to transport oil to warm-water ports on the southern coast. Large quantities of Japanese-made pipe have been shipped to Alaska, although construction of the pipeline has been delayed on ecological grounds.

Import quotas were cut to a total of 40 in October 1971. Of these, 12 were industrial and 28 agricultural. Among items on which quantitative import restrictions were lifted were pork, electronic telephone switchboards and exchanges and some units of computers.

American observers point out that Japanese demand for consumer goods and geater buying power will in time reduce the advantage that Japanese producers of many manufactured goods have over their American counterparts. According to the Commerce Department, for the last

American observers point out that Japanese demand for consumer goods and greater buying power will in time reduce the advantage that Japanese producers of many manufactured goods have over their American counterparts. According to the Commerce Department, for the last two years Japanese wage increases have exceeded pro-

ductivity increases. If this trend continues, the Japanese competitive advantage will be offset eventually and the capital available for reinvestment in more efficient plants and equipment will be reduced.

Finally, Japanese exports account for only 15 percent of U.S. imports. American exports constitute 29 percent of Japan's imports. In Secretary Rogers' words, Americans "need to realize that Japan has not waged and won a war of trade on the United States...." U.S. gross national product is still five times greater than that of Japan. Total textile imports are only about 4 percent of the U.S. market; total U.S. imports in 1970 were about 4 percent of gross national product.

Textiles. The Japanese textile industry announced March 8 that it would voluntarily limit its exports to the United States if other major Asian textile producers—Hong Kong, South Korea and Taiwan—would do likewise.

Chairman Wilbur D. Mills (D Ark.) of the House Ways and Means Committee, which drafted the Trade Act of 1970, played an important backstage role in maneuvering which led to the Japanese proposal. Mills March 8 announced that the voluntary plan made quota legislation unnecessary.

President Nixon rejected the Japanese proposal in a sharp statement March 11. The President said he would press for textile quota legislation, but Congress took no action in the area in 1971.

Pledges from the other producers were not forthcoming, but the Japanese subsequently announced that they would unilaterally place the voluntary restrictions in effect on July 1. The Nixon Administration found the Japanese textile restriction unsatisfactory because it allowed unlimited exports of any type of manufactured textile as long as the over-all quota was observed. Negotiations were underway with the four Asian producers for a formal agreement to limit exports by categories when the Japanese announced their proposal.

While the negotiations were in process, Mr. Nixon announced his new economic policy Aug. 15. The policy included a 10-percent surcharge on foreign imports. The Administration then used the surcharge in its negotiations with the Japanese and the other Asian textile producers. Washington promised to remove the surcharge on textiles covered by the negotiations if the Asian producers agreed to limit their exports to the United States. Confronted with what was widely described as a U.S. ultimatum, the Japanese Oct. 15 signed an agreement limiting synthetic fiber and wool textile exports to the United States. Similar agreements were reached with Taiwan, Hong Kong and South Korea.

Other Inroads. The U.S. Tariff Commission ruled on March 4, 1971, that imported Japanese television sets were being "dumped"—sold at less than fair market value (generally meaning at less than the corresponding price in Japan). This enabled the Treasury Department, under anti-dumping statutes, to impose special import duties on Japanese sets. Japan exported about $250-million worth of television sets to the United States in 1969. Japanese automobiles had 4.7 percent of the U.S. market in 1970; Volkswagen 6.3 percent. But according to a *Wall Street Journal* survey, sales of Japanese cars—which were growing at rapid rates in 1970—were expected to exceed those of Volkswagen in 1971.

New Economic Policy

Some economists argued that the United States could no longer expect to have a favorable trade balance but that services sold abroad and returns from direct investments abroad should ultimately bring the over-all payments position close to balance. Net services produced a surplus of $1.5-billion in 1971. The total inflow to the United States from direct investment in 1970 was $7.9-billion, while the outflow to foreign investors was about $600-million.

Despite these factors the basic 1970 payments position—current account and long-term capital, excluding short-term movements—was in deficit by $3-billion. The over-all position—the official reserve transactions balance—was in deficit by $9.8-billion. Both positions deteriorated substantially in the first half of 1971.

There were four broad reasons for the payments deficits the United States has experienced almost continuously for 20 years:

• Loss of competitive position in exports, due to reduced productivity (output per unit of labor and investment) and also to price inflation.

• Foreign protectionism, chiefly in two forms—imposition of import quotas limiting U.S. exports and the refusal of countries with strong currencies and international payments surpluses to revalue their currencies upward in relation to the dollar (this had the effect of keeping their own prices low in international markets and keeping U.S. prices high).

• Reverse imports, both long-term and short-term investment in foreign countries and also foreign travel by Americans.

• Overseas government expenditures, including the Vietnam war, other international defense spending by the United States (such as the $14-billion-per-year cost of maintaining forces overseas with the North Atlantic Treaty Organization) and military and economic aid to other countries.

The international monetary system was adapted to a situation in which the United States ran continuous deficits and certain other countries—notably West Germany and Japan—enjoyed surpluses for a number of years. The United States has financed its deficits by requiring other countries to hold surplus dollars. While theoretically the dollars which were surplus to the international trade needs of the countries holding them were exchangeable for gold, in fact the U.S. government has pressured its friends and allies to avoid the necessity for exchanging the dollars. Foreigners held about $48-billion in U.S. obligations, nearly five times the remaining U.S. gold reserve of $10.5-billion.

Overseas dollars were a central factor in an unstable system which placed continuous stress on the United States and occasionally overwhelming stress on other countries. West Germany, under a flood of volatile Eurodollars seeking higher interest rates, in May 1971 stopped absorbing them through its central bank in order to maintain the value of the dollar relative to the mark. The government allowed the mark to float upward in value, but it did not formally revalue the mark.

Nixon Measures. Against this monetary background, President Nixon Aug. 15 suspended conversion of dollars to gold and allowed the dollar to float in value, imposed the 10-percent surtax (in addition to existing customs duties) on imports and proposed a tax credit for business for investment in U.S.-produced equipment.

The Japanese objected strongly to the new Nixon policy and at first tried to resist the influence of the floating dollar on the yen. But on Aug. 27 the yen, too, was allowed to float. Still the Japanese central bank continued to buy dollars in order to keep the price up and reduce the appreciation of the yen. The German central bank also recommended buying dollars in late September after the mark had appreciated by about 10 percent.

Japanese View. "It is widely assumed in Japan," Nobuhito Ushiba, the Japanese Ambassador, told an American audience in September, "that President Nixon's new economic program...is de facto directed primarily against Japan." Ushiba summarized the position of his government on the issues which climaxed in the President's Aug. 15 policy announcements:

• Japan has dismantled its trade barriers to an extent comparable to other major trading nations.

• The impact of the new American policy is particularly severe on Japan because of the higher proportion of Japanese exports going to the United States.

• The "cold-blooded export blitz" attributed to Japan by many of its critics is a myth.

• The Japanese takeover of large parts of the American market is also a myth; Japanese exports have a significant share of some parts of the U.S. market while U.S. exports are dominant in some parts of the Japanese market.

• Import barriers will not cure domestic U.S. ailments—inflation, unemployment or lagging exports.

• A protectionist step by one country "invites retaliation from all its partners."

• Lasting solutions to international problems cannot be reached by following the dictates of one nation; they must be reached by a multilateral approach which takes account of the needs and capacities of all nations.

U.S. Response. Addressing the annual meeting of the International Monetary Fund and the World Bank (International Bank for Reconstruction and Development) in Washington in late September 1971, Treasury Secretary John Connally appeared to adopt a conciliatory attitude. He said:

"If other governments will make tangible progress toward dismantling specific barriers to trade over coming weeks, and will be prepared to allow market realities freely to determine exchange rates for their currencies for a transitional period, we, for our part, would be prepared to remove the surcharge."

Connally's condition that market realities be permitted to determine exchange rates was directed at Japan and, to a lesser extent, West Germany. Further, U.S. diplomatic representatives presented Japan and the other textile-producing nations of Asia—Nationalist China (Taiwan), Hong Kong and South Korea—with an ultimatum to limit their textile exports to the United States or face quotas. The Administration claimed Presidential authority to impose quantitative restrictions.

Connally's indication of flexibility in the U.S. position seemed to provide grounds for optimism that the United States would compromise in repairing the international monetary system if other countries also took appropriate action, rather than allow the situation to degenerate into a trade war. Japanese recognition of the need for compromise, expressed by Ushiba, appeared to promise willingness to move partway toward a solution.

HOUSE FOREIGN AFFAIRS SUBCOMMITTEE HEARINGS ON CHINA

The House Foreign Affairs Subcommittee on Asian and Pacific Affairs held hearings on U.S. policy toward Communist China in September 1970. Hearings took place Sept. 15, 16, 22, 23, 24, 29 and 30 and Oct. 6.

The hearings covered the following issues:
- U.S. policy alternatives toward Communist China.
- Chinese military and nuclear policy.
- Sino-Soviet dispute.
- Chinese policy in Southeast Asia.
- Internal Chinese developments.
- Soviet role in Asia.

U.S. Policy Options

Five witnesses testified on U.S. policy alternatives: A. Doak Barnett, Brookings Institution; Professor Fred Greene, Williams College; Professor Robert A. Scalapino, University of California; Professor Allen S. Whiting, University of Michigan and Assistant Secretary of State Marshall Green.

BARNETT'S TESTIMONY SEPT. 15 (Excerpts)

(Barnett called for removal of U.S. travel restrictions to China, placing U.S.-China trade on the same basis as that with other Communist nations, lowering the U.S. military profile in Asia, and approval of the seating of Peking in both the UN Security Council and the General Assembly, provided a seat could be retained for Nationalist China. In the 12 months following Barnett's testimony, all of his recommendations became Nixon Administration policy.

Re-examination of China Policy

The recent change in the over-all U.S. posture toward China has been quite far-reaching in many respects—more so than many Americans realize. It was not very long ago that the United States regarded the Peking regime as "a passing phenomenon" and called upon the whole world to try to isolate and weaken it, yet, in contrast, early this year President Nixon clearly called for normalization of relations with Peking.

In his first report to Congress on foreign policy, Nixon declared that the United States now intends to "take what steps we can toward improved practical relations" with Communist China, and that our aim is the establishment of "a more normal and constructive relationship." He looked forward to the day when Peking will "re-enter the international community," and he declared that "the principles underlying our relations with Communist China are similar to those governing our policies toward the U.S.S.R."

The general thrust of U.S. policy in Asia today, as symbolized by the "Nixon doctrine," is clearly toward a reduced U.S. military role and presence in the region. Implicitly, this appears to assume—justifiably, I believe—that the "China threat" (that is, the threat of Chinese military aggression abroad) is considerably less than it was assumed to be some years ago. The chances of success for this new policy, moreover, may well depend, in considerable part, in the long run, on whether improvement in United States-China relations is eventually possible.

Seven Policy Recommendations

1. **Unofficial Contacts.** The United States has already gone fairly far in liberalizing its travel regulations and attempting to promote two-way nonofficial contacts and travel between the United States and mainland China. In fact, until Peking shows a more positive interest, perhaps there is not a great deal more that Washington can do. In the meantime, however, Americans of a wide variety of sorts should be strongly encouraged to attempt to obtain Peking's permission to travel to China, and persistent efforts should be made to invite Chinese Communist newsmen, scientists, and the like to visit the United States....

2. **Trade.** The time has now come for the United States to take major steps in the trade field. The small steps taken during the past year, opening the first small crack in the two decade-old embargo on trade with mainland China, have been desirable steps in the right direction.

But now the United States should go much further and move to end the embargo on China trade, putting United States-China trade on the same basis as trade with the Soviet Union and other countries (i.e., forbidding the export of a specified list of strategic goods to China but allowing direct trade in all other commodities). The change in U.S. trade policy is long overdue....

3. **UN China Seat.** I also strongly believe that the United States should now move toward a new position regarding the China seat in the UN. The sound position for Washington to adopt, I believe, is for it to indicate, clearly and explicitly, that the United States will approve the seating of Peking in the UN, in both the Security Council and the General Assembly, so long as a seat can be retained for Nationalist China in the Assembly.

In short, the United States should work to achieve acceptance of some sort of formula for "dual representation." Following the precedent set in the UN, in the case of the United Arab Republic (in which Syria and Egypt first merged and then split—and UN membership was adjusted accordingly without involving any question of either admitting a new member or ejecting one), it can and should be argued that the UN should now recognize and accommodate to the fact that, in a de facto sense, two entities now exist on the territory formerly ruled by the one government which existed in China at the time when the UN was founded, and that both of these entities deserve representation.

At present, it is true, both Peking and Taipei oppose the idea of "dual representation." But the hope should be that ultimately both may prove willing to accommodate to the idea, and in devising a specific "dual representation" formula, every effort should be made to maximize the possibility that Peking and Taipei will eventually accept the concept by divorcing the question of representation from issues of sovereignty.

The aim should be to devise a formula that is sufficiently ambiguous so that all parties concerned will be able, if they so choose, to interpret it in their own fashion, and in the light of their own interests—a formula that could allow both Peking and Taipei, for example, to argue that China is still one, yet would permit other nations to view the situation, and interpret the status of the two Chinese regimes, in whatever terms they might choose. The existing triple representation which the Soviet Union enjoys in the UN provides one precedent that may be relevant. As is well known, not only the Soviet Union but also two of its component republics, the Ukraine and Byelorussia, now enjoy representation in the Assembly.

4. **Recognition.** Formal U.S. recognition of Communist China, and official exchanges of diplomatic missions between Washington and Peking, are not likely to be practicable in the near future. Nevertheless, this should be a long-run U.S. aim, since it will obviously be necessary for any genuine "normalization" of relations. For the present, the United States should at least make it entirely clear that it fully accepts, in a de facto sense, Peking's sovereignty over the mainland of China. At the same time, Washington should also make it clear that the United States supports the Nationalist Government as the existing authority on Taiwan but not as the government of all of China.

At Warsaw, the United States should persistently explore the possibilities not only of continuing but of broadening the scope and significance of the American-Chinese ambassadorial-level talks, and if and when it seems feasible, Washington should be prepared to upgrade the level of these talks. In the late 1950s, Peking at one point proposed foreign minister-level talks between the United States and China; the United States should certainly be prepared to hold talks at this level if and when this seems to be practicable in the future.

5. **Military-Security Issues.** It is in the military-security field that some of the most significant changes will have to occur if U.S.-China relations are to undergo real change....

In recent years, Washington has clearly shown greater sensitivity than it did in the 1950s to Chinese apprehensions and fears. On several occasions, in fact, the United States has attempted to reassure Peking that the United States does not wish to threaten China or, for that matter, to threaten the existence of the small Communist nations on its borders.

These have been significant steps in the right direction, but there are various other steps the United States now can and should take, in my opinion.

In the areas immediately on China's borders, for example, the United States should go considerably further than it has to date, to avoid actions which are obviously viewed as irritating, provocative, or hostile by Peking. U.S. patrols along the China coast should be conducted at a greater distance than at present to avoid giving Peking reason for claiming violations of its air space and territorial waters. Overflights over Chinese territory, which violate China's air space, should be ended; essential intelligence regarding China should be obtained by satellites, as in the case of the Soviet Union. And Peking should be reassured that there will not be provocative guerrilla forays against the mainland, for example from the offshore islands.

Most important, Washington should make clear that while the United States will stand very firm in its commitment to defend Taiwan against military attack, American military support to Taiwan is purely defensive. The United States should not only avoid building up

Taiwan in a way that Peking would regard as threatening; it should go further and commit itself to remove all American forces from Taiwan—certainly after the fighting in Vietnam has been halted, but preferably even before then....

6. **Arms Control.** Every effort must be made also, to convince Peking that it is in the Chinese interest to participate in international arms control efforts, even though, realistically speaking, one must recognize that it may be some years before Peking can be persuaded to collaborate.

In the meantime, the United States should, on its part, forgo all special "anti-Chinese" measures (such as "anti-Chinese" area ABM defenses), and it should also, while striving to reach meaningful arms control accords with Moscow, do what it can to allay Chinese fears that the Americans and Russians are collaborating "against the Chinese."

7. **Taiwan.** From Peking's point of view, of course, none of the issues I have mentioned so far gets to the heart of the matter. Peking maintains that the central issue is Taiwan, and for some years it has insisted that this issue must be "solved" before other problems can be dealt with. Clearly, fundamental differences regarding Taiwan will continue to be a very serious obstacle to significant improvement of relations between Washington and Peking. There is no foreseeable prospect, in fact, of any real "solution" to the Taiwan question, since the United States will maintain its commitment to defend Taiwan against military attack, and Peking will continue its commitment to the eventual recovery of Taiwan.

In this situation, should the United States modify or clarify its position regarding Taiwan in any way? Specifically, what position can and should the United States take in regard to the long-range future of Taiwan? In my opinion, the wise course would be for the United States to make clear that, although Washington's defense commitment to Taiwan is firm, the United States is not committed to any particular long-term political outcome in the area....

In sum, over the long run, the United States should neither support nor oppose either a "one China" or a "two Chinas" solution. Instead, it should be prepared to accept either—or some intermediate outcome—if it evolves peacefully. In the meantime, it should continue to protect Taiwan against threats of military attack and should support the Nationalist Government as the existing authority ruling the island....

Vietnam and China

...I strongly believe that it is an error to allow a preoccupation with the immediate problems in Vietnam to push aside such basic long-term problems as how to work actively toward improving relations with Communist China. It is my view, as I have tried to indicate, that we should proceed now to implement major changes in our China policy—without making adjustments in China policy contingent on developments in Vietnam.

Having said this, let me hasten to add that I do not mean to imply that there is no connection between the immediate problems in Vietnam and the long-term problems relating to China. There are certainly interrelationships of many sorts. Continuing conflict, not only in Vietnam, but also in Laos and Cambodia, creates serious obstacles, in addition to many others which are unconnected with Vietnam, to improved United States-China relations.

It was United States intervention (May 1970) in Cambodia, for example, which led Peking to postpone the most recently scheduled session of the Warsaw talks. But the China problem must not be viewed only in relation to immediate problems in Vietnam—any more than problems in Vietnam should be viewed simply in relation to the long-term problems relating to China.

We must frankly recognize that conflict in Vietnam adversely affects United States-China relations. We must also recognize that any eventual settlement in that area must have Chinese support or, at the least, acquiescence if it is to be viable and durable. In short, we cannot ignore the interrelationships between the China problem and problems in Vietnam.

GREENE'S TESTIMONY SEPT. 15 (EXCERPTS)

(Professor Fred Greene of Williams College, an Asian expert and a Johnson Administration State Department official, took a more cautious approach than Barnett. Greene opposed unilateral U.S. policy initiatives regarding China. He said there were "pressures developing" which would lead to a less hostile China in the future; he cited the Sino-Soviet conflict, China's economic needs and the challenge of Japan.)

Limited Prospects for Change

...I think there is very limited prospect for movement with regard to the Chinese, for two very simple and self-evident reasons:

The first is the deep ideological hostility that the Chinese have displayed toward us. This is not simply a matter of form, or a surface belief; it is a fundamental ideological tenet of the regime, and is rooted at the heart of its whole political structure and belief system. Thus, though the Chinese are not as rigid as their popular image of dogmatic fanatics suggests, they are nonetheless committed to an essentially negative posture toward the United States. That is a key to their general orientation in many of their policies, both domestic and foreign, and is not to be given up lightly. They will stick with it for a long time to come.

The second is that in the course of a foreign policy of antagonism, now more than 20 years in duration, which was given a tremendous push forward by the Korean war, has become encrusted with a series of very difficult and bitter specific issues, not the least of which are recognition, and the fate of Taiwan.

Sino-Soviet Dispute

...the Chinese naturally fear a two-front war with two great powers, and, to some extent, believe in the threat of Soviet-American collusion against them. Of course, they also use it as propaganda, but this is sufficiently mixed with genuine concern to have several effects on Chinese foreign policy.

It limits Peking's capability to put pressure on other areas, and puts certain constraints on its ambitions. This has a moderating and sobering influence on what the Chinese think they can do in East Asia. This provides a

very important constraint, without which the Chinese might feel that they had really an open road to power in Eastern Asia. For they feel that is the only indigenous major power in the region, their hegemonial aspirations would be realized were it not for the opposition of the two superpowers.

Thus, the hostile American presence and the Soviet confrontation generate sufficient concern to lead Peking to adopt tactics that do not track with its main course of foreign policy—in order to obviate prospects of a two-front war. For this reason they reopened the Warsaw talks with us and even now try to keep a line open to the United States, if only as a deterrent to the Soviet Union. This is to keep Moscow from feeling that it has a free hand in operating against the Chinese. The Chinese became more forthcoming toward us in the negotiations this last winter, almost proportionate to the extent that they feared a Soviet threat.

Economic Needs

Thinking ahead to the kinds of problems they (the Chinese) are going to face into the future, when they get to the crunch of continued development, the question really emerges: Can they do without very close and sustained relations with the non-Communist industrialized world?

The answer is "No." They have given this answer themselves. When they switched off from the Russians, in economic relations, they immediately switched on with the West Europeans and the Japanese, particularly in trade. The central question really becomes: If the Russians are to be excluded, do the Chinese contain the Americans in a sort of perpetual condition of isolation, and continue to deal with the Japanese and West Europeans? Or will this be an insufficient basis for them to conduct the kinds of economic development that they will need and desire in the future. This must be a matter of grave concern to their long-range planners. The United States is obviously a better prospect, in terms of resources for the long future.

The Rise of Japan

...The Japanese, not having any armed force and embarrassed by the heritage of the Second World War, have been very careful in their dealing with the states of east and Southeast Asia. But as a consequence they therefore become more acceptable, in a political, diplomatic, organizational, economic sense, and the net effect has been a very significant containing influence on the Chinese.

The Chinese thus face multiple challenges, Russian, American and Japanese in east Asia. Unable really to frustrate either of the two great powers, and seeing the Japanese moving up on them in the race for influence at a rapid pace, Peking finds itself in quite a different situation than it may have projected for the future in the euphoric days of the late 1950s or even the early to mid-1960s. This situation requires sober consideration on China's part and justifies the view that, however formidable the difficulties of coming to terms with the Chinese, at the same time there are fundamental reasons why whoever is running the country, has to think in more accommodating terms in dealing with some of the other major powers.

Restraint in Vietnam War

...the Vietnam war did not escalate into an American-China war. I think the Chinese absolutely expected this to happen during the mid-1960s. It didn't happen, and they have been thinking things over ever since; they fully realize that this was not an accident but the consequence of a conscious American policy not to get involved in such a conflict. And this, I think more than anything else, illustrates to both sides the fact that, however much we might threaten one another, we really do not want to engage in war with one another.

The recent move in the easing of travel regulations, the end of the Taiwan patrols, discussions at Warsaw and the like, I think further illustrate this point, as does our very important statement, last year, of not accepting with satisfaction any Russian intimation of use of force against China during the Sino-Soviet border dispute.

Thus, the Americans, without claiming anything from the Chinese, went on record as not being at all pleased with the notion of a Soviet assault on the Chinese. And this is a fine illustration of a case in which unilateral actions, which I generally do not tend to favor, was a good move. Had we acted otherwise and made such a position conditional, it would have been an act of blackmail, saying in effect to the Chinese, "Look, you do something, and I will make this statement." This would have done more harm than good.

China Not Expansionist

...I don't really feel that the Chinese have been aggressive or expansionist in the classical nation state sense. I never have felt that way. They are obviously aggressively using their armed forces around their frontiers, and have been since the accession of power in 1949.

The military occupation of Tibet, the Korean war, the straits confrontation, the Himalaya dispute with the Indians, and the Sino-Soviet difficulties all indicate they are willing and ready to use military power on their frontiers. This may be considered an aggressive posture in the sense of a pugnacious posture, but I don't think it reflects an intent at aggression—for a couple of reasons.

The first is that Chinese are aware that they lack the great power capability to seize and hold a foreign country without having a major war, and they can't conduct a major war in that kind of a context. There is just not the capacity for this.

More important, I think, again ideology plays a role here. It goes violently against Mao doctrine to have Chinese troops occupying a country and converting it to communism in that fashion....

The main feature of Chinese influence abroad in this military sense is helping to create or sustain an indigenous Communist Party which has to carry its own burden and should conduct people's war, and should do so in accordance with Maoist theories of prolonged struggle. But the indigenous elements have to carry most of the work. The Chinese will give them arms, will give them training, will give them support and exhortation, and doctrine, but they have to carry on the burden—and I think that is essentially the way it has been for a long time. I would doubt very much if that is going to change.

SCALAPINO TESTIMONY SEPT. 24 (EXCERPTS)

(Professor Scalapino stressed two principles as a basis for policy in Asia: (1) de facto acceptance of existing states and (2) non-interference in the internal affairs of states. He also discussed the possibility of Japanese rearmament.)

Two Principles of Asian Policy

Two broad principles might well provide the basis for a new approach to international relations in the Asia-Pacific area:

1. Governments in control of a fixed territory, possessing a physical capital, having established institutions of authority, and having de facto control over the people within this area shall be accepted as states.

2. All states shall accept in principle the right of other states to pursue political and socioeconomic theories and institutions of their own choosing. They shall reserve the right on behalf of themselves and their citizens to support or criticize those institutions and theories verbally, and to render or withhold assistance of an economic, political, or military nature to the government concerned. However, they shall not undertake actions of two types: (a) Physical assistance in any form to indigenous groups dedicated to the overthrow of the government; (b) physical intervention on behalf of a government when it is engaged in fighting a civil war, to be defined as a war involving only people whose permanent residence is within the government's territory as defined in point 1.

Implication of Principles

The implications of these policies with respect to China should be clear. As is well known, our policy as adopted in 1950 was essentially that the Chinese Government had a single locus of power legally—namely, in Taipei—and that this was the only Government which we should recognize. That policy has already undergone significant changes. We have refused to support offensive operations against the mainland launched from Taiwan. We have sought to aid in the development of a self-sufficient, increasingly indigenous nation on that island. We have been willing to meet with the mainland Chinese Government at Warsaw, using official representatives. Meanwhile, the validity of our original policy in terms of the realities of Asia and its capacity to provide a common basis of action among ourselves and our allies is increasingly subject to doubt.

Another policy would be to announce that we acknowledge that there is only one China, leaving open the question of who governs China, but by implication at least abandoning the thesis that the people on Taiwan have any rights concerning their own future. The strongest argument for such an action is that it would accord with the present policy of both the Communists and the Nationalists. Indeed, the former insist that it is the sine qua non of any improved relations on a bilateral basis. A modification of this policy would be the so-called one and one-half China policy whereby we would take the position that Taiwan should be an autonomous province with certain "special" political conditions, albeit as a part of China.

China and Taiwan

The problem with these policies is first and foremost that they do not accord with reality, despite the stated positions of both Peking and Taipei. Mainland China and Taiwan are not presently one. Moreover, they are not growing together in any terms—economic, political or cultural. Indeed, they are growing away from each other at a rather extraordinary rate. Consequently, the peaceful unification of China and Taiwan seems a very remote possibility, now or in the foreseeable future, far too remote to enable policy to be based upon it. Meanwhile, we are pledged to oppose any attempt of unification by force, and as long as that pledge is maintained no attempt is likely to be made....

Commitment to Taiwan

(We should) continue our commitments to and our ties with the Republic of China on Taiwan, making it clear that for our part there had been no diminution of our commitment to see that state recognized in the international community, part of the network of international organizations, and fully defended against external attack. We would, moreover, express the hope that all of the people of Taiwan would at some point be allowed to express their wishes as to the political future of their country.

China and Japanese Rearmament

Japan may rearm at a somewhat faster rate than in the past, and—depending upon events in the rest of Asia—she may ultimately acquire nuclear weapons and play a substantial military role at least in the defense of those regions of northeast Asia regarded as critical to her own security. Such developments, however, particularly the latter, are far less certain than many Americans believe. In any case, moreover, their timing could be crucial.

From these facts, Peking's current campaign to portray Japanese militarism as an imminent threat to all Asians, a campaign directed both at southern Asia and at the Japanese people, takes on its significance. This campaign interacts with the strong currents of pacifism manifest within Japanese public opinion to constrict Japanese options, or to retard the application—and scope —of new policies. Meanwhile, Peking justifies its own nuclear program and the pledge to such groups as the North Vietnamese that it will serve as their "great rear base" by asserting that such policies are essential to its national defense and to the advance of "people's democracy."

(Scalapino was questioned by Rep. Lester L. Wolff (D N.Y.) on Japanese rearmament. Wolff said that Japan was "doubling its percentage of expenditure for...defense needs." He asked Scalapino why he "discounted the threat of Japan..." and what effect a U.S. withdrawal from Asia would have on Japan.)

Let me set forth in somewhat greater detail my reservations about the thesis that Japan is going to become a major military force rapidly or inevitably. First, there are certain deeply implanted psychological and political obstacles, particularly manifest in the postwar Japanese generations. Incidentally, I just returned from Japan four days ago, having made a very brief trip. All of

the public opinion polls which I saw indicate great opposition to nuclear weapons and to the use of defense forces outside Japan proper. A majority of Japanese citizens support the present level of defense preparations but there is not a majority in favor of significant increases.

Public opinion is not necessarily controlling in these matters, nor is it necessarily static. Under certain circumstances, I repeat, it is conceivable to me that this particular obstacle, if you wish to call it that, could be removed. It remains true, however, that neither the Japanese people nor, more importantly perhaps, most members of the Japanese political elite today, regard either China or the Soviet Union as an imminent threat to their security. At least among the members of the ruling party to whom I have recently spoken, there is consequently no compelling reason at this point for the assumption of overseas obligations. While they have worries about the international situation, these worries are not of the type, or in the degree, to move them toward a radically different defense policy.

...if we were to withdraw from Asia precipitously or to abandon our commitments, I think there would be a tendency in Japan toward polarization. In that event it is quite possible that the advocates of substantial rearmament and external military commitments would ultimately carry the day—possible but not certain.

WHITING TESTIMONY SEPT. 24 (EXCERPTS)

(Professor Whiting reviewed U.S.-China policy since 1945, discussed Nixon Administration initiatives and recommended five policy steps.)

Mao Asked U.S. Aid in 1945

Some argue that until Mao dies his megalomaniacal vision of leading world revolution makes "U.S. imperialism" China's implacable enemy with whom no relations are possible other than direct and unyielding confrontation. However, neither distant nor recent history supports this prognosis. (In March 1945)...Mao appealed for American economic assistance to modernize China's backward economy, declaring in a secret official interview:

China's greatest postwar need is economic development. She lacks the capitalistic foundation necessary to carry this out alone. Her own living standards are so low they cannot be further depressed to provide the needed capital. America and China complement each other economically...America needs an export market for heavy industry and specific manufactures. She also needs an outlet for capital investment. China needs to build up light industries to supply her own market and raise living standards...America is not only the most suitable country to assist this economic development of China, she is also the only country fully able to participate.

That is a quotation of Mao Tse-tung from the American Foreign Office in 1945.

Chou En-lai later put it more pithily to Ambassador George Marshall. "Of course we will lean to one side. But how far depends upon you." Mao and Chou even sought a secret meeting with President Roosevelt. Following a traditional Chinese desire to "use barbarians against barbarians," they looked for American economic help to offset Russian political leverage. Privately Chinese Communists insisted to American officials that while they shared a common ideology with Moscow they had different policies. These differences already involved control over Outer Mongolia; later they were to include Manchuria and Sinkiang.

A Contest for Influence in Asia

The next two decades of developments do not require recitation here. Despite the determination with which the People's Republic of China and the United States contested for influence in Asia and elsewhere, however, policy in Peking turned once again to the possibility of using Washington as a makeweight against Moscow. In November 1968 the Chinese Ministry of Foreign Affairs responded to the election of President Nixon with an unprecedented formal proposal to discuss "agreement on the five principles of peaceful coexistence."

Although linked to the standard demand for U.S. withdrawal of "Armed Forces from China's territory Taiwan Province and the Taiwan Straits area," it clearly contrasted with previous Chinese attacks on Soviet advocacy of peaceful coexistence as well as with the tenor of Sino-American talks at Warsaw before their suspension in May 1968. As in 1945, it was not love of America but fear of Russia which motivated Chinese policy.

Prospect of Sino-Soviet War

Following Moscow's August 1968 military intervention in Czechoslovakia, Peking suddenly voiced public concern over the buildup of Russian forces in Central Asia, Outer Mongolia, and around Manchuria. A top Sinkiang military official bluntly warned, "Should the Soviet revisionists dare to attack us, we would wipe them out resolutely, thoroughly, wholly, and completely."

The new American administration did not immediately acknowledge the Chinese initiative. Then Peking vacillated in February 1969, canceling the first Warsaw meeting in over a year on a last-minute pretext. But as Sino-Soviet hostility erupted in sporadic border clashes during the spring, Washington awoke to the prospects, positive and negative, which this posed for U.S. policy. In July the State Department permitted limited American tourist purchases of Chinese Communist goods and President Nixon downgraded the Chinese threat in his tour of South and Southeast Asia.

United States Takes Steps

In August Secretary of State Rogers declared a Sino-Soviet war not to be in the U.S. interest. The next month Under Secretary of State Richardson claimed U.S. policy hoped to "bring China out of its angry, alienated shell." Although Sino-Soviet talks began in October, as did renewed Chinese anti-Nixon propaganda, the administration persisted. The U.S. Ambassador at Warsaw pressed for a meeting with his Chinese counterpart despite the latter being only a charge d'affaires.

Washington further loosened the trade embargo by permitting American subsidiaries and affiliates abroad to sell nonstrategic goods to China and to buy Chinese produce for resale in foreign markets. In addition, tourist purchases became wholly unrestricted as did the buying of Chinese goods by American art collectors, scholars, zoos, and museums. In late December the U.S. 7th Fleet quietly stopped stationing ships in the Taiwan Strait, ending a 19-year heritage of the Korean War.

Persistence was rewarded. On January 20, 1970, the first formal Sino-American meeting in over 2 years agreed to hold future talks in the respective embassies. This move anticipated serious discussions, secure from Soviet bloc monitoring devices in Polish-provided facilities. The next session one month later reportedly showed progress. Then, from all indications, Washington balked. Apparently nervous over reactions in Taiwan, it invited Chiang Kai-shek's son and heir for a highly publicized visit in April. Peking did not react in pique but agreed to resume the talks on schedule.

Three days after Peking's announcement, however, President Nixon sent U.S. troops into Cambodia. On May 19, the eve of the next meeting, China again canceled out, ostensibly because of the Cambodian move.

Third Countries Affect Sino-U.S. Relations

These events of 1945, 1968-69 and 1970 underscore the degree to which Sino-American relations are affected by third-country developments. For both Washington and Peking, their mutual relationship is only one of many whose respective importance and impact on United States-China ties change in time. China's interest in negotiations with the United States, whether to worry Moscow or to decrease the risk of simultaneous confrontation on two fronts, lessened in the first half of 1970 as tensions eased along the Sino-Soviet border. Then China's involvement in the Indochina war suddenly increased when Peking became the primary sponsor of the new coalition formally embracing North Vietnam, the Pathet Lao, the National Liberation Front of South Vietnam, and the continuing claimant to rule in Cambodia, Prince Norodom Sihanouk.

Under these circumstances it is clear why Mao issued his major pronounciamento against "U.S. imperialism and their running dogs" on the very day Sino-American negotiations were to have resumed in Warsaw. From the American viewpoint, too, circumstances make changing China policy less attractive now than before. The two sides' interests are now diametrically and explicitly opposed in Cambodia.

New Initiatives Toward China

If we are to be independent of Soviet dictation in our China policy and if we are to keep alive the possibility of policy debate and alternatives in Peking, whether now or after the death of Mao, we should continue and expand upon the changes begun before events in Cambodia created a fresh impasse.

First, the United States should lift all remaining restrictions on nonstrategic trade with China. As the only major industrial nation in the world preventing normal economic intercourse with the mainland, we cannot but appear to the Chinese—whether of Mao's generation or his successors—as determined to obstruct the modernization of that historic civilization.

Second, the United States should lift all remaining restrictions on travel to China. By formally limiting the categories of application to be approved, regardless of how loosely implemented, the Department of State is, in effect, telling China whom it may and may not allow into its country. There is no logical rationale for permitting scholars or journalists to visit the mainland while denying the opportunity to simple tourists.

Third, the United States should revert to our original position on Taiwan whereby—as we avowed and practiced until 1965—we had no military bases there. Ching Chuan Kang, manned by 7,000 U.S. Air Force personnel, provides KC-135 tanker service for B-52's bombing in Indochina and an emergency landing base for the bombers themselves. It is not essential to our defense commitment to the Republic of China. That commitment must, of course, remain credible. This credibility however is more than amply served by the entire U.S. force posture in the Pacific, especially our Polaris/Poseidon nuclear submarines.

Fourth, the United States should avoid any actions by itself or its allies, particularly the Republic of China, which provocatively probe into or move in close proximity to the mainland. Unmanned aircraft reconnaissance flights and seaborne electronic altering of radar defenses communicate a hostile relationship both antithetical and unneccessary to our interests. Far more distance devices should suffice to serve all but the most unusual and exceptional needs, these arising under conditions of rising tension contrary to the norm over the past two decades.

Fifth, we should exert every effort to resume the diplomatic dialogue begun at Warsaw earlier this year. Our two embassies coexist at less publicized points elsewhere. Perhaps an exchange of views can be explored more quietly in one of the African or Asian capitals. In addition, our desire to improve relations can be reiterated through mutually acceptable channels in frequent contact with both sides, such as Rumania, Pakistan, Japan and Canada.

GREEN'S TESTIMONY OCT. 6 (EXCERPTS)

(Assistant Secretary of State, Asian and Pacific Affairs, Marshall Green noted that Peking was attempting to improve its world image in the wake of the Cultural Revolution and cited U.S. policy initiatives taken by the Nixon Administration in an attempt to improve relations with Communist China. He stressed Washington's continuing commitment to Taiwan. His testimony in closed session was released with security deletions by the State Department.)

Peking's New Diplomatic Offensive

Over the past year or so we have witnessed a mounting diplomatic offensive by Peking during which some 28 ambassadors have been sent abroad in contrast to there only being one of their ambassadors at a post during much of the Cultural Revolution.

Peking has recently received a parade of visiting delegations, signed a number of trade agreements and now Premier Chou En-lai is expected to make an extended tour abroad during which he may officiate at the inauguration of the railroad in the East African area which is 1,100 miles long, built with Chinese engineers and funding.

Peking for the first time in many years has shown interest in UN membership, though retaining as a condition for its membership the ouster of the Government of the Republic of China, a condition which we and many other UN members find entirely unacceptable.

Unilateral U.S. Steps on China

As an earnest of our desire to induce a constructive relationship we have taken a series of small unilateral steps on trade and travel:

• In July 1969 we permitted noncommercial tourist purchases of up to $100 of Chinese goods.

• At the same time, we relaxed restrictions relating to travel to permit almost anyone with a legitimate purpose to travel to mainland China on an American passport. (We have validated over 900 passports for this purpose.)

• In December 1969 we permitted unlimited tourist purchases of Chinese goods, enabling tourists, collectors, museums and universities to import Chinese products for their own account.

• In the same month we permitted American controlled subsidiaries abroad to conduct trade in nonstrategic goods with mainland China.

• In April 1970 we announced selective licensing of American-made components and related spare parts for nonstrategic foreign goods exported to China.

• In August 1970 we lifted the restriction on American oil companies abroad bunkering Free World ships bearing nonstrategic cargoes to Chinese ports.

We have other steps under consideration, all of them in the general area of contacts and trade.

So far we have noted very little tangible indication of response from Peking to these moves. (Security deletion.) Peking finds high utility in the so-called "devil's role" in which it has attempted to cast the United States. Our assuming the "devil's role" has utility to Peking for purposes of maintaining domestic cohesion in the face of an alleged foreign threat, as well as in the very vital global context of communism's "anti-imperialist" struggle....

Issue of Taiwan

Our association with the accomplishments of the Government of the Republic of China and its people over the past twenty years and our shared interest in strengthening the security and progressive development of the East Asian region as a whole, together with our treaty commitment to the defense of Taiwan and the Pescadores, are the bedrock of our relationship with the Republic of China today. These considerations are also the basis for our continued support for the Government of the Republic of China internationally. However one may view the Government of the Republic of China's claim to be the only legitimate government of China, the record of accomplishment on Taiwan and the constructive role which that government and the people on Taiwan are playing internationally merit, we believe, a rightful place for the Republic of China in the community of nations.

On this point, of course, we are in basic disagreement with Peking. The People's Republic of China continues to insist that it will "liberate" Taiwan and in the past at least has refused to renounce the use of force in achieving that goal since it regards this as an "internal" matter. Peking also has insisted that there can be no improvement in U.S.-P.R.C. relations until the United States ends what is customarily described as our "occupation" of Taiwan.

It is not clear precisely what Peking seeks in making this demand. In all probability, it seeks the removal of our military presence from Taiwan and the Taiwan Strait area, although it must know our forces on Taiwan are small. (Security deletion.) Our limited military presence is related to Viet-Nam war needs and constitutes no threat to Peking. (Security deletion.) While we may be able to ease this particular point of tension with Peking, we will not want to do so in a manner which would weaken our commitment to the defense of Taiwan and the Pescadores or rupture our close relationship with the Republic of China.

The United States cannot hope to resolve the dispute between these two rival governments. (Security deletion.) We do strongly believe, however, that these issues should be resolved without resort to the use of force.

(Security deletion.) Both our word and our national interest require that we stand by our treaty commitment to the Republic of China and continue to be associated with that government in pursuit of those goals we hold in common. We hope Peking can be persuaded, on this basis, to set aside the issue of Taiwan so that we can explore the possibilities for removing other sources of tension and improving relations between us.

U.S. Responsiveness to Peking

For our part, we will continue to reiterate our willingness to remain responsive to any indications of reduced hostility from Peking, to cooperate in removing tensions and to enter into a constructive dialogue eventually leading to more normal relations. We will attempt to convince Peking that we are not seeking to "contain and isolate" China and that we favor China's emergence from isolation.

Meanwhile we shall weigh carefully and deliberately any additional steps which will result in net advantage to the overall United States interest. One area, for instance, in which we must constantly weigh the advantages against the disadvantages is in the matter of trade in nonstrategic goods. It is no secret that a number of friendly nations, notably Japan, Great Britain, West German, France, Australia and Canada derive considerable comfort from the fact that they do not have to contend with United States competition in China's growing trade with non-Communist countries.

Some of the steps we have taken, or may take in the future, with a view to improving relations arise from our recognition of changed circumstances since the time of the Korean war. Some of the restrictions relating to travel and trade, for instance, today result in little or no restraint on the Chinese and constitute disadvantages to us. Others are designed simply to untie our hands, so that we may be in position better to bargain with the Chinese on a basis of reciprocity. Finally, some of our courses of action may stem from the increasing quadrilateral nature of Sino-Soviet-Japanese-U.S. relationships.

We do not, for example, seek to exploit the hostility between the Soviet Union and the People's Republic of China. Each is highly sensitive about our efforts to improve relations with the other, but we cannot allow these

apprehensions to deter us from seeking agreements with either of them where those agreements are in our interest....

Peking's Changing Views on UN

(In discussion with Subcommittee Chairman William T. Murphy (D Ill.), Green explained that Communist China had modified its conditions for UN membership.)

Mr. Green. You (Murphy) raised the question about their admission to the United Nations. You see, in the past their position has been very rigid. I was looking at what Chen Yi had said back in 1965. He said when he was asked what conditions there should be for the entry of Communist China, People's Republic of China, in the UN—

Mr. Murphy. Pardon me. He is the Foreign Minister?

Mr. Green. Yes. He said—

The UN must oust the Chiang Kai-shek clique, must cancel its 1951 resolution condemning China and North Korea as aggressors and adopt a resolution condemning the United States as an aggressor. Furthermore, the UN Charter must be reviewed and revised...by all countries, big and small; all independent states should be included in the UN; and all imperialist puppets should be expelled.

Those are rather wide conditions for entry into the UN. That was 1965.

Now in 1970, though, there has been a change in their tone at least; and this year, in particular, they are not laying down all of these conditions. They are still talking of course, about the ejection of the Republic of China, but on these other conditions they are not saying very much, and it seems that they are making a serious bid this year, probably for the first time, to be a member of the United Nations, at the expense, however, of the Republic of China. That, of course, is the major condition.

Sino-Soviet Dispute

Two witnesses addressed the Subcommittee Sept. 16 on the implications of the Sino-Soviet dispute and its consequences for U.S. policy. The two witnesses were Professor Donald S. Zagoria, Columbia University, and Thomas W. Wolfe, Rand Corporation.

ZAGORIA'S TESTIMONY SEPT. 16 (EXCERPTS)

No other single development since the end of World War II has had such a profound impact on international relations as the Sino-Soviet schism. Moreover, that schism is likely to have lasting significance much like the split in the Christian Church during the Middle Ages.... The following are some of the most important effects of the split:

• The effort to contain China has become the major theme of Soviet policy in Asia. This has created a new triangular balance which provides both the non-communist and the communist countries of Asia with much more room for maneuver than there was in the bilateral balance. India, for example, has utilized both Soviet and American support against China while enjoying greater leverage on both superpowers. North Vietnam has similarly been able to enjoy the competitive support of both Russia and China against the United States while increasingly asserting its independence of both.

- In part because of the threat from China, Russia has become more interested in preventing the spread of nuclear weapons. The whole series of U.S.-Soviet agreements on nuclear weapons since 1963 has in part been motivated by a common desire to check the only nuclear power that is a potential danger to both superpowers.

- Also, because of the threat from China, Russia has shown greater determination to become a major Asian sea power, to develop military capabilities that might be used to support Asian proxies against either China or the United States, and to bolster the will of smaller Asian countries to resist Chinese pressure. Russia has established diplomatic relations with Malaysia (March 1967) and Singapore (June 1968) and openly proposed a system of "collective security" in Southeast Asia.

- Under ideological challenge from Peking, the Russians have been under pressure to demonstrate to the communist world that they are as good revolutionaries as the Chinese, an objective that conflicts with their desire to avoid increased tensions with the United States....

- The net effect of the split on Russia has been greatly to weaken its power, influence and prestige and to force it to contemplate the long-range danger of a hostile, xenophobic nuclear power on its border.... While this has not yet led to a major transformation in Soviet policy in Europe, it may well reduce Soviet willingness to provoke crises in Europe.

- In part because of the "Russian threat," China has demonstrated what may prove to be more than a passing interest in improved relations with the United States.

- As a result of the split, China has completely reoriented its foreign trade pattern away from the communist world and towards the West.

- As a result of the split, China has sought to increase its power and influence in Africa, Asia and Latin America, to encourage revolutionaries there, and to isolate both superpowers from the underdeveloped countries. This effort has not been very successful because of China's limited resources. Only in Asia can China compete with the two superpowers successfully.

- The net effect of the split on China has been to deepen its already considerable isolation, and to weaken it economically and militarily....

- The ideological and political unity of the communist world has been shattered. The dream of Marxist internationalism lies buried on the Amur. Soviet power and influence in Eastern Europe is now maintained largely by force or the threat of force. Major conflicts between communist states and parties are possible. As a result, the extension of communist power is no longer automatically in the interests of either Moscow or Peking.

- The three big powers—Russia, China and the United States—fear a combination of the other two against them. This provides the possibility of greater diplomatic flexibility for all three.

Future of the Sino-Soviet Dispute

Turning now to the likely future development of Sino-Soviet relations over the next decade, it seems to me that there are three possibilities. One is armed conflict on a major scale. A second would be some kind of limited reconciliation. And a third would be a protracted cold war.

Of these three possible futures, it seems to me that the last, a protracted cold war, is the most likely. I think a hot war is unlikely, because it seems to me that the Soviet Union is unlikely to provoke war with China so long as Mao lives, because a significant number of Soviet leaders seem to be convinced that a post-Mao Chinese leadership will be more amenable to reconciliation.

But even after Mao dies, the Soviet fear of getting bogged down in an internal land war, and the fear of Chinese retaliation, is likely to outweigh the arguments for preemptive war in Moscow.

China, for its part, is unlikely to provoke a major war with Russia, because I think it is well aware of the overwhelming Soviet nuclear preponderance.

The second possibility, a limited reconciliation, is more likely than war. But it still seems to me, on the whole, improbable. Mao's death would remove the biggest single obstacle to such a reconciliation. But, whatever the nature of any post-Mao government in China, the Soviet Union would have to contemplate the fact that it would be a Chinese Government with a deep sense of wounded national dignity, long-standing grudges against and suspicious of Russia, and in control of an independent and growing nuclear force....

Impact of U.S. Policy

The most likely of the three alternatives—a protracted Cold War between Russia and China—will make more or less permanent the triangular balance of power that has replaced the bipolar balance. While such a triangular balance will afford each of the three powers greater room for maneuver, it will also be inherently more unstable. A certain degree of paranoia will be present in each of the three powers, each of them fearful of a combination of the other two against it....

Out of fear of Russia, China will want better communications with the United States. While for the moment Peking's interest in reopening the Warsaw talks with the United States are guided largely by tactical considerations, they could develop into something more serious provided the United States demonstrated a genuine willingness to reach a detente. Such an effort would require the elimination or reduction of many of the military bases presently surrounding Peking, an end to U.S. opposition to China's entry into the United Nations, and a demilitarization of the Taiwan Straits. At the same time, Washington should keep Moscow informed of its efforts to reach an accommodation with Peking, so as to assure the Russians that this detente need not come at Soviet expense.

Similarly, Washington should continue efforts to stabilize the arms race with Moscow and to relax tensions throughout the world while assuring Peking that such efforts are not directed against its legitimate interests.

WOLFE'S TESTIMONY SEPT. 16 (EXCERPTS)

Soviet Policy: Avoid War

The top item on the Soviet agenda...will remain that of averting outright war with China. Though the arsenal of modern arms at Soviet disposal would doubtless permit "surgical" strikes at vital Chinese installations, the prospect of becoming bogged down in a "people's war" in China is not one which even the most ardent Soviet hawks can relish, not to mention the political and economic costs that a full-scale war with China would entail.

To be sure, the possibility of a Soviet-Chinese war depends in part on just how intractable the issues between the two are. As some observers see it, for example, the Chinese are driven by the inexorable pressure of a huge population, now approaching a billion, to expand China's food-producing and economic base. Hence, China's irredentist claims on lands wrenched from her by the "unequal treaties" with Tsarist Russia. Recovery of these lands (which, incidentally, are but thinly populated by about one-fourth of the Soviet Union's 240 million people), would help feed China's teeming population and enhance her prestige as a great world power. The Russians, by the same token, can be said to be determined to preserve a commanding power position in Asia and to suffer emotional affront at the suggestion that the Soviet Far East be dismembered. Given also probable concern in Moscow that relative Soviet military advantage may diminish with each passing year as China acquires more of the attributes of a nuclear power, it is certainly possible that the ingredients of a major war are inherent in the situation. On the other hand, however, despite a long historical record of conflict and rivalry, Russia and China have never fought a major war. The border negotiations into which they entered after the inflamed crisis of 1969 may again exemplify a built-in tendency on both sides to stop short of war.

So far as Soviet resort to military force against China is concerned, it seems to me that the Soviets are more likely to confine themselves to veiled threats of the use of major force or to minor applications of force along the Sino-Soviet border—in keeping with what might be termed a "coercive diplomacy"—than to undertake substantial military action against China. Under circumstances of internal turmoil in China where a breakdown of central Communist authority appeared imminent, I would also suppose that the Soviets might intervene in China's northern provinces on the pretext of having been invited to restore order and preserve Communist control—a variation on the theme of the "Brezhnev doctrine" of intervention applied in the case of Czechoslovakia....

(The Sino-Soviet dispute) could range at the one extreme from a durable rapprochement between the Communist rivals to a devastating war between them at the other. Neither of these outcomes would be likely to serve our own interests, it seems to me. Rather, a situation in which the Soviet Union and China continue to eye each other warily and to limit their collaboration essentially to steering clear of resolving their differences by war would seem most likely to afford us the maximum latitude in our policies toward both of these powers.

Exploiting the Sino-Soviet Split

(Rep. Clement J. Zablocki (D Wis.) asked Zagoria and Wolfe if the United States should "exploit the conflict by actively intervening or playing one off against the other....")

Wolfe....we should not in an egregious way attempt to exploit the situation. I think our best posture toward the world is to present ourselves as interested, first of all, in keeping these two from fracturing the peace of the world, as both of them have said in their statements to each other, moving down the path toward the use of nuclear weapons....

We should have no illusions that our dictate to either one of them is going to settle their quarrel. This is an affair between themselves. At the same time, we should try to convince them that we are not trying to actively exploit one against the other....

...the policy of trying to be evenhanded, between the two, is one that best serves American interests.

Zagoria. I am not sure that I would use the word "exploit," in a sense that we should develop a policy that can be applied to either maximize or minimize the strain between these two countries, because I think that the leverage that we have on this relationship is a rather minimal one. And I think that it grows out of problems that are, to a certain extent, beyond our control.

However, it is certainly a conflict which looms in the background of every major foreign policy decision we are likely to make. So I would say that it is a factor that has to be taken into account in our overall foreign policy.

For example, we are now facing a question of ABMs. There may be arguments for building ABMs when one looks at the Russian-American relationship. There may be more arguments against it when one looks at the Chinese-American relationship. One would therefore have to weigh those two contradictory problems.

I think the major way in which we can adapt to the Sino-Soviet dispute is by improving our relationship with China, thereby no longer letting the Soviet Union take our relationship with China for granted—while at the same time not encouraging paranoia in the Soviet Union, that is, without encouraging the Soviet Union to believe that we are engaged in some sort of gang up against them....

Military and Nuclear Policy

Two witnesses addressed the Subcommittee Sept. 23 on Chinese military and nuclear policy. The two witnesses, Morton Halperin, Brookings Institution, and William Whitson, Rand Corporation, stressed the defensive nature of the Chinese military capability.

HALPERIN'S TESTIMONY SEPT. 23 (EXCERPTS)

United States-Taiwan Threat

Basically there is a common acceptance in the leadership of the notion that China is threatened by external enemies. In the earliest period it was, of course, the Chinese Nationalists on Taiwan aided by the United States who appeared to pose a threat. In the middle 1950s with the doctrine of massive retaliation and with the security treaties which the United States negotiated with the Chinese Nationalists and with a number of other Asian nations the leadership began to fear the possibility of an American attack or large-scale American support for a Chinese-Nationalist attack.

USSR: Primary Threat

More recently, of course, the Soviet Union has come to be seen as the primary threat to Peking. Throughout the period of Communist rule in China the dominant fact in military calculations and military arguments has been the acceptance of the notion that China was threatened, that she had real enemies that might launch military attacks against her.

The second fundamental notion closely related to the first is that the primary purpose of Chinese military capability should be to deter an invasion, if that is possible, or to defeat it or neutralize it if it cannot be deterred. This means that arguments in Peking are primarily about what are the best forces, what is the best strategy to prevent the Russians, the Americans or the Chinese Nationalists from attempting to invade and conquer parts of China, and how should one deal with such invasions if they occur in contrast to conceivable debates about what territory might be invaded, or how military forces can be used overseas.

In fact, there has been a consensus on the part of the leadership that use of Chinese military power beyond its borders ran very high risks of provoking either American or Soviet counterattack and that therefore it should be avoided except in very extreme circumstances....

If one looks at the structure of Chinese military capability, the kind of forces they have, their limited mobility, their limited sea and airlift capability, it is clear there has been general agreement on the part of those making military policy that the use of the forces beyond China's borders was not a primary objective; in fact, it was to be avoided at the risk of provoking the Americans or Russians.

Taiwan Not Threatened

...Despite the fact that the elimination of the Chinese Nationalist rival claim to power has always been an objective, they have not, to this day, begun to develop the military forces which would be necessary for an invasion of Taiwan. So it appears to be the case that the Chinese Nationalists alone can defend Taiwan. Certainly the 7th Fleet can defend Taiwan. The Chinese simply have not developed an airlift capability, they have not developed the amphibious capability to launch a military attack on Taiwan. The period is now long enough and the other modern jet aircraft, medium range missiles, nuclear weapons makes it clear that this is not a limitation of technology but rather a choice arising at least in part out of the shared view among the Peking leadership that the way to incorporate Taiwan into China is by political propaganda, and psychological means, certainly not by military attack....

Chinese Nuclear Strategy

There has always been acceptance on the part of the Peking leadership that China as one of the great powers had to have nuclear weapons. The issues they were concerned with were how fast, what kind of nuclear capability, how much aid to accept from the Russians. But on the basic notion that China as a great power had to have a nuclear capability thing, there has been no dispute at all, nor do I think there has been any dispute over the notion that the primary role over the Chinese capability other than this political, psychological one of saying, "We are a great power, we have nuclear weapons," was a deterrent role; that is, to prevent or to try to prevent an American or Soviet nuclear attack.

All of the Peking leadership realizes the destructive power of nuclear weapons. There was a belief, which the Russians were spreading for their own reasons several years ago, that Peking did not understand nuclear war, that the Chinese believed that a nuclear war might even be a desirable thing because it would spread revolution.

I think in fact there is nothing to that at all. The leadership has recognized the great destructive power of nuclear weapons right from the time of Hiroshima, which we know was a traumatic experience to them, and that they continue to be concerned about the destruction that can be done to China by nuclear war and to attach high priority to preventing such a war.

They do believe that to stress the destruction that nuclear war would bring to China can only encourage the Americans or the Russians to attempt to blackmail them or to threaten them....

So I think it is quite natural one finds in the Chinese statements very little discussion of the destructive power of nuclear weapons and certain statements about how revolution would go on even if nuclear war occurs. Underneath that there is the fundamental recognition of the great destructive power of nuclear weapons and the desire to avoid nuclear war, but also a belief that the way to avoid being attacked is to build up one's own military strength and one's own nuclear capability.

WHITSON'S TESTIMONY SEPT. 23 (SUMMARY)

Whitson stressed the defensive orientation of Chinese military policy. He said that major trends in Chinese domestic affairs "constrain(ed) the ability of the Chinese to project military power beyond their borders." Among the factors he cited were the following:

• The Chinese economy—Whitson said the Chinese leadership would have "difficulty in taxing" regional resources for military purposes. He said that "heavy industry would not "grow very fast during the 1970s and that therefore military modernization will proceed but will tend to emphasize obsolescent equipment rather than radical new equipment."

• Chinese military theory—Chinese military planning, said Whitson, placed internal considerations above foreign priorities. The Chinese army command "reflect(s) the...perspectives of...the long march generations—that is, those people who entered the Red Army before July 1937. These people have really had experience first in combining political and military tools for the achievement of local objectives...because they were forced to do so during the years when they were developing a political military style...they are familiar with general purpose forces or theater operational weapons. They are much less acquainted with more sophisticated weapons or the joint use of those weapons, such as armored, artillery and airborne operations. My guess would be that the demand for more sophisticated weapons will be limited to a small number of people at the center, including those organizations responsible for research and development."

China and Southeast Asia

Two witnesses, Harold C. Hinton, George Washington University, and Wayne A. Wilcox, Columbia University testified Sept. 22 on China's policy in Southeast Asia. Both witnesses said that China did not constitute a military threat in Southeast Asia.

HINTON'S TESTIMONY SEPT. 22 (EXCERPTS)

In spite of its extensive ambitions and superior overall power, Peking suffers from many limitations on its actual or potential influences on South Asia. Indian sources often overstate the degree of threat that China poses to the region. Access of any kind to South Asia is difficult for China, and it is impossible for Peking to apply more than a fraction of either its military or non-military power to the region at any one time.

Even the least difficult land route, via the Chumbi Valley through Sikkim, is not an easy one, and the sea approaches are dominated, at least potentially, by the U.S. 7th Fleet. Due to a marked strengthening of the Indian Army since 1962, the possibility of India going nuclear if pressed too hard, and still more, to the evident determination of both the United States and the Soviet Union to prevent a serious Chinese threat to South Asia, the risks of direct Chinese military action against India, even on the limited scale of 1962, would be great and probably excessive. This applies to both conventional and nuclear threats. Direct pressures, furthermore, would probably tend to unite rather than divide the victim, as was the case in India in 1962...

Peking's easy and obvious line, in its effort to increase its influence in South Asia, has been to exploit the tension between India and Pakistan, in the absence of which Chinese leverage on the region would be almost negligible. This tendency has been especially strong since Sino-Indian tension escalated to the level of armed conflict in 1962.

China gave Pakistan virtually the only external support it received during the Indo-Pakistani War of 1965, and since then China has been supplying Pakistan with significant amounts of military equipment, although not enough to counterbalance the Indian buildup. Peking's ties with Rawalpindi are sufficiently important to inhibit it so far from significant support for dissidence in Pakistan, in East Bengal, for example.

WILCOX'S TESTIMONY SEPT. 22 (EXCERPTS)

When one looks at Chinese conventional forces, they are best judged against the opposition that they face. The Indian military forces now number about 1 million men, and since 1962 have been equipped with modern weapons. Indian armor is better than the Chinese have available, and it is easily deployable in the Indian plains. The Indian Air Force has excellent ground support in the Su-7 and HF-24 fighter-bombers. The equipment of the Indian forces and the topography of the Himalayas gives them almost no offensive capability for mounting a Tibetan operation but, on the other hand, this combination presents formidable defense advantages for India.

...China does not appear to have relevant military capabilities, under present conditions, to convert its large military investments into political power in South Asia. Military assistance and psychological-ideological subversion capabilities are both limited in effect and in possible use, and both are effective only when translated by third parties into actions which may or may not be in the Chinese interest.

Internal Chinese Developments

Three witnesses addressed the subcommittee Sept. 29 on Chinese internal, economic and political developments resulting from the Cultural Revolution. The witnesses were Lucian W. Pye, Massachusetts Institute of Technology; Alexander Eckstein, University of Michigan and Franz Michael, George Washington University. The following excerpts from their testimony focus on the foreign policy implications of internal developments.

PYE'S TESTIMONY SEPT. 29 (EXCERPTS)

As Communist China tidies up after the state of disarray of the Cultural Revolution, we should prepare for the new phase in China's relations with the world. For the United States this phase will be marked, in my judgment, by a troublesome paradox that will tax the maturity of American public opinion.

On the one hand, it is highly likely that Peking will shortly be interested in some very modest and highly tentative openings for relationships with the United States and I suspect that we too will be interested in actively exploring the possibilities for more flexibility in our mutual relations.

On the other hand, domestically the Chinese are probably entering a period of more conspicuous repression which may have some ugly dimensions. Consequently the image of China may become not just that of an uninhibited revolutionary power but also that of an increasingly harsh, but somewhat paralyzed, authoritarian regime. This tendency toward repression at the local level is related to a state of weakness and uncertainty at the capital, which in turn may also leave China incapable of sustained foreign relations.

In short, the United States and China can move gradually but perceptably toward more constructive and accommodating relations, but at the same time Chinese domestic practices may become more offensive to liberal and humane values and Peking may be too weak and uncertain to implement novel foreign efforts....

Internationally, the Cultural Revolution, coming as it did on the heels of the Sino-Soviet split, committed China irrevocably to treating Moscow and Washington as essentially equal foes. Specifically, Mao Tse-tung made it unmistakably clear to his domestic opponents that the Vietnam war and the entire American involvement in Asia were less dangerous for the true revolutionaries of Peking than the Moscow regime with its intolerable "revisionist" ideology. Consequently the most intensive and far-reaching purge in the history of Chinese Communism legitimized the novel ideological perspective that "imperialism" could be balanced by "revisionism" as equally threatening foes of proletarian revolutionaries....

Thus, the Cultural Revolution as the culmination of the Sino-Soviet split has set the stage for China to treat with "imperialists" if such actions will counter the threat of the "revisionists." The ideological basis has thus been established for Communist China to participate in a three-way balance of power involving Moscow, Washington and Peking.

From a historical perspective this consequence of the Cultural Revolution converges with a gradual change in Washington's appreciation of Peking. When the Sino-Soviet bloc seemed firm and monolithic, Washington properly recognized Peking as a major threat to the peace and stability of Asia; as the split developed, the danger declined; and then the extreme disruptions of the Cultural Revolution so weakened China as to make her almost irrelevant in East and Southeast Asia; but as Peking has stiffened against Moscow and engaged in border clashes that have produced mass redeployments and substantial new Russian investments in conventional forces, Washington can properly feel less antagonistic toward Peking.

ECKSTEIN'S TESTIMONY SEPT. 29 (SUMMARY)

Eckstein, an economist, said that the Chinese economy made progress between 1949 and 1959 but stagnated in the 1960s. Following the Cultural Revolution, he discerned a return to economic rationality and a stability in all aspects of Chinese policy, foreign and domestic. "In this context, dealings with China have once more become more feasible. Therefore, this is the time to continue the active pursuit of policies initiated by our government over a year ago. It is incumbent upon us to seek out and facilitate all avenues of contact ranging from simple travel to commercial, scientific, journalistic and diplomatic dealings with the People's Republic."

MICHAEL'S TESTIMONY SEPT. 29 (EXCERPTS)

Sino-Soviet Reconciliation

...(Chou En-lai's) foreign policy has two features: (1) a defusing of the Sino-Soviet conflict, which may potentially lead to a rapprochement between Moscow and Peking; (2) an increased militancy against the United States, expressed by the so-called Asian United Front and formulated in the Peking-Pyongyang negotiations and the new agreements with the Southeast Asian Communist regimes of North Vietnam, and the exiled Sihanouk.

On the first item, the easing of Sino-Soviet tensions, I disagree with the often expressed view that the conflict between Moscow and Peking—under whatever form—is here to stay. Soviet policy is clearly directed toward coaxing China back into the Communist commonwealth, whether by military threat or action or by diplomatic pressure. The Soviet action in Czechoslovakia, the Brezhnev doctrine, and the massive buildup of Soviet military forces along the Chinese border dramatized by the bloody frontier incidents of last year came as a shock and a warning to Peking.

Mending of Sino-Soviet Conflict

These demonstrations of Soviet toughness may have speeded up or even caused the shift in Chinese foreign policy and the strengthening of Chou's position. The first apparent success of the tough Soviet policy was the beginning of Sino-Soviet negotiations in October of last year (1969), following personal contact between Kosygin and Chou En-lai at the Peking airport. Military tension still continued at the end of last year and into this year but has clearly declined since the new policy initiatives of Chou in April of this year.

Since then there have been no more major ideological accusations from either side. Nor have there been more frontier incidents. With the appointment of new Chinese and Soviet ambassadors in Peking and Moscow, relations begin to be normalized. Most of all, the decline of the Mao cult, previously described, has removed the chief bone of contention between Moscow and Peking, which was Mao's claim to personal leadership of the world revolution....

Militancy Against the United States

The other aspect of the new Chinese policy, the increased militancy against "U.S. imperialism and its lackeys"—our allies in Japan, South Korea, Taiwan, Southeast Asia and the Near East—is a complementary aspect of this new policy in Peking. Because of Communist setbacks in Southeast Asia, the military threat of the of the new staff negotiations between Peking, Pyongyang, and Hanoi may not prove to be quite so serious as the present confrontation in the Near East. What is certain to emerge from this policy is a new Communist initiative in the political warfare in Asia.

Soviet Policy in Southeast Asia

Foy Kohler, former U.S. ambassador to the Soviet Union, and Vladimir Petrov, professor at George Washington University testified Sept. 30 on Soviet policy in Southeast Asia. In their prepared statements both witnesses stressed that Southeast Asia was of marginal and declining interest to the Soviet Union. In the following questions and answers they discussed the future of the Sino-Soviet dispute.

Kohler said that Sino-Soviet rivalry was national in character rather than ideological. "One must remember," he said, "that the longest unsettled frontier in the world today is that between the Soviet Union and China, over 4,000 miles of direct border, plus 2,000 miles of Mongolian border, that the Soviets are pledged to defend. These borders lie in lands that the Chinese...(claim) were unfairly taken by Czarist Russia and in fact, Mao has staked out a claim for them, just simply said that he has not presented his bill yet."

Petrov said that "China is still viewed by the Soviet government and Soviet political elite as potentially a friendly power in world affairs." Petrov did not see the possibility of Sino-Soviet "unified action" in the "foreseeable future." "What I can see," he said, "is a parallel action against what both of them perceive to be a common enemy.... A great deal of unhappiness is bound to continue between Moscow and Peking. Nevertheless, we will find ourselves on the receiving end of their hostility."

EXCERPTS FROM 1971 SENATE HEARINGS ON CHINA

The Senate Foreign Relations Committee held hearings June 24, 28 and 29, 1971 on five resolutions (S J Res 48 and S Res 18, 37, 82 and 139) concerning U.S. relations with the Chinese People's Republic (Communist China).

The resolutions were:

• S J Res 48, introduced by Frank Church (D Idaho) and Charles McC. Mathias Jr. (R Md.), to withdraw authority granted to the President in 1955 to use armed force to protect Nationalist China from attack on Taiwan and neighboring islands.

• S Res 18, by Mike Gravel (D Alaska), providing that the two Chinas should be encouraged to reach agreement on unification and that the United States should support entry of mainland China into the United Nations and the Security Council.

• S Res 37, by Jacob K. Javits (R N.Y.), providing that the United States should seek to permit Communist China to join the United Nations and to relax tensions through trade, cultural exchanges, loosening of travel restrictions and other actions leading ultimately to restoration of diplomatic relations while maintaining support of Nationalist China as a UN member.

• S Res 82, by George McGovern (D S.D.), providing that the United States should support Communist China membership in the United Nations and the Security Council and take other steps to improve relations with China.

• S Res 139, by Edward M. Kennedy (D Mass.), providing that Communist China should be given full United Nations membership, that the United States should not try to preserve membership for Nationalist China and that admission should not be delayed until questions of unification of China and U.S. recognition are settled.

Only S J Res 48 would have the force of law; the others would be advisory only. *(Later action on S J Res 48, p. 26)*

Senators Church, Mathias, Gravel, Javits, McGovern and Kennedy testified June 24 in favor of their resolutions. Rep. Patsy T. Mink (D Hawaii) called for placing Taiwan under the UN Trusteeship Council. Sen. Peter H. Dominick (R Colo.) testified June 28 criticizing all proposed resolutions.

Academic specialists on China testified June 25, June 28 and June 29. Most of the experts supported closer ties with Peking but differed on the extent to which the interests of Nationalist China should be compromised. Those testifying included Jerome Alan Cohen, Harvard Law School; Marc Mancell, Stanford University; James C. Thomson Jr., Harvard University; Allen S. Whiting, University of Michigan, and Stanley Lubman, University of California.

Subjects covered by these witnesses:

• Cohen—legal implications of U.S. policy on representation of China at the United Nations, the status of Taiwan and diplomatic recognition of Peking. *(p. 71)*

• Whiting—early postwar attempts by Communist China to establish good relations with the United States, the Taiwan problem, U.S. policy alternatives. *(p. 76)*

• Mancell—Taiwan. *(p. 75)*

• Thomson—Four power Asian politics, Taiwan. *(p. 76)*

• Lubman—Trade with China. *(p. 79)*

Testimony by Members of Congress

CHURCH'S TESTIMONY JUNE 24 (SUMMARY)

Congress in January 1955 passed the Formosa Resolution (H J Res 159—PL 84-4) authorizing President Eisenhower to use armed force to protect Nationalist China. In February 1955, the Senate approved both the Southeast Asia Collective Defense (SEATO) Treaty and the Mutual Security Treaty with Nationalist China.

Congress did not reserve the right to withdraw its grant of authority from the President, providing instead that it would expire when the President determined. The threat of an invasion of Taiwan has dwindled, fears of Communist China have diminished and the United States has reduced restrictions on trade with and travel to China. The United Nations may admit China within a year or two.

There is a chance to create a reopening to the East, an initiative which would be advantageous to both the United States and Asian nations. It might also mean the difference between peace and war in Asia.

Politically it is important that the United States move toward an opening to the East. It is constitutionally important to revoke this grant of authority to commit U.S. forces. It is important constitutionally that commitments be embodied in treaties rather than in sweeping resolutions. It is essential to national security that, except for situation demanding instant reaction, future involvements in combat result only from the joint action by the President and Congress envisaged in the Constitution.

JAVITS' TESTIMONY JUNE 24 (EXCERPTS)

There have been subtle indications that Peking—without relinquishing its longstanding claims—may well prefer to avoid a serious diplomatic confrontation with the U.S. over the status of Taiwan, at least at this time. The emphasis in Peking's recent statements regarding Taiwan has been on the withdrawal of U.S. military forces from Taiwan—rather than on earlier demands for a repudiation of the U.S.-Republic of China defense treaty, or for the immediate handover of Taiwan. If Peking is willing to "bend" on Taiwan, the chances for finding a new Chinese representation formula would be enormously increased.

Peking's emphasis on the removal of U.S. forces stationed on Taiwan may well be related to its fear that the potent U.S. nuclear capacity on Okinawa will be transferred to Taiwan, pursuant to the return of Okinawa to Japan. Peking may also be seeking to test the "sincerity" of the Nixon doctrine, with its emphasis on the pull-back and non-involvement of U.S. forces in Asian nations on China's periphery....

The U.S. has already ceased patrols of the Taiwan Straits by units of the Seventh Fleet—a measure initiated during the Korean War. Peking responded favorably and quickly. I see no reason why the U.S. cannot declare its intention to remove its forces from Taiwan concurrently with the withdrawal of U.S. forces from Vietnam. Such a demonstration of U.S. flexibility and sensitivity to Peking's military fears could help promote further flexibility in Peking.

...I would urge the Administration to issue a declaration of intent to withdraw U.S. forces from Taiwan, concurrently with the withdrawal from Vietnam—as an important and timely element in the effort to defuse the Chinese representation status of Taiwan issues before the pressure of time locks us (and Peking) into our old positions of confrontation in the UN this fall....

GRAVEL'S TESTIMONY JUNE 24 (EXCERPTS)

Until we dispose of the question of our...reservations about Taiwan's status, I think it is idle to call for diplomatic relations with the People's Republic.

What I am saying is that I am for eventual recognition of the Peoples Republic even at the cost of abandoning dreams of an indepdent Taiwan as well as ending relations with the Republic of China....

I am asking the U.S. to abandon its claim to a right to interfere with China's reunification. It is this claim which first justified the 1950 renewal of our military intervention in China's civil war and our continued military presence in and around Taiwan.

McGOVERN'S TESTIMONY JUNE 24 (EXCERPTS)

Peking...has neither in being nor in production the offensive capability, either in amphibious landing capacity, airdrop or bombers, to mount an effective attack against defenses as solid as those on Taiwan.... Under such circumstances it is clear that we can, without fear of the consequences, fully remove our forces from Taiwan and from the Taiwan Straits and terminate our military assistance to the Nationalist government. We can do so without abrogating our defense commitment to Taiwan, since the 1954 agreement can in no way be construed to demand further action than that required to deter attack. Hence the door is open to end in very real terms our involvement in China's civil war. I believe we should move speedily to do so, thus clearly placing the burden of achieving a solution where it must eventually reside in any case—in the hands of negotiators representing Peking and Taipei.

As my resolution proposes, the People's Republic of China should assume the China seats in the United Nations, and that decision should not await resolution of the status of Taiwan by the parties involved.

We should meanwhile end our diplomatic challenge to the legitimacy of Peking's authority on the mainland, by announcing our willingness to establish diplomatic relations with that government as the sole government of China and to withdraw such recognition from the Taiwan regime.

KENNEDY'S TESTIMONY JUNE 24 (EXCERPTS)

My view on the issue of UN representation is clear, and it is shared, I believe, by many members of the Senate, the academic community, and the American people at large. As I urged in 1969, it can be stated in three simple propositions:

First, the People's Republic of China should be granted its legitimate seat in the United Nations as the sole government of China, not only in the General Assembly, but also in the Security Council and in all the other principal and subsidiary organs of the United Nations.

Second, the United States should make no effort to impose a formula for dual UN representation on the People's Republic of China and Taiwan, unless those two governments themselves agree to such a formula.

Third, the resolution of the issue of United Nations representation need not await the resolution of the other complex issues dividing the United States and the People's Republic of China, such as the question of the future of Taiwan, or the question of diplomatic relations between the United States and the People's Republic of China. The time has come for the People's Republic to take its seat in the United Nations as the government of China, whether or not these other issues are settled....

MINK'S TESTIMONY JUNE 24 (EXCERPTS)

...If the United States attempts to seat Taiwan as a separate nation in the United Nations as part of the new arrangement, rejection by the People's Republic is a certainty. While some seem to speak favorably of this "two China" approach, this proposal is unrealistic.

...Of course, we cannot merely abandon the people of Taiwan even if we discontinue our support of the Nationalist regime. After 21 years of existence separated from the continent of China, we cannot ignore the growth of a new generation of Taiwanese. It should be clear, however, that if the Nationalist government is no longer the government of China because the People's Republic of China is the recognized sole and legitimate government of the Chinese people, then it follows that the Nationalist government has no rightful dominion over the people of Taiwan.

I believe that the solution for this most difficult problem can be found by treating the territory of Taiwan like the territories over which Japan had dominion prior to World War II which after the war were placed under UN trusteeship....

DOMINICK'S TESTIMONY JUNE 28 (SUMMARY)

Dominick said none of the resolutions is capable of resolving the basic schism between Taiwan and Peking. The resolutions try to settle a matter in which the United States can have little influence, given the present attitudes of the Chinese governments. The resolutions would only alienate an old ally unnecessarily and perhaps weaken its international position.

Testimony by China Experts

COHEN'S TESTIMONY JUNE 25 (EXCERPTS)

Cohen discussed the legal implications of U.S. policy on representation of China at the United Nations, the status of Taiwan and diplomatic recognition of Peking.

United Nations

...Following the lead of Senators McGovern and Kennedy, (the United States)...should genuinely welcome Peking into the UN by supporting a proposal similar to the Albanian resolution, but less objectionably phrased. If that choice should be deemed "unrealistic," rather than resort to dual representation, it would even be preferable for the United States to maintain its present support for Taipei, but without twisting arms, for this too would assure Peking's entry, albeit in unattractive circumstances.

There is...another option that is both "realistic" and attractive—that is for the U.S. to guarantee Peking's entry into the UN by abstaining from the vote on the Albanian resolution. Abstention would obviously cause more serious deterioration in our relations with Taipei than would sponsorship of dual representation, but this will be inevitable as we gradually move toward the establishment of diplomatic relations with Peking. And, unlike dual representation, which entails great cost and yields little benefit, abstention, by assuring Peking's presence in the UN, would produce clear long-range benefit to both the world community and ourselves.

Diplomatic Relations With Peking

...Although less immediate than the UN question, it (diplomatic relations) is equally important if the United States is to place Sino-American relations on the same long-term basis as Sino-Soviet and Soviet-American relations in a serious effort to reduce tensions in Asia....

How does Peking view the problem?

Some students of China's foreign policy suggest that, if Washington were to announce its willingness to open negotiations regarding recognition and establishment of diplomatic relations, the People's Republic would almost certainly either ignore or reject the offer. Actually, it all depends upon what Washington has in mind. Even Alf Landon came out for "recognition" a few years ago, but, of course, he didn't mean that the U.S. should withdraw recognition from the Nationalist regime. If that is all we would mean, such an offer would be fatuous in Peking's view, and that of many other capitals including Taipei, and it certainly would deserve no response.

The consistent practice of twenty-two years leaves no doubt that Peking and Taipei regard themselves as competing, mutually exclusive representatives of the same territorial community, the state of China, and that is the way they have been regarded by the rest of the world. No country has simultaneously maintained relations with both regimes.

If we indicate that we are prepared to negotiate withdrawal of recognition from Taipei and its conferral upon Peking, there is a very high probability that Peking will at least be willing to enter into serious discussions. For even if such negotiations were only to conclude with establishment of diplomatic relations—without settling the status of Taiwan, Peking would have important incentives to attain this result. It would strike a heavy blow against the Nationalist government, because many of the countries that have retained diplomatic relations with the Nationalists would follow our lead. Moreover, withdrawal of our recognition from Taipei would terminate our defense commitment to the Chiang regime and our military assistance to it, although the U.S. could, of course, maintain a military umbrella over Taiwan in some other form.

Recognition Formula. There are various formulae that Washington and Peking could use to announce their establishment of diplomatic relations without determining the status of Taiwan. Recent precedents are worth noting. Peking's joint communique with Canada of October 13, 1970 stated:

> The Chinese Government reaffirms that Taiwan is an inalienable part of the territory of the People's Republic of China. The Canadian Government takes note of this position of the Chinese Government.

Two days later, however, a joint communique establishing relations between the People's Republic and Equatorial Guinea made no mention of Taiwan. But Equatorial Guinea recognized Peking as the "sole legal government representing the entire Chinese people," a phrase that did not appear in the Canadian communique. Although this phrase was probably meant to include the people on Taiwan, technically—at least for a state that does not acknowledge Taiwan as Chinese territory—it would leave open the question whether the people on Taiwan are to be regarded as Chinese. It is interesting that when Austria established relations with Peking a month ago nothing was said about Taiwan, nor was "the entire Chinese People" formula invoked. Austria simply recognized Peking "as the sole legal Government of China."

Yet, as Premier Chou En-lai's June 21 interview with American newsmen reminds us, we should not delude ourselves into believing that Peking will readily agree to establish relations until Washington at least tacitly concedes that Taiwan is Chinese territory. The relation of the United States to the Taiwan problem is far different from that of Canada, Equatorial Guinea, Austria or any other country. To understand this we should briefly examine the background of the dispute over Taiwan.

Status of Taiwan

Taiwan is populated almost entirely by people who are ethnically, linguistically and culturally Chinese. Although Taiwan had been Chinese territory for centuries, the Imperial Chinese Government did not pay a great deal of attention to its affairs until the latter part of the nineteenth century, when efforts by Japan and then France to take the island by force led China to appreciate the importance of Taiwan to China's national defense. As part of a series of governmental reforms on the island, Taiwan became a regular province of China in 1885. Following the Sino-Japanese war of 1894-5, however, China was forced to cede the island to Japan by the Treaty of Shimonoseki.

During World War II, in the Cairo Declaration of 1943, the President of the United States, the Prime Minister of the United Kingdom and the President of China issued a joint declaration that "(it) is their purpose...that all the territories Japan has stolen from the Chinese, such as Manchuria, Formosa and the Pescadores, shall be restored to the Republic of China." In the 1945 Potsdam Proclamation the heads of the three governments agreed that "(the) terms of the Cairo Declaration shall be carried out...." Just before the end of the war against Japan, the Soviet and French governments formally adhered to the Potsdam Proclamation.

The Japanese Instrument of Surrender accepted the terms of the Potsdam Declaration, and Japanese forces on Taiwan carried out instructions to surrender to the

Chinese army. On October 25, 1945, China announced to the world that it had resumed sovereignty over Taiwan and the neighboring Pescadores islands, which were "again incorporated into the territory of China." Shortly thereafter, China informed foreign governments that the people on Taiwan as well as overseas Taiwanese had resumed Chinese nationality and were to enjoy the same legal status as other Chinese nationals. Taiwan again became a province of China. None of these public acts by China elicited protests from other governments.

From 1945 until the Korean War, Taiwan was plainly regarded as having become Chinese territory once again, a fact that was eventually expected to be confirmed in the peace treaties that would formally conclude World War II. Following Chiang Kai-shek's defeat on the mainland and flight to Taiwan in late 1949, a great national debate occurred over whether it would be wise, legal and moral for the United States to intervene to protect Taiwan against the anticipated Chinese Communist effort to "liberate" the island. This debate culminated on January 5, 1950, when President Truman, in keeping with the Cairo and Potsdam Declarations, solemnly announced that for the previous four years the United States and the other Allied Powers had accepted the exercise of Chinese authority over Taiwan, that the island was Chinese territory, and that we would "not pursue a course which will lead to involvement in the civil conflict in China." The President stated:

> The United States Government has always stood for good faith in international relations. Traditional United States policy toward China, as exemplified in the open-door policy, called for respect for the territorial integrity of China.

That afternoon Secretary Acheson elaborated on the President's policy statement in a press conference that is well worth quoting. He said:

> The Chinese have administered Formosa for 4 years. Neither the United States nor any other ally ever questioned that authority and that occupation. When Formosa was made a province of China nobody raised any lawyer's doubts about that. That was regarded as in accordance with the commitments.
>
> Now, in the opinion of some, the situation is changed. They believe that the forces now in control of the mainland of China, the forces which undoubtedly will soon be recognized by some other countries, are not friendly to us, and therefore they want to say, 'Well, we have to wait for a treaty.' We did not wait for a treaty on Korea. We did not wait for a treaty on the Kuriles. We did not wait for a treaty on the islands over which we have trusteeship.
>
> Whatever may be the legal situation, the United States of America, Mr. Truman said this morning, is not going to quibble on any lawyer's words about the integrity of its position. That is where we stand.
>
> Therefore, the President says, we are not going to use our forces in connection with the present situation in Formosa. We are not going to attempt to seize the island. We are not going to get involved militarily in any way on the island of Formosa. So far as I know, no responsible person in the Government, no military man has ever believed that we should involve our forces in the island.

The Department of State subsequently informed the House of Representatives that "the Allied Powers including the United States have for the past 4 years treated Formosa as part of China." It specifically rejected the possibility of holding a plebiscite on Taiwan under United Nations or other auspices, stating:

> For the United States Government at this date, to seek to establish a non-Chinese administration on Formosa...would be almost universally interpreted in mainland China and widely interpreted throughout Asia as an attempt by this Government to separate Formosa from China in violation of its pledges and contrary to its longstanding policy of respecting the territorial integrity of China. The important point from the standpoint of our interests in Asia, including mainland China, is not the technical justifications which we might urge for taking such steps but rather the way such action on our part would be viewed by the people of Asia. In this connection we do not wish to create a Formosa *irredenta* issue about which the Chinese Communists could rally support within China and with which they could divert attention from Soviet actions in the North. We must not place ourselves in the unenviable position of the U.S.S.R. with regard to the integrity of China and must remain free to take the position that anyone who violates the integrity of China is the enemy of China and is acting contrary to our own interests.

This clear-cut view of the United States and the other Allied Powers suddenly changed upon the outbreak of the Korean War. Without any public warning whatever, on June 27, 1950, President Truman dramatically reversed our policy. He did not refer to the Korean conflict as an attack by North Korea upon South Korea but as an attack by "Communism." Therefore, he concluded—in one of the most momentous leaps of logic of the century, the occupation of Taiwan by "Communist forces" would be a direct threat to the security of the Pacific area and American forces. "Accordingly" the President ordered the Seventh Fleet to prevent any Communist attack on Taiwan and to prevent any Nationalist attack on the mainland.

The President did not seek to justify American intervention as action taken during a civil war at the request of what we regarded to be the legitimate government of China, nor did he even claim that Generalissimo Chiang had agreed to our action. He simply announced that "The Seventh Fleet will see that this is done." The last sentence of his statement provided a different legal rationalization of our surprising conduct: "The determination of the future status of Formosa," the President said, "must await the restoration of security in the Pacific, a peace settlement with Japan, or consideration by the United Nations."

This unanticipated announcement that the status of Taiwan was yet to be determined came as a rude shock to both the Communist and Nationalist regimes. Overnight, what had been Chinese territory became territory that was still subject to the Allied Powers; what had been the binding commitment of the Cairo Declaration became merely a "statement of intention;" what had been a civil war became an international conflict.

The United States then sought to erect a legal superstructure for post-war relations in East Asia that reflected its new legal position. The 1951 Treaty of Peace with Japan merely stated that "Japan renounces all rights, title and claim to Formosa and the Pescadores," and did not prescribe the *de jure* status of these territories. Although the 1952 Treaty of Peace between the Republic of China and Japan "recognized" that all pre-1941 treaties between China and Japan had become void as a result of the war, it also simply "recognized" Japan's renunciation of Taiwan and the Pescadores without clarifying the question of sovereignty. The 1954 Mutual Defense Treaty between the United States and the Republic of China defined Taiwan and the Pescadores as territory of China for purposes of the treaty, but the contemporaneous Exchange of Notes described the islands as territory that the Republic of China "effectively controls."

Thus the United States for the past twenty years has been in the anomalous, but little-understood, position of recognizing as the government of China a regime whose almost exclusive territorial base it refuses to acknowledge as Chinese territory. The tiny islands of Quemoy and Matsu in Amoy harbor are the only territory occupied by the Nationalists that is undisputedly Chinese. *(Map p. 20)*

The Nationalist regime has had to tolerate this humiliation because the United States insisted that only by "freezing" the status of Taiwan could it justify dispatching the Seventh Fleet to protect the island and taking steps at the United Nations to keep the island out of hostile hands. The new Communist government, however, has had no reason to tolerate what it has understandably regarded as cynical legal legerdemain. Indeed, it has consistently complained that American intervention in the Taiwan strait constitutes aggression against China's territorial integrity.

Both Chinese governments claim that the outbreak of war in 1941 abrogated the Treaty of Shimonoseki and restored Taiwan to China. They also claim that China's unprotested reintegration of Taiwan at the close of the war in accordance with the Cairo and Potsdam declarations completed the transfer of territory and that no peace treaty was needed. A strong argument has also been made by the Nationalist government that Japan's renunciation of Taiwan in the 1951 and 1952 peace treaties constituted implicit acquiescence in the claims of the *de facto* occupant, the Republic of China. On the other hand, one can also argue, as have the United States, some of its wartime allies and spokesmen for the Taiwan is undetermined....

The critical question, of course, is not whether Taiwan should or should not be deemed as having already been legally restored to China. The critical question is one of American good faith, as President Truman and Secretary Acheson recognized prior to the Korean War. Is the United States going to renege on its solemn pledge to restore Taiwan to China and thereby repudiate its oft-proclaimed respect for China's territorial integrity? We have heard a great deal in recent years about the importance of preserving the credibility of American commitments. Have we conveniently forgotten this commitment? The People's Republic has not, nor have Chinese of other political persuasions.

Outlook for Diplomatic Ties

For these reasons we cannot be sanguine about the prospects for the establishment of diplomatic relations between Washington and Peking unless Washington is prepared to confirm, if only tacitly, that Taiwan is Chinese territory. It is one thing for the People's Republic to establish relations with certain other states without obtaining their acquiescence, but the United States has been responsible for the political, legal and military actions that have kept Taiwan separated from the mainland. Peking may well fear that, if it establishes relations without at least obtaining Washington's implicit

agreement in principle on the territorial question, it will have forfeited its chances to achieve national unification.

What would be the implications of Peking's insistence upon settling the status of Taiwan at the time of establishing diplomatic relations? I have already pointed out that by severing relations with the Nationalist regime the United States would terminate the 1954 Mutual Security Treaty to defend Taiwan, a treaty that in any event provides for its termination by either party upon one year's notice. So long as we do not acknowledge Taiwan to be Chinese territory, however, there would at least be the legal possibility of maintaining our protection of the island in some other form. Should we couple establishment of relations with tacit recognition that Taiwan is Chinese territory, we would, of course, no longer have any basis for our intervention.

Peking's insistence that we recognize Taiwan as part of China does not necessarily mean that the People's Republic intends to take Taiwan by force or that it insists upon gaining actual control over the island in the near future by other means. We cannot expect Peking formally to renounce the use of force against the Nationalist regime, just as we have not expected the Nationalists to do so against their Communist rivals, for such a renunciation would imply that Taiwan is not part of China. Governments may commit themselves to renounce the use of force in international affairs but not in domestic matters.

Peking plainly has not built up the military capability required to launch an invasion across the Taiwan strait. Moreover, the Nationalist government has a substantial military capacity for defending Taiwan for the foreseeable future. Chinese statesmen are not naive. The leaders in Peking are well aware that the United States is unlikely to establish relations at the price of stimulating another major bloodletting in Asia. They also know that a costly military expedition against Taiwan would leave Peking badly exposed on its vast northern frontier, would galvanize Taiwanese nationalism and would quicken the pace of Japan's rearmament.

Given the political momentum that would be developed by entry into the UN and by U.S. diplomatic recognition, and given the opportunities that Peking would then enjoy for political and economic maneuvers to "heighten the consciousness" of the people on Taiwan, understandably Peking might feel confident that it eventually would be able to achieve the peaceful integration of Taiwan.

What it insists upon for the immediate future is the defeat of Chiang diplomatically, an end to American intervention in the Chinese civil war, and recognition of China's territorial integrity in principle. Once the principle is respected, if only tacitly, Peking can be expected to behave in a flexible manner toward Taiwan, just as it has toward Hong Kong and Macao.

What, after all, might be the precise outcome of the long and arduous negotiations over the establishment of relations? It is impossible to predict the terminology upon which the parties might eventually agree. Clearly the People's Republic will accept no limitations upon Chinese sovereignty. One can envisage a joint communique that explicitly or implicitly acknowledges Taiwan to be Chinese territory but that takes note of Taiwan's distinctive development, its autonomous characteristics and the lack of any necessity to reintegrate it into China through warfare or in the immediate future. More probable would be a tacit or perhaps even secret understanding that at least for a substantial period of time, such as twenty years, there would be no resort to force against Taiwan....

If I am correct in believing that some significant degree of change in our China policy seems inevitable and that the cost of such change in our relations with Taipei will be great, the changes that we carry out ought to be calculated to enhance the likelihood that we will thereby attain our goal—the improvement of relations with the People's Republic. Of course, neither Peking's entry into the UN, nor the establishment of diplomatic relations guarantees any immediate relaxation of Sino-American tensions, but these steps are essential prerequisites of significant relaxation. After heading in the wrong direction for over twenty years, we should at least get back to the starting post.

MANCELL'S TESTIMONY JUNE 28 (EXCERPTS)

The Problem of Taiwan

American co-belligerency in the Chinese civil war was accompanied by direct interference in the affairs of the island of Taiwan, Chiang Kai-shek's refuge after his defeat in China. American economic and military aid enabled Chiang to impose his regime on a population which, as early as 1947, revolted against the corrupt Chinese Nationalist administration of the island. Under the leadership of Chiang Kai-shek and his son, Chiang Ching-kuo, the government of this East Asian "bastion" of the "Free World" has continuously perpetuated itself in despotic power, denied the overwhelming majority of its people basic civil rights, and—on the ground that until it regained control of all China no national elections could be held—has refused to permit itself to be judged democratically at the polls. American military and economic aid to Taiwan has freed the resources of the regime for the development of an elaborate mechanism of internal secret police control, which is reenforced by denial of freedom of the press, freedom of speech, and freedom of assembly.

Because of American support for and involvement with Chiang Kai-shek's regime, the question of Taiwan is the major impediment to the development of Sino-American relations today. As knotty as the Taiwan problem may be, the United States is capable of taking certain specific steps which, while not resolving the problem, will open the doors to serious negotiations.

First, the seating of the People's Republic of China in the United Nations as the legitimate representative of China will lead to a redefinition of the international status of the regime currently installed in Taipei. Chiang Kai-shek's regime may choose to leave the United Nations completely or to apply for membership as the government of Taiwan, rather than of China. In this case Peking, as a United Nations member, would be in a position to argue her case in turn before the international community....

Second, the United States must recognize officially that the legal status of the island of Taiwan itself is yet to be defined. The problem is open for negotia-

tions without foreclosing any of several possible resolutions of the problem.

Third, the United States must make it perfectly clear to the People's Republic of China that it has no intention of using Taiwan as a base for American military activities in the Far East consequent upon our withdrawal from Vietnam and the return of Okinawa to Japanese control.

Fourth, the United States must cease to be a co-belligerent in the Chinese civil war (1) by ending all military aid to the Taipei regime, (2) by adopting the position suggested in S J Res 48 (repealing the 1955 Formosa resolution), and (3) by abrogating the (1954) Mutual Security Treaty.

Finally, the United States must begin to develop formulae that will enable it to recognize the People's Republic of China without prejudging the eventual disposition of the Taiwan issue. All other steps are preparatory for this one. For instance, to recognize that China has a special interest in Taiwan would simply be acknowledgement of a political, geographical, and historical reality in the Far East. To state that Taiwan's future relationship with China is a matter for negotiation between the government of the People's Republic and "local authorities" on Taiwan would prejudge neither the identity of the "local authorities" nor the eventual disposition of Taiwan itself. However, only direct discussions with Peking about the establishment of diplomatic relations will determine whether such formulae can serve as the basis for recognition.

The measures proposed here will inevitably have profound effects within Taiwan itself. For two decades the native Taiwanese majority of the island's population, together with liberal groups among the Chinese minority, have felt that opposition to Chiang Kai-shek was doomed because of American support for the regime. A new American position denying the regime's legitimacy and American support for it would open the way for the development of mechanisms through which the island's population could participate in the determination of its future. To deny them participation so that we may maintain an American presence in the Far East would be a continuation of past policy and would inhibit relations with Peking. To accede to Chinese Communist possession of the island as a price for diplomatic relations without a free expression of the wishes of the island's 14,000,000 people would be rank opportunism.

American recognition that the future of Taiwan is a matter for negotiations between Peking and Taipei would permit the exploration of several possible solutions to the Taiwan problem, ranging from political independence for Taiwan to its total incorporation into China. America's moral responsibilities in this matter can go no further than insuring that the Taiwanese themselves play a major role in determining their own future. However, that responsibility cannot be exercised directly; our own participation in the Chinese civil war and our conduct of the war in Southeast Asia leave us no political or moral capital with which to participate in the determination of Taiwan's future. Therefore, the United States must plan to abstain from future interference in the island's affairs and must promote a political solution through the offices of the United Nations, in which the People's Republic will be a full member. In the same way, American economic aid to Taiwan, which may become necessary as we withdraw from the Chinese civil war, will have to be channeled through international organizations in which China participates.

THOMSON'S TESTIMONY JUNE 28 (EXCERPTS)

Four Power Asian Politics

...The old stereotype of the United States and Japan, on the one side, pitted against the Soviet Union and China, on the other, is clearly an anachronism. While ideologies may die hard, nationalisms have inevitably begun to supersede them. Central to the change, of course, is the Sino-Soviet conflict—long apparent to trained observers but only belatedly accepted by our policy-makers as a permanent fact of life. Also central to the change is the spectacular re-emergence of Japan as an independent force in its own right. A further factor in the change—harder to evaluate than the others—is at least the new aspiration embodied in the so-called Nixon Doctrine: namely, gradual American withdrawal from that grandiose role of East Asian gendarme that our victory over Japan and the ensuing Cold War seemed to force upon us.

So Russia and China must be seen as independent entities. So Japan must be similarly viewed. And so the United States seeks to recede from a forward posture of over-commitment to the region. Four powers, four sets of national interests, are coming into focus. Here are the makings of both instability and balance—a new situation of both danger and opportunity, discerned, one can be certain, in all four capitals.

....I welcome and applaud the significant substantive steps that the Nixon Administration has taken in the past two years in the areas of rhetoric, travel, and trade....While applauding the Administration's recent initiatives, however, I would strongly urge that they now move further. And this brings me, as I suggested at the outset, to the potential significance of these hearings. It is my hope that the Congress may encourage—or perhaps, more accurately, prod—the Administration to follow the logic of its own proclaimed desire to "normalize" America's relations with the People's Republic of China.

Some months ago several of us were told by a high Administration official that Washington's policy aspiration was to "normalize" its relations with Peking "while preserving our relationship with our old friend and ally, the Republic of China on Taiwan." I would respectfully submit that that is an unrealistic and unrealizable aspiration. Foreign policy-making often forces hard choices; and on the Peking-Taipei matter a hard choice is certainly at hand. It need not, however, be quite as hard a choice as some tend to suggest....

Our highest immediate priority should be the engagement of the People's Republic of China in the international order. That means, specifically, seeing to it that the People's Republic is granted its rightful seat in the United Nations—as the heir to the seat called "China" in both the General Assembly and the Security Council....

Taiwan Problem

But what of Taipei, that other claimant to the seat called "China?" One used to hope, in recent years, that some formula for "dual representation"—"two Chinas," or "one China, one Taiwan"—might somehow be workable. Such arrangements appeal to our Wilsonian spirit. My own evolving view, however, is that such a formula is not now workable, given the deep-seated feeling of virtually all Chinese everywhere that "China" is indivisible, and given also the positions of the two relevant "Chinese" governments. Indeed, dual representation could easily become a formula for the continued exclusion of Peking— or even of both claimants. I therefore move to the conclusion that Peking's seating—our proper paramount objective in clearly ordered priorities—will probably require Taiwan's ouster.

Let me be clear on the implications of what I have just said. The expulsion of Taiwan from the United Nations will not end Taiwan's existence as a separate state. It will not terminate Washington's recognition of the Taipei government. It will not terminate our mutual defense treaty. Nor will it necessarily preclude Taiwan's admission to the United Nations at some future date under some arrangement agreeable to the authorities in both Peking and Taipei. It will only mean that for the time being Taiwan will exist outside the United Nations— like West Germany, Switzerland, and several others.

Peking's entry into the United Nations is, then, the first step, one of overriding importance. And from that step can follow, even in the absence of diplomatic relations, a widening of Sino-American contacts, discussions, and negotiations on a broad agenda of subjects—arms control and disarmament, peace in Indochina, scientific and technical cooperation, trade, cultural and educational exchanges, and the modalities of diplomatic recognition.

As we begin to explore such issues, it is quite possible that both powers will find sufficient common ground, common language, and mutual face-saving devices to permit a temporary by-passing of the Taiwan issue. It is quite possible that American military disengagement from Taiwan—already under way—and American assurances that Taiwan's future is for the people on both sides of the Straits to decide, can gradually open the way to fuller Washington-Peking conversations and even diplomatic relations. Peking, while adamant on Taiwan's ultimate future, has proved to be somewhat flexible in what it demands of other foreign powers on the subject. And Chinese ingenuity on both sides of the Taiwan Straits may—thanks to time and mortality—provide a longer-term accommodation (perhaps through mainland "sovereignty" and island "autonomy," as John K. Fairbank has suggested) that will defuse the issue while assuring the indivisibility of China.

WHITING'S TESTIMONY JUNE 28 (EXCERPTS)

I should like to develop three basic points. First, Peking's recently expressed interest in improving relations with the United States is not new. Mao Tse-tung and Chou En-lai tried as early as World War II to reach an understanding with our government. Second, precisely because this is not a new policy suddenly arrived at, the Chinese are unlikely to feel an improvement of relations is so urgently necessary as to abandon such long held interests as their claim to Taiwan and their professed support for world revolution. If we insist on renunciation of these interests, Mao and Chou will leave this twenty-one year impasse to their successors. Third, the time to move toward the establishments of diplomatic relations is now, while we can still negotiate with experienced leaders who have determined China's policies over two decades. Moreover there is still sufficient stability on Taiwan under Chiang Kai-shek to make a negotiatory posture credible. Postponement of this effort does not promise any easier settlement should Mao be succeeded by a regime dominated by the military, while Chiang's death may well trigger internecine struggles in Taiwan.

Background

(Whiting reviewed efforts by Mao Tse-tung in January 1945 and in 1968-1969 to establish improved relations with the United States as a counter weight to exclusive Soviet pressure on China. His testimony on this point was similar to his presentation in 1970 before the House Foreign Affairs Subcommittee on Asian and Pacific Affairs. *(See p. 61, 62)*

...Chinese Communist concern over relations with Russia has led to exploration for improved relations with the United States. However, while this (1971) spring's developments stem from Chinese decisions made in the context of 1968-69, the same strategic considerations and sense of threat do not still prevail in Peking, three years later. On the contrary, the slow steady improvement in Sino-Soviet relations is manifested by the mutual return of ambassadors and agreement for increased trade. No significant border incidents appear to have occurred since August 1969. Nonetheless the basic asymmetry in Chinese relations with the two superpowers remains to be corrected. Peking has persisted in signalling its interest in negotiations with Washington, responding to statements and steps by President Nixon and Secretary Rogers which express their desire to dismantle the barriers of confrontation erected during the Korean War. Chinese negotiators at Warsaw were sufficiently forthcoming in February 1970 for President Nixon to characterize discussions there as showing "slight progress." After suspending talks in May because of the Cambodian incursion, Mao Tse-tung ostentatiously hosted "our American friend" Edgar Snow from last August to this February....

With the Warsaw talks in suspense, however, it remained for Washington, to lift all restrictions on travel before further forward movement on Peking's part was possible. So long as the State Department restricted by categories or individual authorization those persons whom the People's Republic could admit, sensitivity over China's sovereign right to choose its own visitors precluded any response to the earlier easing of U.S. travel restrictions. But once Peking could invite whomever it wished, the way was open for the flow of American newsmen, scientists, and others.

The relatively minor but dramatic breakthrough in travel highlights a major aspect of Chinese policy. Although strategic considerations may argue for improving relations with the United States, tactical implementation requires appropriate American moves which conform with Peking's sense of priorities and propriety. If this entails delay and risks eventual failure, Chinese policy has been willing to accept the consequences. Compromise may be forthcoming on a mutual basis where fundamental issues are not involved. But nothing in the past or present pattern of events suggests Mao or his colleagues see improved American relations to be so urgently necessary as to warrant a speedy resolution of outstanding issues on terms obviously favorable to us. On the contrary, delay may bring developments that improve Peking's bargaining position. Thus while the Chinese sense of threat from the Soviet military buildup has clearly diminished since 1969, Peking's prospects in the United Nations have taken their brightest turn in years, with last fall's majority vote supporting expulsion of Taiwan's representatives.

Taiwan Issue

This should caution against any false sense of euphoria concerning the immediate future of Sino-American relations. Mao's objectives today remain remarkably similar to those of 1945: to detach American support from Chiang Kai-shek and to deal freely with all governments, unconstrained either by exclusive ties of dependence or externally imposed barriers to diplomatic relations. At a minimum, the People's Republic of China insists on its rightful place in the United Nations as the sole representative of the Chinese people. Eventually, Peking hopes to extend its authority over Taiwan, ending the civil war *inter alia*.

A continuity of policy objectives, however, does not necessarily require the means of policy to remain constant over time. Mao's military options for recovering Taiwan disappeared in June 1950 when President Truman interposed the U.S. Seventh Fleet in the Taiwan Strait, following the North Korean invasion. Any serious thought of regaining that option must have ended in December 1954 when President Eisenhower concluded a Treaty of Mutual Assistance with Chiang Kai-shek. This may explain why the People's Liberation Army has never developed the necessary air and sea lift capacity to mount an invasion across the more than one hundred miles of ocean which separate Taiwan from the mainland. Facing more than 300,000 highly trained Taiwanese combat troops defending their homeland with $2.4-billion of U.S. military assistance, Mao Tse-tung is prevented by more than our treaty from pursuing his Taiwan objectives by the use of force. The respective capabilities of the two sides in the Taiwan Strait flatly rule out a successful invasion by the People's Liberation Army. Although Peking's negotiators may continue to reject any American demand for a formal renunciation of force, this option has been tacitly abandoned for twenty years. Only the off-shore islands, lying within a few miles of the Chinese coast and still occupied by Chiang's troops, face a credible threat of military attack in the foreseeable future. To avoid any ambiguity concerning a possible U.S. commitment to defend these islands, I support the (Church) resolution....*(p. 70)*

Thus Peking must rely on political means to achieve its ends. Yet Peking's subversive capability has dwindled sharply as compared with 1950. The two million mainland refugees are no longer a demoralized, bankrupt mass in an alien land. Nor has Mao dared to encourage a strong Taiwanese insurgency among the twelve million native inhabitants for fear of losing control to a genuine independence movement. The only alternative is negotiation with those in control of the island. In the past secret messages to high officials on Taiwan have probed this possibility. On occasion, Chou-En-lai has openly discussed a possible ministerial appointment for Chiang Kai-shek. Basically, however, Peking's strategy towards Taiwan has resembled a shadow-play manipulated behind a screen of slogans which effectively shields both the directors and the details from external view.

Negotiating Opportunities

...We need not wait "for the dust to settle" before attempting negotiations. On the contrary, we should explore these possibilities while Mao and Chou remain in command. There is little evidence on which to estimate the degree to which their successors may be willing and able to negotiate in their place, but we cannot afford optimism on this count. Before the Cultural Revolution many China specialists foresaw a post-Mao regime dominated by a younger, sophisticated, pragmatic elite which would relate to the outside world in a more relaxed and less revolutionary fashion. This is no longer a convincing image. More likely is a post-Mao regime of considerable fluidity as factions jockey for power. Basic control will probably lie with the military, as civilian organizations and institutions will attempt to refashion the system according to coalitions of interest. The result may be several years of a more inward and less ideologically oriented regime, but it is also likely to be less experienced and self-confident in foreign policy than what we face today. Under these circumstances compromise may be more, not less, difficult to negotiate, particularly on sensitive issues affecting national prestige and security.

In addition to the uncertainties of a post-Mao regime on the mainland, the odds favor an increased instability on Taiwan after the passing of Chiang Kai-shek. No single figure combines Chiang's symbolic and real authority. Any serious struggle there, either among mainlanders or by the Taiwanese, can so complicate our involvement as to make negotiations with Peking impossible until the struggle is resolved. With these future uncertainties on both sides, the time for attempting to resolve the impasse in our relations is now.

It may be objected that we cannot be certain Peking is willing to compromise. That is obviously true. Two counter-objections are relevant, however. First, determining Peking's willingness to compromise is the job of diplomacy not of academic analysts or outside observers. We won't know unless we try to find out. Second, we do know that although Peking has publicly pledged for twenty years to "Liberate Taiwan" it has never seriously attempted to do so. This impressive ability to defer attainment of proclaimed goals may also encompass a willingness to examine alternative means of realizing them. Presumably Peking knows it must negotiate with the authorities on Taiwan because they—not the United States—control the situation there. Moreover the incentives to negotiate are strong. Taiwan is a valuable economic prize so long as its international investment and trade assets remain intact. Taiwan's foreign trade promises to exceed that of mainland China this year or next. In addition, the longer the island remains separate the greater are the prospects for the twelve million Taiwanese to win ascendancy and eventual independence. These calculations may persuade policy-makers in Peking to adopt a gradualist approach, perhaps along the historical precedents of earlier decades suggested by Professor John

Fairbank's formula of "autonomy within sovereignty." Whatever Taiwan's ultimate resolution, we can be certain it will not be dictated in Washington or at the United Nations.

U.S. Policy Alternatives

Negotiations between the two sides in the Taiwan Strait are unlikely to begin tomorrow. But they may never have any serious prospect unless the United States divests itself of the military and intelligence interests which prevent Peking and Taipei from believing our disclaimers of intent to keep the island out of communist control. So long as thousands of American military personnel remain there with facilities for our Strategic Air Command and the Seventh Fleet, so long as Taiwan serves as an American intelligence base directed against the mainland, we share common interests with one side in the Chinese civil war. Moreover, it is the Nationalists, not the Communists, who have maintained the more aggressive and provocative posture in this war. Chiang's batteries on Quemoy block the largest harbor between Hong Kong and Shanghai. His espionage and sabotage teams from the offshore islands repeatedly raid nearby coastal areas. His airfields launch intelligence collection aircraft. Our involvement in these operations, either explicit or implicit, belies our claim that we wish the People's Republic no harm.

We must end all assistance, direct and indirect, to the military establishment of the Republic of China if we are serious in our express desire to improve relations with the People's Republic. This does not mean we simply hand Taiwan over to mainland rule. The armed forces there are fully capable of defending themselves against any foreseeable threat for years to come. Should the military balance eventually change and no settlement ensue, the lead time necessary for Peking to develop and deploy amphibious capability sufficient to threaten Taiwan gives us ample opportunity to reintroduce military assistance if this should be dictated by our commitments and interests at that time. Until then, we must make clear that Taiwan's continued separation is not a function of our military presence and intelligence interests, but results from the inability of both sides to negotiate a mutually satisfactory agreement.

Indeed, we should explicitly declare that we recognize both sides now agree Taiwan is part of China but its final, formal adherence depends upon arrangements between the authorities in Taipei and Peking. In the absence of such arrangements we obviously must deal with those in control of their respective territories without prejudice to the sovereignty and claims of the People's Republic of China. Should no agreed arrangement ever emerge, the people on Taiwan may redefine their status, at which time we would have to re-examine our position as, presumably, would Peking. In the meantime, we should accept the People's Republic in the United Nations as the sole representative of China, ruled uninterruptedly and exclusively by that government since 1949. More than one hundred China scholars in more than fifty American colleges and universities support this position. Resolutions toward this end have been introduced by Senators George McGovern, Mike Gravel and Edward Kennedy. We should also try to settle such matters as the blocked accounts which we have withheld from Peking against claims for American property confiscated after the establishment of the People's Republic. We should try to arrange mutual representation in both countries at the highest official level that can be agreed upon to serve the needs of trade and travel between the United States and the People's Republic. Diplomatic contacts should explore these and related problems through specially designated representatives in Ottawa or perhaps later at the United Nations.

Nuclear Politics

...A nuclear-free zone in Asia was once supported by the People's Republic, admittedly before it possessed nuclear weapons. However this does not preclude an effort to test its feasibility now, at least for northeast Asia. In addition to mutual pledges against their first use, agreements prohibiting the stationing of nuclear weapons in the region would strengthen Japanese opposition to acquiring an independent nuclear capability. The advent of still another nuclear power is sufficiently ominous in its implications to warrant the most determined effort by all concerned to forestall that eventuality.

Essential to any agreement on arms limitations is not only a convergence of interest but some symmetry of compromise. A nuclear-free zone in northeast Asia offers both factors. On the one side, we would pledge not to station nuclear weapons in South Korea; Japan would pledge not to develop its own nuclear capability or permit us to station weapons in any of its territory, including Okinawa. We, of course, would not station our Polaris/Poseidon fleet in the area. On the other side, the People's Republic would not position nuclear weapons within 1200 miles of Tokyo, excluding them from most of northeast and east China. Hopefully the Soviet Union would join the agreement, removing its nuclear weapons from adjacent territory.

Admittedly this is an imperfect scheme since it only removes part of the threat or incentive which might impel the Japanese to develop an independent nuclear capability. It would safeguard Tokyo against attack by a Chinese IRBM (intermediate range ballistic missile) but not an ICBM (intercontinental ballistic missile). Similarly it would protect an important segment of China's industrial base against a nearby threat but leave it exposed to our more distant strike forces on Guam and in the United States. However, any improvement over an uncontrolled arms race is worth striving for, particularly if we can convince the leaders in Peking that we are genuinely interested in foreclosing further nuclear proliferation. Even should negotiations prove long, arduous, and perhaps in the end futile because of technical or other complications, they can provide an important forum for communication between governments. Toward this end American scholars and scientists should endeavor to establish a Chinese counterpart to the Pugwash conferences which have facilitated informal, confidential exchanges between American and Russian specialists in arms control.

Fortunately, not all our common interests require formal implementation. For one, China's acquisition of nuclear weapons offers us the best safeguard against a surprise Soviet attack we can ever hope to achieve. It is inconceivable that Peking would permit Moscow to eliminate our countervailing nuclear power, leaving Russia to dictate whatever terms it wished on the threat of striking elsewhere as it had at the United States. No Chinese government could hope for independence under such a Soviet nuclear hegemony. Thus Peking's growing nuclear arsenal, designed to deter attack against China, also deters attack against the United States. The requirements for a Soviet strike against various future Chinese weapons systems simultaneous with an attack against the United States, sufficiently successful to prevent unacceptable retaliatory damage, make such a move virtually impossible to plan. Nor can any prior agreement guarantee Chinese passivity in the face of an unprecedented act with such far-reaching consequences.

Our minds may still be too dulled by decades of dogma on China to grasp the full implication of the new nuclear world that is emerging. But at least we can see that in the very near future a "hot line" to Peking will be as necessary as one to Moscow. Moreover if agreement between the two superpowers on defensive systems is limited by the capability of a third power which sees the two as conspiring against it, then we must strive to bring that third power into separate or joint negotiations. In the nuclear age we can neither preserve the *status quo* of power nor can we manage global change in uneasy partnership with Moscow....

LUBMAN'S TESTIMONY JUNE 29 (EXCERPTS)

Trade With China

The resumption of trade between the United States and China should continue to be encouraged. Trade offers some economic advantages to each nation; it promises to increase the knowledge each country has of the other, it would symbolize the intent of the two nations to improve their relations, and it would begin to create the economic links which form part of the very substance of normal international relations.

However, resumed trade and a new American trade policy will not meaningfully improve Sino-American relations until the United States adopts new policies on the fundamental political issues which separate China and the United States.

Those new policies should include support of the claim of the People's Republic to represent China in the United Nations, commencement of negotiations on the establishment of diplomatic relations, recognition of the Peking government as the government of China, strict avoidance of a "two China" policy, and an American commitment to allowing the future of Taiwan to be resolved by the Chinese people themselves.

The present Administration has indicated to China a willingness to re-examine, and move toward normalizing, Sino-American relations. The Administration's initiatives have in large measure focused on trade, particularly in the recent partial lifting of the long-standing trade embargo. Although the precise extent of the Chinese response may not be known for some time, the initial Chinese reaction has not been unfavorable. On June 24th, Robert Keatley of the *Wall Street Journal* reported from Peking that Premier Chou En-lai has stated that requests by Americans to attend the Canton Trade Fair later this year would be "considered." With Sino-American trade enjoying a new prominence in official and public attention, I think it appropriate in these hearings to consider the expectations Americans should entertain about that trade and the extent of the contributions it might make to Sino-American relations.

It is important that American expectations be realistic, because over the past twenty years, during which there has been no direct trade between the two nations, a new China has become a member of the international community, with ways of doing business uniquely her own. Some of those business practices may limit rather than expand contacts, and must be understood before trade begins so that disappointments will be avoided.

My views on the desirability and the future outlines of Sino-American trade are based on study of China's commerce with other Western nations. That commerce has increased markedly since 1960—roughly a quarter of China's trade is with Western Europe—and it furnishes a body of experience that suggests what normalized Sino-American economic relations might be like. I am not here concerned with the economic benefits of trade, which would most likely be minor so far as the United States is concerned, at least in the near future. Rather, I intend to discuss the nature and quality of the relationships which develop out of trade, and the increased knowledge of China that trade makes possible, even if unevenly and within considerable limits.

Bureaucratic Problems of Trade

At the outset, I note some institutional problems. Most Western businessmen are allowed to come to China only to attend the semiannual Canton Trade Fairs at which the Chinese conclude most of their foreign trade transactions. At these Fairs, Westerners negotiate with representatives of trading corporations, which stand between the West and the ultimate Chinese end-users or suppliers. Westerners at Canton who meet only these unique middlemen often do not know the identity of the Chinese enterprises they represent. This situation has long been characteristic of trade with the Soviet Union and Eastern Europe, although in recent years the European Communist nations have begun to allow limited direct contacts between Westerners and their domestic enterprises. A fortunate minority of Westerners have gone to Shanghai and Peking to negotiate the large transactions which are beyond the scope of the Canton Fairs.

Americans who deal with the Chinese will find, like other Western traders before them, that Chinese business practices sometimes vary from standard Western practice. The bureaucratic complexities of Chinese planning processes cause negotiations to be protracted and they also make development of markets for new Western products difficult. As a result, it is next to impossible for Westerners to introduce new products at the Canton Fair with the expectation of making quick sales. Purchases of Western products are most likely approved long before the Fair by the end-user and the ministry to which it is responsible; in addition, purchases depend on prior allocations of scarce foreign exchange. As a result, Chinese negotiators come to Canton with a "shopping list," from which departures on short notice are extremely difficult. Westerners have to bombard the Chinese trading corporations with technical literature and sam-

ples, and wait for expressions of interest which may come only after many months if at all. Also, the Chinese have not always been eager to style, design, package and label their products for Western markets. Since the Cultural Revolution, however, some Western buyers have indicated that the use of Western labels—which the Chinese usually insist include their brand names—has reappeared.

Americans will also find that some standard Chinese contract clauses vary from Western ones. Some examples are of special note. Contracts under which the Chinese buy from abroad, for instance, typically include a clause which provides for inspection of the quality, quantity, specifications and weight of the goods by Commodity Inspection Bureaus, which have offices in every major Chinese port and major transport center. The clauses often further provide that certified findings of the Bureaus are to be taken as final. Other characteristic clauses on quality in contracts for the purchase of capital goods may contain very rigorous guarantees of quality and workmanship, and may further stipulate that the seller guarantees "satisfactory performance" for a lengthy period of time.

Contracts with foreign sellers, especially those involving capital goods such as machinery, also often contain penalty clauses, under which the seller may be liable for delay in delivery regardless of whether he was at fault or the buyer suffered losses as a result of the delay. The penalty normally varies with the delay and is computed as a percentage of the contract price up to a stated maximum.

With the Chinese emphasis on prompt delivery of Western goods given teeth by the penalties that may be imposed for delay, Western sellers have been concerned to define the conditions under which they may be excused for delay for reasons beyond their control of the type normally subsumed in international practice under the concept of *force majeure*. However the Chinese have sometimes been reluctant to define the circumstances which they consider to be included under *force majeure*, making sellers uncertain of the protection afforded them by a vaguely worded contract clause.

A unique aspect of the China trade is the Chinese attitude toward settling disputes, which embodies a strong preference for negotiated solutions. The Chinese may negotiate stubbornly at great length about claims which some traders say could be handled expeditiously in ordinary trade. The informal contacts between traders which often help to make possible compromises are lacking in the China trade, with its focus on the Canton Fairs. Also, under most Chinese contracts the insurer is the People's Insurance Company of Peking (the Chinese normally buy F.O.B. a Western port and sell C.I.F.); the trading corporations appear to be reluctant to allow losses to fall on the Chinese insurer. As a result, they sometimes go to very great lengths to try to get a Western seller to admit that damage to cargo occurred as a result of defective packaging, *i.e.* before delivery, and to bear the loss. In addition, the Chinese are reluctant to settle a claim on a basis which would be variance from the surveys of cargo conducted by their Commodity Inspection Bureaus.

Also, like other Communist nations China avoids litigation in Western courts; Chinese standard form contracts have long included clauses specifying arbitration in

Peking as the ultimate means of dispute resolution; only rarely have they consented to clauses calling for arbitration elsewhere, as in Stockholm. Yet they seem to consider resort to arbitration, even their own, as "an unfriendly act." Some observers remind us that Chinese have traditionally held litigation in low esteem, and Chinese negotiators have indeed expressed to Westerners their distaste for law courts. Pertinent also, perhaps, is Chinese recollection of how Western law was used to aid Western penetration in the nineteenth century. At any rate, the Chinese prefer to settle disputes "amicably through negotiation...."

Chinese Trading Attitudes

Other problems in Sino-Western commercial relations are caused by differences in attitudes, especially Chinese suspicion and distrust of the West. The record of Western commercial intercourse with China in the nineteenth and early twentieth centuries would hardly encourage the Chinese to think that Western businessmen had Chinese interests at heart; trade with the West has historically meant exploitation by the West....

These Chinese attitudes may significantly affect business negotiations. For instance, when the Chinese purchase machinery or complete plants, they may be most reluctant to give a Western seller the full information he may need to assure himself that his product will perform up to specifications. The Chinese are apparently concerned to avoid disclosing "economic intelligence." Yet when particular operating conditions cause less than fully satisfactory performance of a Western product—a difficulty which could have been avoided if the Western seller had been informed of these conditions—the Chinese may press a claim for alleged defects.

Chinese attitudes also critically affect their approach to importing the advanced Western technology which they recognize to be important to Chinese modernization. Chinese determination to avoid dependence on other nations has provoked intense unwillingness to allow foreign investment in China, and will surely bar American investment in the foreseeable future. At the same time, they recognize that China must adapt Western technology to Chinese needs; the purchase of Western producer goods, including entire plants, will continue to be the favored vehicle for importing Western technology.

The negotiations for these purchases have often proven to be extremely time-consuming. They represent major uses of scarce foreign exchange for the Chinese, who often attempt to combine the most up-to-date knowledge and equipment with indigenous equipment, which is apparently substituted whenever possible for more expensive Western types. These concerns prompt the Chinese to ask for extremely detailed price and cost breakdowns and technical information. The cooperativeness and patience of the Western seller is thus extremely important in this type of transaction, which if consummated may involve a relationship of several years in duration and the presence of Western technical personnel in China.

Thus far I have stressed some of the respects in which the China trade presents distinctive aspects which have proven unfamiliar to Western traders. However, I again emphasize my strong belief that the China trade has proven profitable and challenging to Western traders, and that it promises to prove so to Americans as well....

Generally speaking, the Chinese record on adherence to contract specifications, on timely payments and on quality of merchandise, appears to be excellent, despite unique contract clauses and practices which require Western traders eventually to take the Chinese at their own word. In many cases, the Chinese record on settlement of claims is also good. Politics has sometimes intruded to influence the choice and treatment of customers, but political interference with contracts has been rare.

JOINT ECONOMIC SUBCOMMITTEE

The Joint Economic Subcommittee on Priorities and Economy held hearings Aug. 9, 10 and 11, 1971, on defense priorities. Three witnesses discussed China policy: Jerome Alan Cohen, Harvard Law School (Aug. 10); John K. Fairbank, Harvard University; and Allen S. Whiting, Michigan University (Aug. 11).

Cohen said that "President Nixon's professed belief that the United States will be able to establish diplomatic relations" with Peking "while retaining diplomatic relations with the Republic of China on Taiwan may well represent the most recent example of persistent American failure to understand...China's Communist leaders." To succeed in "establishing diplomatic relations" the United States, he said, "may" be required to "not only recognize...(Peking) as the only legitimate government of China but also to acknowledge, implicitly if not explicitly, that Taiwan is Chinese territory and that the United States, at some point if not immediately, will cease its intervention in the Chinese civil war."

Fairbank said that historically China had not been an expansionist power. "Their military tradition is defensive and throughout most of their history has been concerned with inner Asia, where the Russians now pose a menace to their frontiers. Predecessors of the Russians were, first, the Huns in the period B.C. and then, later, the various Mongol tribes, leading up to the Mongol conquest of China in the 13th century. This record of conquest of China from inner Asia...has led to a Chinese strategic concern on the landward side of their realm. Their concern for Russia today carries on this tradition. The Great Wall was built in the period before Christ to mark this frontier and help keep those foreigners out of China. There was no menace from the ocean, and no tradition of defense by naval power. All of this land-minded defensiveness has resulted in China having a very weak naval tradition." "The Chinese," said Fairbank, "are never going to threaten us in this country. The problem is how to stay in contact with East Asia and still stay out of trouble with the East Asian peoples on their home ground. For this the requirements are less military than diplomatic, less material than psychological-intellectual."

Whiting discussed U.S. support for Taiwan and clandestine military activity against mainland China carried out "for twenty years" by the Chinese Nationalists "with the knowledge and support of the United States...." The sources of much of the material he presented were the Senate Foreign Relations subcommittee hearings on U.S. policy contained in the publication of the Pentagon Papers on U.S. involvement in Vietnam by *The New York Times* and other newspapers in June and July 1971.

PRESIDENTIAL STATEMENTS ON CHINA POLICY: 1968-1973

During the 1968 and 1972 presidential campaigns and his first four years in the White House, President Nixon made numerous official statements on U.S. relations with the People's Republic of China. Many of these were a specific part of Nixon Administration efforts at rapprochement with the Communist Chinese. The statements touched on such areas as trade, travel, nuclear power, Sino-Soviet relations, membership in the United Nations, the Vietnam war and the President's proposed visit to mainland China. Following is a compilation of principal statements through May 1973:

1968 Campaign

Statements made by Richard M. Nixon during the 1968 presidential campaign:

U.S. POLICY

Any American policy toward Asia must come urgently to grips with the reality of China. This does not mean, as many would simplistically have it, rushing to grant recognition to Peking, to admit it to the United Nations and to ply it with offers of trade—all of which would serve to confirm its rulers in their present course. It does mean recognizing the present and potential danger from Communist China, and taking measures designed to meet that danger. It also means distinguishing carefully between long-range and short-range policies, and fashioning short-range programs so as to advance our long-range goals.

Taking the long view, we simply cannot afford to leave China forever outside the family of nations, there to nurture its fantasies, cherish its hates and threaten its neighbors. There is no place on this small planet for a billion of its potentially most able people to live in angry isolation. But we could go disastrously wrong if, in pursuing this long-range goal, we failed in the short range to read the lessons of history.

The world cannot be safe until China changes. Thus our aim, to the extent that we can influence events, should be to induce change. The way to do this is to persuade China that it *must* change: that it cannot satisfy its imperial ambitions, and that its own national interest requires a turning away from foreign adventuring and turning inward toward the solution of its own domestic problems.

Only as the nations of non-communist Asia become so strong—economically, politically and militarily—that they no longer furnish tempting targets for Chinese aggression, will the leaders in Peking be persuaded to turn their energies inward rather than outward. And that will be the time when the dialogue with mainland China will begin.

For the short run, then, this means a policy of firm restraint, of no reward, of a creative counterpressure designed to persuade Peking that its interests can be served only by accepting the basic rules of international civility. For the long run, it means pulling China back into the world community—but as a great and progressing nation, not as the epicenter of world revolution.

The dialogue with Communist China must come, I think, during the two terms of the next president. I do not believe we should recognize Communist China now or admit it to the United Nations, because that would be in effect putting the seal of approval on Communist China's present very aggressive course against India and against our forces of course in Vietnam and against all of its neighbors.

A strong Japan and a strong group of free nations around the perimeter of China will have more effect on mellowing the Chinese Communist leaders than anything else we could do. Because once the Chinese Communist leaders realize that there is a risk in trying to break out, then the Chinese leaders will have to turn inward and solve some of their own problems.

I think that the Chinese Communist leaders will change their policies when they realize that by not being belligerent toward the United States and toward their neighbors in Asia, including the Indians and all the rest, that by turning inward and trying to work for their own people, that they have a much greater possibility to have a better life for their own people.

The answer is that trade with China, recognition of China, admitting it to the UN, should come only when the Chinese Communists indicate by deeds that they want to be a part of the civilized family of nations and not an outlaw nation.

RECOGNITION

I would not recognize Red China now and I would not agree to admitting it to the UN and I wouldn't go along with those well-intentioned people that said, 'Trade with them,' because that may change them. Because doing it now would only encourage them, the hardliners in Peking and hardline policy that they're following. And it would have an immense effect in discouraging great numbers of non-communist elements in Free Asia that are now just beginning to develop their strength and their own confidence.

NUCLEAR WEAPONS

At the end of this century, Communist China will have a billion people that will have unlimited atomic weapons and it can be exporting them all over the world, and it is essential that whoever is the next President of the United States develop policies now that will get Communist China to change so that we can open a dialogue with them.

EXPANSIONIST POLICY

We have to realize, looking down the road, that Communist China within six years, seven years, at the very least, will have a significant nuclear capability. And Communist China will be outside of the nuclear club. Therefore, whoever is elected president this next time has to be thinking now as to how we develop the power around the perimeter of China which will convince the Communist Chinese leaders that they will not gain—as a matter of fact, that they will run very great risks—in the event that they attempt to expand through the area of the Pacific as they have been attempting to expand in their sorties against India and other countries who are their neighbors.

EVOLUTION

Red China will change as they are convinced by what happens in the settlement of Vietnam. They will be convinced, as they see the strength of Japan and the other free countries on the perimeter of China growing economically and eventually, probably militarily. They will then become convinced that their best interests will be served by turning inward rather than outward. Then the dialogue will begin. Then Red China, as it changes and becomes a civilized member of the community of nations, will be recognized and will be admitted to the United Nations.

1969

During 1969 President Nixon made no formal statements on China but responded to questions on China at three news conferences.

IMPROVING RELATIONS

The following is an excerpt from the President's Jan. 27 news conference:

Q. Mr. President, now that you are President, could you be specific with us about what your plans are for improving relations with Communist China, and whether you think they will be successful or not?

The President. Well, I have noted, of course, some expressions of interest on the part of various Senators and others in this country with regard to the possibility of admitting Communist China to the United Nations.

I also have taken note of the fact that several countries—including primarily Italy among the major countries—had indicated an interest in changing its policy and possibly voting to admit Communist China to the United Nations.

The policy of this country and this Administration at this time will be to continue to oppose Communist China's admission to the United Nations.

There are several reasons for that. First, Communist China has not indicated any interest in becoming a member of the United Nations.

Second, it has not indicated any intent to abide by the principles of the UN Charter, and to meet the principles that new members admitted to the United Nations are supposed to meet.

Finally, Communist China continues to call for expelling the Republic of China from the United Nations and the Republic of China has, as I think most know, been a member of the international community and has met its responsibilities without any question over these past few years.

Under these circumstances, I believe it would be a mistake for the United States to change its policy with regard to Communist China in admitting it to the United Nations.

Now, there is a second immediate point that I have noted. That is the fact that there will be another meeting in Warsaw. We look forward to that meeting. We will be interested to see what the Chinese Communist representatives have to say at that meeting, whether new changes of attitude on their part on major, substantive issues may have occurred.

Until some changes occur on their side, however, I see no immediate prospect of any change in our policy.

CHINA THREAT

The following is an excerpt from the President's Feb. 6 news conference:

Q. Mr. President, you know the ABM system was planned originally to protect us against the threat of a nuclear attack by Red China early in the 1970s. Does your information indicate that there is any lessening of this threat, or greater, or just where do we stand on that?

The President. First, I do not buy the assumption that the ABM system, the thin Sentinel system, as it has been described, was simply for the purpose of protecting ourselves against attack from Communist China.

This system, as are the systems that the Soviet Union have already deployed, adds to our over-all defense capability. I would further say that, as far as the threat is concerned, we do not see any change in that threat, and we are examining, therefore, all of our defense systems and all of our defense postures to see how we can best make them consistent with our other responsibilities.

TRADE AND TRAVEL RESTRICTIONS

The following is an excerpt from the President's informal remarks to newsmen in Guam July 25 during Mr. Nixon's Asian trip:

Q. Mr. President, it has been suggested that we have relaxed trade and travel restrictions to China as a backdrop to your Asian trip, and that this may cause some disquiet in those countries which fear Communist China. Can you say whether there was any connection between your trip and those relaxations, and what accounted for the timing of them?

The President. No. As a matter of fact, suggestions for relaxing restrictions vis-a-vis Communist China—incidentally, suggestions going considerably beyond those that I adopted—have been before the National Security Council for the past 3 months. As far as these two matters that you refer to, one, of course, as you know, dealt simply with the purchase by tourists of commodities of $100 or less; the more significant one dealt with the travel restrictions. I have always felt that with Communist China or with any country in the world, that an exchange of persons is very valuable for us, and I would trust also for them.

This is a policy I have announced previously, and it is one that I was simply implementing at this time. It had no relationship to the timing of this trip. I see no reason why any of the countries should be concerned.

Q. Could you give us your evaluation of Red China's economic-political capability of inspiring further wars of liberation in the Asian nations? Are they able to continue that?

The President. Red China's capacity in this respect is much less than it was 5 years ago, even 10 years ago. Because of its internal problems, Red China is not nearly as effective in exporting revolution as it was then. I think a pretty good indication of that is the minimal role that Red China is playing in Vietnam as compared with the Soviet Union.

Three years ago, Red China was furnishing over 50 percent of the military equipment, the hardware, for the North Vietnamese. Now it is approximately 80-20 the other way around.

There may be other reasons for that coming about, but part of it is that Red China has enough problems within.

Another point I would make in that respect that bears on this, how things have changed in Asia: In 1953, in country after country that I visited—and I was in every one that we are visiting here and all the others as well, the ones that Secretary (of State William P.) Rogers is going to visit on that trip—among most of the intellectual leaders and among many government leaders, there was a real question as to what was the best path for progress, a question as to whether communism, as it was developing in Red China, a Communist system, was a better way to progress, or whether a non-Communist system was the better way.

Now, one of the significant developments that has occurred over these past 16 years, with all the bad things that have occurred, including the war in Vietnam, has been that that situation has reversed itself. The appeal of the Communist philosophy, for example, in Pakistan, in India, in Indonesia, in Japan, in any one of these countries, is less today than it was 16 years ago, 10 years ago, 5 years ago.

On the other hand, I would have to say that the effectiveness of subversive activities in many of these countries has not abated to the same extent. It can be on the upgrade. But as we look at the whole of Asia today, it is significant to note that what we have going for us more than anything else is this enormous rate of growth in non-Communist Asia as compared with Communist Asia. You compare Hong Kong with Communist China, you compare Taiwan with Communist China, you look at Japan with 100 million people, with a greater GNP than China with 700 million people, looking clear around the perimeter, from Japan through India, we find that free Asia's record of growth is a very significant factor in affecting the thinking of those who have to make the determination as to which path they are going to take.

1970

The following is excerpted from the President's Feb. 18 message to Congress on U.S. foreign policy in the 1970s.

The Chinese are a great and vital people who should not remain isolated from the international community. In the long run, no stable and enduring international order is conceivable without the contribution of this nation of more than 700 million people.

Chinese foreign policy reflects the complexity of China's historical relationships with the outside world. While China has the longest unbroken history of self-government in the world, it has had little experience in dealing with other nations on the basis of equal sovereignty. Predominant in Asia for many centuries, these gifted and cultural people saw their society as the center of the world. Their tradition of self-imposed cultural isolation ended abruptly in the Nineteenth Century, however, when an internally weak China fell prey to exploitation by technologically superior foreign powers.

The history inherited by the Chinese Communists, therefore, was a complicated mixture of isolation and incursion, of pride and humiliation. We must recall this unique past when we attempt to define a new relationship for the future.

Nor can we underestimate the gulf of ideology between us, or the apparent differences in interests and how we interpret world events. While America has historic ties of friendship with the Chinese people, and many of our basic interests are not in conflict, we must recognize the profound gulf of suspicion and ideology.

The principles underlying our relations with Communist China are similar to those governing our policies toward the USSR. United States policy is not likely soon to have much impact on China's behavior, let alone its ideological outlook. But it is certainly in our interest, and in the interest of peace and stability in Asia and the world, that we take what steps we can toward improved practical relations with Peking.

The key to our relations will be the actions each side takes regarding the other and its allies. We will not ignore hostile acts. We intend to maintain our treaty commitment to the defense of the Republic of China. But we will seek to promote understandings which can establish a new pattern of mutually beneficial actions.

I made these points to the leaders I met throughout my trip to Asia, and they were welcomed as constructive and realistic.

We have avoided dramatic gestures which might invite dramatic rebuffs. We have taken specific steps that did not require Chinese agreement but which underlined our willingness to have a more normal and constructive relationship. During the year, we have:

• Made it possible for American tourists, museums, and others to make non-commercial purchases of Chinese goods without special authorization.

• Broadened the categories of Americans whose passports may be automatically validated for travel in Communist China, to include members of Congress, journalists, teachers, post-graduate students, scientists, medical doctors and representatives of the American Red Cross.

• Permitted subsidiaries of American firms abroad to engage in commerce between Communist China and third countries.

The resumption of talks with the Chinese in Warsaw may indicate that our approach will prove useful. These first steps may not lead to major results at once, but sooner or later Communist China will be ready to re-enter the international community.

Our desire for improved relations is not a tactical means of exploiting the clash between China and the Soviet Union. We see no benefit to us in the intensification of that conflict, and we have no intention of taking sides. Nor is the United States interested in joining any condominium or hostile coalition of great powers against either of the large Communist countries. Our attitude is clearcut—a lasting peace will be impossible so long as some nations consider themselves the permanent enemies of others.

1971

During 1971 the President made several formal statements on China and responded to questions on China at news conferences.

CHINA POLICY

The following statement is excerpted from the President's second annual message to Congress on foreign policy, Feb. 25.

We are prepared to establish a dialogue with Peking. We cannot accept its ideological precepts, or the notion that Communist China must exercise hegemony over Asia. But neither do we wish to impose on China an international position that denies its legitimate national interests.

The evolution of our dialogue with Peking cannot be at the expense of international order or our own commitments. Out attitude is public and clear. We will continue to honor our treaty commitments to the security of our Asian allies. An honorable relationship with Peking cannot be constructed at their expense.

Among these allies is the Republic of China. We have been associated with that government since its inception in 1911 and with particular intimacy when we were World War II allies. These were among the considerations behind the American decision to assist the Government of the Republic of China on Taiwan, with its defense and economic needs....

In that connection, I wish to make it clear that the United States is prepared to see the Peoples Republic of China play a constructive role in the family of nations. The question of its place in the United Nations is not, however, merely a question of whether it should participate. It is also a question of whether Peking should be permitted to dictate to the world the terms of its participation. For a number of years attempts have been made to deprive the Republic of China of its place as a member of the United Nations and its Specialized Agencies. We have opposed these attempts. We will continue to oppose them....

TRADE AND TRAVEL RESTRICTIONS

The following statement announcing changes in U.S. trade and travel restrictions with Communist China was made April 14:

In my second annual Foreign Policy Report to the Congress on February 25, 1971, I wrote, "In the coming year, I will carefully examine what further steps we might take to create broader opportunities for contacts between the Chinese and American peoples, and how we might remove needless obstacles to the realization of these opportunities."

I asked the Under Secretaries Committee of the National Security Council to make appropriate recommendations to bring this about.

After reviewing the resulting study and recommendations, I decided on the following actions, none of which requires new legislation or negotiations with the People's Republic of China:

• The United States is prepared to expedite visas for visitors or groups of visitors from the People's Republic of China to the United States.

• U.S. currency controls are to be relaxed to permit the use of dollars by the People's Republic of China.

• Restrictions are to be ended on American oil companies providing fuel to ships or aircraft proceeding to and from China except on Chinese-owned or Chinese-chartered carriers bound to or from North Vietnam, North Korea, or Cuba.

• U.S. vessels or aircraft may now carry Chinese cargoes between non-Chinese ports and U.S.-owned foreign flag carriers may call at Chinese ports.

• I have asked for a list of items of a nonstrategic nature which can be placed under general license for direct export to the People's Republic of China. Following my review and approval of specific items on this list, direct imports of designated items from China will then also be authorized.

DIPLOMATIC RELATIONS

The following statements are excerpted from the President's discussion with six editors at the American Society of Newspaper Editors annual convention April 16:

Q. Do you think that we can anticipate an establishment of diplomatic relations with the People's Republic of China in your first administration rather than your second?

The President. What we have here is the result of a long process that began in my own thoughts even before 1968, the spring of 1968, when I answered that question at this convention. I wrote an article for *Foreign Affairs*... in which I pointed out that we could not have what will be by the end of the century a billion of the most creative and able people in the world isolated from the world and that whoever was President of the United States had to develop a policy which would bring the isolation of a billion Chinese from the rest of the world to an end.

I also pointed out that that was a long-range goal. The long-range goal of this administration and of the next one, whatever it may be, must be two things: one, a normalization of the relations between the Government of the United States and the Government of the People's Republic of China, and two, the ending of the isolation of Mainland China from the world community....

I think the steady ordered process that we have engaged on now begins to bear fruit. I will just conclude with this one thought:

...I hope sometime I will be able to go to China. I am not sure that it is going to happen while I am in office. I will not speculate with regard to either of the diplomatic points. It is premature to talk about a change of our policy with regard to the United Nations.

However, we are going to proceed in these very substantive fields of exchange of persons and also in the field of trade. That will open the way to other moves which will be made at an appropriate time.

CHINA POLICY QUESTIONS

The following statements are excerpted from the President's April 29 news conference:

Two-China Policy

Q. Mr. President, the Commission on the United Nations that you appointed, headed by your 1960 Vice Presidential running mate, has come out rather strongly for a two-China policy.... I wonder if tonight you could say how you feel about those proposals?

The President. Well, Mr. Cormier, that recommendation by that very distinguished committee, of course, is being given consideration in the high councils of this Government, and I am, of course, considering it along with recommendations which move in the other direction.

I think, however, that your question requires that I put, perhaps, in perspective much of this discussion about our new China policy. I think that some of the speculation that has occurred in recent weeks since the visit of the table tennis team to Peking has not been useful.

I want to set forth exactly what it is and what it is not.

First, as I stated at, I think, one of my first press conferences in this room, the long-range goal of this administration is a normalization of our relationships with Mainland China, the People's Republic of China, and the ending of its isolation from the other nations of the world. That is a long-range goal.

Second, we have made some progress toward that goal. We have moved in the field of travel; we have moved in the field of trade. There will be more progress made.

For example, at the present time I am circulating among the departments the items which may be released as possible trade items in the future and I will be making an announcement on that in a very few weeks.

But now when we move from the field of travel and trade to the field of recognition of the Government, to its admission to the United Nations, I am not going to discuss those matters, because it is premature to speculate about that....

I would just summarize it this way: What we have done has broken the ice. Now we have to test the water to see how deep it is.

I would finally suggest that—I know this question may come up if I don't answer it now—I hope, and, as matter of fact, I expect to visit Mainland China sometime in some capacity—I don't know what capacity. But that indicates what I hope for the long term. And I hope to contribute to a policy in which we can have a new relationship with Mainland China.

Policy Alternatives

Q. Sir, in your first answer on China, you said that you were considering suggestions for a two-China policy, along with suggestions that move in the other direction. Could you expound a little bit on what you mean by that?

What is the range of alternatives?

The President. Mr. Bailey, what I meant to convey was that both within the administration and from sources outside the administration, there are those who favor a two-China policy; there are those who favor universality in the United Nations; there are those who favor a one-China policy, either Mainland China or Taiwan China.

Now, all of these are positions that are taken. I am not suggesting that they are lively options as far as I am concerned. What I am saying is that this is a very complex problem. I will make the decision after advising with the Secretary of State and my other chief advisers in this field, and when I make it, I will announce it, but I am not going to speculate on it now because I emphasize this is a very sensitive area and too much speculation about it might destroy or seriously imperil what I think is

the significant progress we have made, at least in the travel area, and possibly in the trade area, looking to the future.

TRADE AND TRAVEL

Excerpts from the President's remarks to southern media representatives at a background briefing on May 25:

A few weeks ago you all, of course, covered in your newspapers, on your television and radio programs, the developments with regard to China, Mainland China.

In a recent press conference, you may recall that I said that, when asked about what this meant, I said we must realize that what happened was significant, not simply the visit of the table tennis team—that had some significance and, of course, great interest because of its rather bizarre character as far as we are concerned—but because in the field of travel and in the field of trade, in the field of exchange of persons and in the field of trade, to put it more precisely, we see a very significant change occurring for the first time since the Government which presently is in power in Mainland China, the People's Republic of China, that Government and the Government of the United States have found two areas, exchange of persons and travel, where again, on a precise step-by-step basis, they are beginning to have a different relationship than they had previously. As I put it, what we have done really is broken the ice; now we have to test the water to see how deep it is. More steps will be taken on our part and on their part when it is to the reciprocal interest of both to do so.

I do not suggest that any steps are presently being contemplated on either side. That would not be in the interest of having that come about. But I do say that the very fact that the United States and the Government of Mainland China, the People's Republic of China, have finally moved in these limited areas toward a relation of normalcy gives us hope that not immediately—not within a year, for example—but looking to the future, that 800 million Chinese will not be isolated from the rest of the world.

UNITED NATIONS POLICY

The following statement is excerpted from the text of President Nixon's June 1 news conference:

Q. Mr. President, since April you have been considering policy studies on the China question, easing trade with China, and representation at the United Nations. Can you say where these stand now, please?

The President. With regard to the United Nations question, a significant change has taken place among the members of the United Nations on the issue of admission of Mainland China. We are now analyzing that situation in consultations with the Republic of China on Taiwan and with third countries.

After we have completed our analysis, which I would imagine would take approximately 6 weeks, we will then decide what position we, the Government of the United States, should take at the next session of the United Nations this fall, and we will have an announcement to make at that time with regard to that particular problem.

A number of various options are open to us.

With regard to trade, the various agencies have now completed their review of the situation and have submitted their recommendations to me. And on June 10th, I will make an announcement releasing a wide variety of items which previously had been banned. These are all non-strategic items in which trade can be conducted with Mainland China.

Let me put all of this in context by saying that there are only two areas where we have moved. They are significant, however, in themselves. In the area of opening the door to travel and opening the door to more trade, we have made significant movement. I think what, however, we should realize is that we still have a long way to go.

As I recall, there is a Chinese proverb to the effect that a journey of a thousand miles begins with a single step. We've taken two steps, but the important thing is that we have started the journey toward eventual, a more normal relationship with Mainland China, and eventually, and this is vitally important, ending its isolation and the isolation of 700 million people from the rest of the people of the world. This we think is a goal well worth pursuing.

TRADE CONTROLS

Statement by the White House Press Secretary on the lifting of trade controls between the United States and the People's Republic, June 10:

On April 14, the President announced that he would shortly open the possibility of trade between the United States and the People's Republic of China. That announcement followed a series of moves begun in 1969 to end the strict isolation between the United States and China. Today, President Nixon is announcing the details of the trade controls which he is now lifting.

The United States will permit the free export to China of a range of nonstrategic U.S. products. These include most farm, fish and forestry products; tobacco; fertilizers; coal; selected organic and inorganic chemicals; rubber; textiles; certain metals such as iron, zinc and tin; agricultural, industrial and office equipment; household appliances; electrical apparatus in general industrial or commercial use; certain electronic and communications equipment; certain automotive equipment and consumer goods.

President Nixon has also decided to permit the free export of grains to China as well as to the Soviet Union and Eastern Europe. In the past, these exports have been governed by regulations that have hindered the export of grains to these countries.

The President has also decided that the Government will examine requests for the export of other items to the People's Republic of China, and permit those transactions which are consistent with the requirements of U.S. national security.

The United States will also permit for the first time commercial imports from China, while keeping the possibility of future controls on these imports if necessary.

President Nixon looks upon these measures as a significant step to improve communications with a land of 800 million people after a 20-year freeze in our relations. The President will later consider the possibility of further steps in an effort to reestablish a broader relationship with a country and people having an important role for future peace in Asia.

White House announcement of termination of controls on certain nonstrategic United States exports to China and decision to permit imports from China, June 10.

The President announced today the first broad steps in the termination of U.S. controls on a large list of nonstrategic U.S. exports to the People's Republic of China. In the future, a range of U.S. products listed on the attached sheet may be freely sold to China under open general export licenses without the need to obtain Department of Commerce permission for each specific transaction.

The items to be released from trade controls have been recommended by the NSC Under Secretaries Committee chaired by the Department of State. They include most farm, fish and forestry products; tobacco; fertilizers; coal; selected chemicals; rubber, textiles; certain metals; agricultural, industrial and office equipment; household appliances; electrical apparatus in general industrial or commercial use; certain electronic and communications equipment; certain automotive equipment and consumer goods.

The President has also decided to terminate the need to obtain Department of Commerce permission for the export of wheat, flour and other grains, to China, Eastern Europe and the Soviet Union, suspending the 50 percent U.S. shipping requirement for these items.

Items not on the open general license list may be considered for specific licensing consistent with the requirements of U.S. national security. The Department of Commerce and other agencies will continue to review our export controls.

The President has also decided to permit all imports to enter from China under a general license, while retaining standby authority for future controls if necessary. Imports from the People's Republic of China will be subject to the tariff rates generally applicable to goods from most Communist countries. They will also be subject to the normal conditions governing our imports from all sources such as cotton textile controls and antidumping and countervailing duty legislation.

OUTLOOK ON CHINA

Excerpts from the President's remarks to media executives at a background briefing in Rochester, N.Y., on June 18:

Let me put it in perspective this way: As far as Mainland China is concerned, it is at present not a major nuclear power. It at present is not a major economic power. Japan, with one-fifth of the population of Mainland China, has one and a half times as much GNP as Mainland China.

But looking down to the end of this century, to the kind of a world that we leave for our children, we will have a billion Chinese who, because they are Chinese— not because they have a Communist government—are among the most creative and dynamic people in the world —a billion Chinese.

If we have those billion Chinese people outside the world community, living in isolation, isolated, of course, by the Soviet Union, as is the present case, and isolated from the other major power, the United States, with Japan in the middle, you can see what the prospects for peace in the Pacific might be, how dim they might be, and you can also see what the dangers might be, regardless of what agreements the Soviet Union and the United States might make to reduce tensions that we might have regardless of what might happen in other parts of the world. Therefore, anyone in a position of responsibility at this time in the United States must look to that future and in a careful, measured way, as we are, move toward a normalization of relations—and it will not come quickly —and toward a time when Mainland China will not be isolated from the world community.

CHINA ISOLATION

Excerpts from the President's remarks to news media executives during a background briefing in Kansas City, Mo., on July 6:

Let me be very, shall I say, limited in what I would discuss on this particular issue, because we should not consider that more has happened than has happened. What we have done is simply open the door—open the door for travel, open the door for trade.

Now the question is whether there will be other doors opened on their part. But at least the doors must be opened and the goal of U.S. policy must be, in the long term, ending the isolation of Mainland China and a normalization of our relations with Mainland China because, looking down the road—and let's just look ahead 15 to 20 years—the United States could have a perfectly effective agreement with the Soviet Union for limitation of arms; the danger of any confrontation there might have been almost totally removed.

But Mainland China, outside the world community, completely isolated, with its leader not in communication with world leaders, would be a danger to the whole world; that would be unacceptable, unacceptable to us and unacceptable to others, as well.

So, consequently, this step must be taken now. Others must be taken, very precisely, very deliberately, as there is reciprocation on the other side.

But now let's see how this all fits into the economic program I mentioned a moment ago, and the economic challenge. The very success of our policy of ending the isolation of Mainland China will mean an immense escalation of their economic challenge, not only to us, but to others in the world.

I again come back to the fundamental point: 800 million Chinese, open to the world, with all the communication and the interchange of ideas that inevitably will occur as a result of that opening, will become an economic force in the world of enormous potential.

So, in sum, what do we see? What we see as we look ahead 5, 10, and perhaps 15 years, we see five great economic superpowers: the United States, Western Europe, the Soviet Union, Mainland China, and, of course, Japan.

...First in terms of its (China's) economic capacity at the present time, a pretty good indication of where it is is that Japan, with 100 million people, produces more than Mainland China with 800 million people. But that should not mislead us, and it gives us and should give none of the potential competitors in the world markets. Mainland China, any sense of satisfaction that it will always be that way, because when we see the Chinese as people—and I have seen them all over the world, and

some of you have, too, whether in Hong Kong or Thailand or Singapore or Bangkok, any of the great cities, Manila, where Chinese are there—they are creative, they are productive, they are one of the most capable people in the world, and 800 million Chinese are going to be, inevitably, an enormous economic power, with all that means in terms of what they could be in other areas if they move in that direction.

PRESIDENTIAL VISIT

The complete text of President's remarks broadcast to the nation announcing his acceptance of an invitation from Premier Chou En-lai to visit China. July 15:

Good evening:

I have requested this television time tonight to announce a major development in our efforts to build a lasting peace in the world.

As I have pointed out on a number of occasions over the past 3 years, there can be no stable and enduring peace without the participation of the People's Republic of China and its 750 million people. That is why I have undertaken initiatives in several areas to open the door for more normal relations between our two countries.

In pursuance of that goal, I sent Dr. Kissinger, my Assistant for National Security Affairs, to Peking during his recent world tour for the purpose of having talks with Premier Chou En-lai.

The announcement I shall now read is being issued simultaneously in Peking and in the United States:

"Premier Chou En-lai and Dr. Henry Kissinger, President Nixon's Assistant for National Security Affairs, held talks in Peking from July 9 to 11, 1971. Knowing of President Nixon's expressed desire to visit the People's Republic of China, Premier Chou En-lai on behalf of the Government of the People's Republic of China has extended an invitation to President Nixon to visit China at an appropriate date before May 1972.

"President Nixon has accepted the invitation with pleasure.

"The meeting between the leaders of China and the United States is to seek the normalization of relations between the two countries and also to exchange views on questions of concern to the two sides."

In anticipation of the inevitable speculation which will follow this announcement, I want to put our policy in the clearest possible context. Our action in seeking a new relationship with the People's Republic of China will not be at the expense of our old friends.

It is not directed against any other nation. We seek friendly relations with all nations. Any nation can be our friend without being any other nation's enemy.

I have taken this action because of my profound conviction that all nations will gain from a reduction of tensions and a better relationship between the United States and the People's Republic of China.

It is in this spirit that I will undertake what I deeply hope will become a journey for peace, peace not just for our generation but for future generations on this earth we share together.

Thank you and good night.

PURPOSE OF VISIT

Excerpts from the President's remarks at ceremonies marking the dedication of the Rathbun Dam near Centerville, Iowa, on July 31:

Also, as you have heard, I am planning a journey to Mainland China. The purpose of that journey involves not just peace for my generation, but even more, it affects peace for generations to come because looking far to the future we cannot have a peaceful world if 800 million of the most creative, able people in the world, one-fourth of all the people in the world, are isolated from the rest of the world.

So that is why I believe the President of the United States should take the first step to establish a new communication with that one-fourth of the world's people who live in Mainland China so that we can have a better chance for peace in the generations to come.

VIETNAM WAR

The following statement is excerpted from the text of President Nixon's Aug. 4 news conference:

Q. Mr. President, can you tell us any more about your forthcoming trip to China, when it is likely to occur, and can you give us your assessment of what effect you think this will have on ending the war in Vietnam?

The President. As far as the timing is concerned, I cannot add to what I said in the original announcement. It will be before May 1. The time will be worked out sometime within the next 2 to 3 months, I would assume, and a considerable amount of preparatory activity must take place, setting up the agenda, setting up the numbers in the official party.

These are matters, of course, that must be discussed and worked out before the time of the visit is finally announced.

Second, and I know a number of you are interested in who is going, that is a matter still to be decided. It was raised by Dr. Kissinger and by Premier Chou En-lai in their conversations, and will be worked out by mutual agreement.

As far as our party is concerned, it will be a small working party. The only ones that presently are definitely going are, of course, the Secretary of State and Dr. Kissinger and myself. Beyond that, whatever others will be added will be determined by mutual agreement between the parties concerned.

Now, as to the effect the visit will have and the conversations will have on Vietnam, I will not speculate on that subject. I will only say that as the joint announcement indicated, this will be a wide-ranging discussion of issues concerning both governments. It is not a discussion that is going to lead to instant detente.

What it really is, is moving, as we have moved, I believe, in the situation with regard to the Soviet Union, from an era of confrontation without communication to an era of negotiations with discussion. It does not mean that we go into these meetings on either side with any illusions about the wide differences that we have. Our interests are very different, and both sides recognize this, in the talks that Dr. Kissinger had, very extended talks he had with Premier Chou En-lai. We do not expect that these talks will settle all of those differences.

What is important is that we will have opened communication to see where our differences are irreconcilable to see that they can be settled peacefully, and to find those areas where the United States, which today is the most powerful nation in the world, can find an agreement with the most populous nation in the world which potentially in the future could become the most powerful nation in the world.

As we look at the peace in the world for the balance of this century, and for that matter the next century, we must recognize that there cannot be world peace on which all the peoples in the world can rely, and in which they have such a great stake, unless there is communication between and some negotiation between these two great superpowers, the People's Republic and the United States.

I have put this in general terms because that is the understanding of the People's Republic, Premier Chou En-lai, and it is our understanding that our agenda will be worked out at a later point; before the trip it will be very carefully worked out so that the discussions will deal with the hard problems as well as the easy ones.

We expect to make some progress, but to speculate about what progress will be made on any particular issue, to speculate, for example, as to what effect this might have on Vietnam, would not serve the interests of constructive talks.

UNITED NATIONS

The following statement is excerpted from the President's Sept. 16 news conference:

Q. Mr. President, on the subject of the United Nations debate over China, some critics of your new policy on the UN, and I refer specifically to Dr. Walter Judd who made a statement yesterday, are saying that the expulsion of the Nationalist Government would not be legal under the Charter without a vote of the Security Council making such a recommendation to the General Assembly.

Now, recognizing that we hope they will not be expelled, can you address yourself to the legalities of the question, what the administration's position is on that?

The President. Mr. Bailey, we spent many months looking into the legality of the situation, and in fairness to Dr. Judd, I should say that there are different legal opinions that you can get with regard to what action is needed for purposes of expulsion and whether Security Council action is required as well as the other.

We, however, have reached the conclusion that the position we presently take, which has been stated by the Secretary of State and by Ambassador Bush, is the legally sustainable one.

To put also our policy in clear perspective, we favor the admission and will vote for the admission of the People's Republic to the United Nations and that will mean, of course, obtaining a Security Council seat.

We, will vote against the expulsion of the Republic of China and we will work as effectively as we can to accomplish that goal.

Beyond that, I would have no further comment at this point.

Q. When you say you favor the obtaining of a Security Council seat by the People's Republic, that implies that the Republic of China would be removed from the Security Council.

The President. Our analysis indicates that this is really a moot question. In the event that the People's Republic is admitted to the United Nations, the seat in the Security Council would go to the People's Republic and that, of course, would mean the removal of the Republic of China from the Security Council seat.

The statement that was made yesterday simply reflected the realities of the situation in the United Nations.

PRESIDENTIAL CHINA TRIP

Excerpts from the President's remarks during a session with 10 members of the Economic Club of Detroit on Sept. 23:

Q. Mr. President, is news of current developments in Mainland China likely to change any of your travel plans? And the second part of the question is, just what do you expect to realize from your proposed visit to Mainland China?

The President. I do not expect the current developments to change our travel plans, and those plans will be announced, incidentally, at an appropriate time in due course.

With regard to what we intend to accomplish, I think it is important for us to put it in the context of what we cannot accomplish and do not expect. Some rather naive observers have assumed that because I was going to Mainland China, that the differences between Mainland China and its 800 million people and its Government and that of the United States—that those differences would evaporate. They will not.

There are very deep differences between the United States and the Government of Mainland China—the People's Republic of China. Premier Chou recognized those in his public statements and in more detail in his private meetings with Dr. Kissinger. Those differences, however, now will be discussed.

They will be discussed by the President of the United States and by the leader of the People's Republic of China. There have been no conditions on either side, but we have agreed to talk about those differences.

Now, let me tell you why I think that is important. Ten, 15 years from now, there will be between 900 million and a billion people in Mainland China. Ten or 15 years from now, they will be a very significant nuclear power.

For Mainland China and its 900 million or a billion people at that time to be out of the family of nations, isolated from the rest of the world, would be a danger to the rest of the world which any man who is President of the United States at this time should try to avert if he can. What I am trying to do is simply to open a dialogue, move toward more normal relations, so that these differences which will continue to exist between our two countries—so that we will talk about them and not fight about them, now or 15 years from now.

MEETING CHINESE LEADERS

Excerpts from the President's remarks during a media briefing for Northwest editors and publishers and broadcast executives in Portland, Ore., Sept. 25:

Q. Mr. President, you said in Detroit you would meet with the leader of Red China. Do you expect that to be Mao Tse-tung?

The President. In any meeting that occurs with a leader of a Communist country, a meeting must occur not only with the head of government, which in this case of course would be Chou En-lai, the Premier, but it must also occur with the Chairman of the Communist Party in that country.

1972

During 1972 President Nixon traveled to Communist China. The Chou En-lai and Nixon toasts in Peking and the final communique from that historic trip are printed elsewhere in his book. (p. 2, 6)

RATHER INTERVIEW

Excerpts from President Nixon's televised interview with CBS White House correspondent Dan Rather on Jan. 2, 1972:

Mr. Rather. Mr. President, you have raised the subject of China, and I am sure it comes as no surprise to you that I would like to talk with you about that. Everyone is interested. You have also mentioned that you hope to reach your goals in the war this year, 1972; that everything seems to have been pointed in the direction of climaxing in this election year: besides your ultimate goals in the war, victory over inflation, driving down unemployment, agreement for the strategic arms limitations, trips to Peking and Moscow.

Is all of this coincidental, the timing, or is it, as some of even your friends say, some of the timing must be politically motivated?

The President. Well, that is a very legitimate question, and I understand why many would feel that it was politically motivated. After all, when you look at the bombing halt of 1968, I know many on our side felt that that was politically motivated, at least the timing of it. I, of course, never made such a charge, and would not, and I don't think you would, because I think President Johnson was interested in doing everything that he could while he was President, and before the election, to start some negotiations in Paris.

But I realize that anyone who sits in this office is one that is going to be charged with having a political motivation for everything that he does. But just let me point this out: Let me say that if I could have ended the war the day I came into office, in a way that would not have encouraged this kind of aggression in other parts of the world, that would not have resulted in what I would have thought—and I thought then and think now—would have been a disastrous blow to America's foreign policy leadership in the world, believe me, I would have done it.

Anyone who signs, as the President does, letters to the next of kin of men killed in war has, as his constant thought in his mind, the first time he wakes up in the morning and the last time as he goes to sleep at night, when he goes to bed, he has in mind what can he do to bring that war to an end in a way that isn't going to bring on other wars, or in a way that will discourage other wars.

So as far as the Peking visit and the Moscow visit are concerned, we could have had a Moscow summit when we first came into office. It would have been a failure, just as the Glassboro summit was a failure. When summits are not well planned, when they have for their purpose just cosmetics, they raise great hopes and then there is a great thud when they fall down....

Now, the Chinese summit is one that I, as you may recall, wrote about in 1967. You may not recall it, because in 1967 there weren't many who thought I would be sitting here now, and certainly I wasn't sure.

Mr. Rather. Frankly, I didn't think that you would be.

Mr. President. And that makes you not a bad prophet, either. But looking at the situation in 1967, I wrote an article for *Foreign Affairs*. As you know, I traveled very extensively while I was out of office, and much more freely than I can travel now. But in that article, I raised the lid on what many think was the biggest surprise in history when I made the 90-second-announcement that we were going to go to China.

I said then that the United States, looking to the future, had to find a way to open communinations with the leaders of 750 million people who lived in Mainland China, and so the long process began. If we could have had it in 1969 or 1970, if it could have been properly prepared, we would have done so; but I can assure you it wasn't delayed because I was thinking, "Well, if I could just have it before the New Hampshire primary, in the year 1972, what a coup."

And the other side of that is, you see, it takes two to work out this neat little conspiracy that someone set up. Does anybody suggest the Soviet Union is interested in my reelection; that the Chinese would set their summit so that I could do well at that time of year?

Mr. Rather. Well, I don't know—

The President. The answer, of course, is that I would doubt if that were the case. I don't mean that they would be against my reelection; but I am simply suggesting that those of us who make decisions in offices like this, certainly we think politically. We have that responsibility. We are leaders of our party; we are leaders of our country. But the country comes first.

I can assure you ending the war in Vietnam, building a lasting peace through opening to China, limiting tensions between the United States and the Soviet Union— those decisions have no political connotations whatever. If we could have done it earlier, we would have done it. And if this is not the right time to do it, we would have postponed it.

Mr. Rather. Well, that raises the question, Mr. President, that has always bothered me about summitry and I know from your writings before you became President, just before you came to this office, about the dangers of summitry. Doesn't it give the Communists in both capitals, Peking and Moscow, a bargaining advantage to bargain with you at the summit in the middle of an American election year? Wouldn't it have been better to say we either have the summits in both cases before our election year starts or postpone them a few months until after the election so as not to give the Communists this bargaining advantage?

The President. Well, first, peace is too important to postpone, and I will elaborate on that for just a moment if I can, after I cover the second part of the question. The second part of the question deals with the whole problem of summitry and whether or not it is a good idea. You raised that point and I think I should respond to it. Sum-

mits which are held for the sake of having summits are a very bad idea, but when you are dealing with governments which have basically one-man rule—and that is true of the Soviet Union, it is true of the People's Republic of China—then for the major decisions summitry sometimes becomes a necessity. I became convinced that with regard to China and with regard to the Soviet Union that it lould serve our interests and their interests in avoiding those confrontations that might lead to war, in building a world of peace, to meet, and the timing was such that it had to be now. To postpone it might have meant that something could have occurred in between so it would not be held at all. And as I have already pointed out, we could not arrange to have it earlier.

Now, second, with regard to the bargaining position, let me make one thing—It seems to me in that connection is very possibly a misunderstanding. Let me get the misunderstanding out of the way. When I go to meet with the leaders of the People's Republic of China, with Mr. Chou En-lai, with Mr. Mao Tse-tung, and later on with Mr. Brezhev and Mr. Kosygin, I can assure you that there is not going to be any bargaining advantage due to my desire to affect our election campaign. And I say that not to be sanctimonious, not to be pious, but because I know what is riding. What is riding here is the future for generations to come, and the wrong kind of an agreement with the Soviet Union, one, for example, in the arms control field that would give them an advantage and make us the second strongest nation in the world, the wrong kind of an agreement with the Chinese, one that would discourage our friends in non-Communist Asia, that kind of an agreement, and so forth, would be one that simply would not be worth making.

Let me say, any President—it would not be just me, any President—would not want to win an election at that cost, and I certainly will not. I am going into these meetings, I can assure you, well prepared, and I will go well prepared and I will go there to defend the interest of the United States, to negotiate as well as I can, to reduce the differences, recognizing that there are basic philosophical differences between us and the two Communist powers. But unless we talk about those differences eventually we may end up fighting about them, and that will be the end of civilization as we know it....

CHINA ITINERARY

Excerpts from President Nixon's news conference of Feb. 10, 1972, seven days before departing on his journey:

Ladies and gentlemen, before going to your other questions, I would like to make an announcement with regard to the details of the trip to Mainland China. This will not cover all the details, but it will at least cover those that have been announced at this time.

The official party will be announced from Florida, Key Biscayne, on Saturday the 12th. Of course, as you know, we have already announced that Dr. Kissinger, the Secretary of State, Mrs. Nixon and I will be going, and the other member of the official party at that time will be announced from Washington.

On Monday, I have an event that I think has already been announced, a meeting with Andre Malraux, and I am giving a dinner that night for him to which several Congressional leaders will be invited, as well as members of the official party, the Secretary of State and Dr. Kissinger.

In mentioning Andre Malraux, I do not want to reflect on many of the other experts—and there are many experts in this field of China whose books have been brought to my attention. I do not want to indicate I have read them all, but I have been exposed to a great number. I asked him to come because there was an interesting coincidence.

In 1969, when I met with President de Gaulle in Paris, Mr. Malraux at that time was the Minister of Culture in the de Gaulle Cabinet. We had a discussion prior to dinner on the subject of China generally, and I was particularly impressed with his analysis of the leaders. His book, at least one he has writte, but his book—the one I particularly refer to was his *Anti-Memoirs*. I commend it to you not only for what it tells about China and its leaders, but also about France, its problems, and the whole World War II and post-World War II era.

I give you this only to indicate the breadth of the kind of briefings that all of us who are going to participate in the talks are trying to undertake. It is very different from the other meetings that we have had at the highest level with other governments. I have visited virtually all of the other countries, just as I have visited the Soviet Union.

But here it is essential to do an enormous amount of homework just to come up to the starting line. I don't want to say after having read as much as I have, and as much as I will be reading between now and the time we arrive, that I will be an expert, but at least I will be familiar with the men with whom we will be meeting and the problems that may be discussed.

Tuesday and Wednesday will be used primarily to finish up on many of the domestic matters that are, of course, the subject of matters that I will be discussing with Secretary Connally and Mr. Ehrlichman over the weekend, and also for further briefings from members of the NSC staff and the State Department on the China trip.

The time of departure has now been set. It will be 10:00 o'clock Thursday morning, the 17th, from Andrews. We will fly directly to Hawaii. We will spend Thursday night and all day Friday in Hawaii.

The following morning, Saturday morning, on the 19th, the press plane will go directly to Mainland China, stopping in Shanghai first, and arriving in Peking. The Chinese Government is arranging this so the members of the press can be on the ground prior to the time I will be arriving.

On that same day Saturday, the 19th, the Presidential plane, the Spirit of '76, will fly to Guam, and we will stay overnight in Guam and then take off the next day, Monday, for Shanghai and Peking, arriving in Peking Monday morning at approximately 11:30 a.m. The date, of course, is the 21st there and the 20th here. As you know, we cross the International Date Line on the way.

A couple of other points that I know have been raised in briefings and that I can only cover generally:

With regard to agenda, both governments have decided that we will not make any announcements on agenda items prior to the meetings. The agenda will be covered by a joint communique that will be issued at the conclusion of our talks and consequently, questions on agenda, what will be discussed and so forth, on the part of both sides, will not be answered either before we get there or during the course of the meetings, unless the two sides decide, while we are meeting, that an agenda item can properly be discussed or disclosed.

With regard to the itinerary itself, the itinerary, generally as you know, has been announced for three cities. With regard to what we do in each city, it is being kept flexible and no final decisions have been made and none will be announced at this time.

Mrs. Nixon's itinerary will be much more public than mine. And she will have an opportunity, which I hope many of you also will have, those of you who are going, to visit a number of institutions, places of interest in Peking and Hangchow and Shanghai. She, as you know, having traveled to perhaps more countries than any First Lady, is looking forward to this with a great deal of interest and I think as she demonstrated on her trip to Africa, her events, I think, will be worth covering.

One side note, and I am sure all of you who have been studying, as I have, will have noted this, is that one development in the 20th century China which is very significant, is the enormous elevation in the status of women. Total equality is now recognized and looking back over Chinese history, that is, of course, a very significant change.

Consequently, I think that Mrs. Nixon's activities will be significant for us in the United States to see their schools and other institutions and how they compare with ours and the other countries that we visit.

As far as my agenda is concerned, there will not be a great deal of what I would call public—well, to put it perhaps rather plainly—sightseeing. There will be some. I mean actually I would hope to see some of the points of interest and the Chinese Government is arranging for some, but we have both agreed that this visit is one, taking place as it does at this time, in which first priority must be given to our talks and sightseeing and protocol must come second. And consequently, we have agreed that we will not get frozen into any extended travel within the cities which we will be visiting, in the event that that might interfere with an extended conversation that might be taking place.

I do not want to suggest here what the length of the talks will be, but, necessarily because we are in truth at a beginning, they will be much longer, both with Mr. Chou En-lai and Mr. Mao Tse-tung than with the leaders of other governments that we have visited, because there we are not starting at the beginning. We have the opportunity to come immediately to matters of substance.

Finally, in order to perhaps put the trip in context, you have heard me discuss it in various speeches that I have made. I really haven't much to add, because as I pointed out, the agenda items will be decided at the beginning of the meetings, but they will be published at the end of our meetings and by communique.

But I think we could say this, this trip should not be one which would create very great optimism or very great pessimism. It is one in which we must recognize that 20 years of hostility and virtually no communication will not be swept away by one week of discussion.

However, it will mark a watershed in the relations between the two governments; the post-war era with respect to the Peoples Republic of China and the United States, that chapter now comes to an end from the time that I set foot on the soil of Mainland China, and a new chapter begins.

Now, how the new chapter is written will be influenced, perhaps influenced substantially, by the talks that will take place. On our side and we believe also on their side we hope that the new chapter will be one of more communication and that it will be a chapter that will be marked by negotiation, rather than confrontation and one that will be marked by the absence of armed conflict. These are our hopes.

We, of course, will now see to what extent those hopes can be realized in the first meetings.

I will go to any other questions.

Q: Mr. Malraux is quoted as having said that he is sure the first question Mao will ask you is will you provide aid to China and the rest of the trip, the success of the talks, will be determined by your answer. Can you give us any indication if that is true?

The President: That gets into the area that I will decline to comment upon, because it involves the agenda items. I cannot really predict with much confidence as Mr. Malraux perhaps can, as to what Mr. Mao Tse-tung's questions will be.

So, consequently, I don't believe it would be proper to comment now on a question that has not yet been asked by him. If it is asked, I will have an answer.

Dialogue or Negotiation

Q: Mr. President, do you look upon your meeting with Chou En-lai and Mao Tse-tung as dialogue or negotiation?

The President: They will be primarily dialogue. Here a very subtle but definite distinction is made between the talks that will take place in Peking and the talks that will take place in Moscow.

In the talks on Moscow there are certain subjects that we have been negotiating about and those subjects, therefore, will be negotiated, although, of course, there will be dialogue as well, dialogue is an essential part of negotiation.

In the case of Peking, there will necessarily have to be a substantial amount of dialogue before we can come to the point of negotiating on substantive matters. I should emphasize, too, that it has already been pointed out by Dr. Kissinger when he returned, that when we speak of these matters that they will be primarily bilateral matters. Beyond that, however, I will not go.

RETURN FROM CHINA

The following statements are excerpted from the President's remarks on his return to Washington, Andrews Air Force Base, Feb. 28, 1972:

...When I announced this trip last July, I described it as a journey for peace. In the last 30 years, Americans have in three different wars gone off by the hundreds of thousands to fight, and some to die, in Asia and in the Pacific. One of the central motives behind my journey to China was to prevent that from happening a fourth time to another generation of Americans.

As I have often said, peace means more than the mere absence of war. In a technical sense, we were at peace with the People's Republic of China before this trip, but a gulf of almost 12,000 miles and 22 years of noncommuni-

cation and hostility separated the United States of America from the 750 million people who live in the People's Republic of China, and that is one-fourth of all the people in the world.

As a result of this trip, we have started the long process of building a bridge across that gulf, and even now we have something better than the mere absence of war. Not only have we completed a week of intensive talks at the highest levels, we have set up a procedure whereby we can continue to have discussions in the future. We have demonstrated that nations with very deep and fundamental differences can learn to discuss those differences calmly, rationally, and frankly, without compromising their principles. This is the basis of a structure for peace, where we can talk about differences rather than fight about them.

The primary goal of this trip was to reestablish communication with the People's Republic of China after a generation of hostility. We achieved that goal. Let me turn now to our joint communique.

We did not bring back any written or unwritten agreements that will guarantee peace in our time. We did not bring home any magic formula which will make unnecessary the efforts of the American people to continue to maintain the strength so that we can continue to be free.

We made some necessary and important beginnings, however, in several areas. We entered into agreements to expand cultural, educational, and journalistic contacts between the Chinese and the American people. We agreed to work to begin and broaden trade between our two countries. We have agreed that the communications that have now been established between our governments will be strengthened and expanded.

Most important, we have agreed on some rules of international conduct which will reduce the risk of confrontation and war in Asia and in the Pacific.

We agreed that we are opposed to domination of the Pacific area by any one power. We agreed that international disputes should be settled without the use of the use of the threat of force and we agreed that we are prepared to apply this principle to our mutual relations.

With respect to Taiwan, we stated our established policy that our forces overseas will be reduced gradually as tensions ease, and that our ultimate objective is to withdraw our forces as a peaceful settlement is achieved.

We have agreed that we will not negotiate the fate of other nations behind their backs, and we did not do so at Peking. There were no secret deals of any kind. We have done all this without giving up any United States commitment to any other country.

In our talks, the talks that I had with the leaders of the People's Republic and that the Secretary of State had with the office of the Government of the People's Republic in the foreign affairs area, we both realized that a bridge of understanding that spans almost 12,000 miles and 22 years of hostility can't be built in one week of discussions. But we have agreed to begin to build that bridge, recognizing that our work will require years of patient effort. We made no attempt to pretend that major differences did not exist between our two governments, because they do exist.

This communique was unique in honestly setting forth differences rather than trying to cover them up with diplomatic doubletalk.

One of the gifts that we left behind in Hangchow was a planted sapling of the American redwood tree. As all Californians know, and as most Americans know, redwoods grow from saplings into the giants of the forest. But the process is not one of days or even years; it is a process of centuries.

Just as we hope that those saplings, those tiny saplings that we left in China, will grow one day into mighty redwoods, so we hope, too, that the seeds planted on this journey for peace will grow and prosper into a more enduring structure for peace and security in the Western Pacific.

But peace is too urgent to wait for centuries. We must seize the moment to move toward that goal now, and this is what we have done on this journey.

As I am sure you realize, it was a great experience for us to see the timeless wonders of ancient China, the changes that are being made in modern China. And one fact stands out, among many others, from my talks with the Chinese leaders. It is their total belief, their total dedication, to their system of government. That is their right, just as it is the right of any country to choose the kind of government it wants.

But as I return from this trip, just as has been the case on my return from other trips abroad which have taken me to over 80 countries, I come back to America with an even stronger faith in our system of government.

As I flew across America today, all the way from Alaska, over the Rockies, the Plains, and then on to Washington, I thought of the greatness of our country and, most of all, I thought of the freedom, the opportunity, the progress that 200 million Americans are privileged to enjoy. I realized again this is a beautiful country. And tonight my prayer and my hope is that as a result of this trip, our children will have a better chance to grow up in a peaceful world....

1973

Following is the portion of President Nixon's March 15, 1973, news conference at which he announced plans for the U.S. liaison office in Peking:

The President: Be seated, please.

Ladies and gentlemen, I have an announcement with regard to our liaison office in Peking.

The office will open approximately on May 1, and Ambassador David Bruce will be the Chief of the Liaison Office. In the office will be approximately a total complement of 20, of whom 10 will be what we call the expert level; the others, of course, for the support level.

The two top assistants, top deputies to Ambassador Bruce—however, we should note I call him Ambassador, but his title will be Chief of the Liaison Office—will be Mr. Jenkins from the State Department, who, as you know, is one of our top experts on Chinese-American relations in State; and Mr. Holdridge from NSC, who is the top man in NSC advising in that area there.

We selected these two men because Mr. Jenkins and Mr. Holdridge not only are experts in Chinese, they are bilingual, incidentally, in both Chinese and American; speak it well. I remember both assisted in translations when I have been there. But in addition to that, they are men who have from the beginning been participating in the new initiatives between the People's Republic and

the United States. They have accompanied Dr. Kissinger on his trips.

A word about why Ambassador Bruce was selected. We call him out of retirement because I thought it was very important to appoint a man of great stature to this position. The Chinese accepted that view themselves, and we expect soon to hear from them as to the appointment of the man they will have as his opposite number here in Washington. Another reason that I selected Ambassador Bruce was because of his great experience. All of you know that he has been Ambassador to Britain and Ambassador to Germany, Ambassador to France, and also headed our delegation in Paris on the Vietnam talks in 1971 and '72, in the early parts of '72.

A third reason, perhaps, has even greater significance. Many of you in this room were on the trip to China, and sometimes I suppose the feeling must have developed, "Well, this is a one-shot deal." I never considered it that, and all of you who reported on it did not consider it that. It was the beginning, we trust, of a longer journey; a journey in which we will have our differences, but one in which the most populous nation in the world and the United States of America can work together where their interests coincide for the cause of peace and better relations in the Pacific and in the world.

It is necessary that this be, therefore, a bipartisan enterprise in the highest sense of the word.

Mr. Bruce, as you know, while he has not been engaged in partisan politics, as such, is a Democrat. He has served four Presidents with equal distinction, Democratic Presidents as well as Republicans, and we believe that appointing him as head of the delegation indicates our intention that this initiative will continue in the future, whether the Presidency is occupied by a Democrat or a Republican. Of course, I am not making any predictions as to what will happen when I leave.

But that is the end of my announcement. We will now go to your questions.

FOREIGN POLICY MESSAGE

Excerpts from the introduction to President Nixon's annual foreign policy message to Congress, released May 2, 1973:

In January 1969, America needed to change the philosophy and practice of its foreign policy....

The weight of China rested outside the international framework. This was due partly to its own attitude and its preoccupation with internal problems, and partly to the policies of the outside world, most importantly the United States. In any event, this Administration inherited two decades of mutual estrangement and hostility. Here the problem was not one of a fluctuating relationship but rather of having no relationship at all. The People's Republic of China was separated not only from us but essentially from the world as a whole.

China also exemplified the great changes that had occurred in the Communist world. For years our guiding principle was containment of what we considered a monolithic challenge. In the 1960's the forces of nationalism dissolved Community unity into divergent centers of power and doctrine, and our foreign policy began to differentiate among the Communist capitals. But this process could not be truly effective so long as we were cut off from one-quarter of the globe's people. China in turn was emerging from its isolation and might be more receptive to overtures from foreign countries.

The gulf between China and the world distorted the international landscape. We could not effectively reduce tensions in Asia without talking to Peking. China's isolation compounded its own sense of insecurity. There could not be a stable world order with a major power remaining outside and hostile to it....

This Administration's Approach

Peace could not exclude a fourth of humanity. The longer-term prospects for peace required a new relationship with the People's Republic of China. Only if China's weight was reflected in the international system would it have the incentive, and sense of shared responsibility, to maintain the peace. Furthermore, the time was past when one nation could claim to speak for a bloc of states; we would deal with countries on the basis of their actions, not abstract ideological formulas. Our own policies could be more flexible if we did not assume the permanent enmity of China. The United States had a traditional interest in an independent and peaceful China. We seemed to have no fundamental interests that need collide in the longer sweep of history. There was, indeed, rich potential benefit for our two peoples in a more normal relationship.

So we launched a careful process of private diplomacy and public steps to engage the People's Republic of China with us and involve it more fully in the world. We did so, confident that a strong, independent China was in our national interest; resolved that such a process need not—and would not—be aimed at any other country; and looking for a reciprocal attitude on the part of the Chinese....

The Past Year

This past year we realized major results from our previous efforts. Together they are shaping a durable peace. Three years of careful groundwork produced an historic turning point in our relations with the People's Republic of China. My conversations with Chinese leaders in February 1972 reestablished contact between the world's most powerful and the world's most populous countries, thereby transforming the postwar landscape. The journey to Peking launched a process with immense potential for the betterment of our peoples and the building of peace in Asia and the world. Since then we have moved to concrete measures which are improving relations and creating more positive conditions in the region. China is becoming fully engaged with us and the world. The process is not inexorable, however. Both countries will have to continue to exercise restraint and contribute to a more stable environment.

UNITED NATIONS VOTES ON CHINESE REPRESENTATION

The following table indicates the relative strength of the move for Chinese Communist representation in the UN General Assembly during the years 1950-1971: The China question was on the provisional agenda for the 1964 session but did not come to a vote because of the UN stalemate over peace-keeping assessments.

The votes on the issue:

Year		For	Against	Abstentions
1950	(a) Indian resolution to seat Chinese Communists Rejected	16	32	10
	(b) USSR resolution to unseat Chinese Nationalists Rejected	10	38	8
1951	Moratorium (U.S. resolution not to consider any changes in Chinese representation) Adopted	37	11	4
1952	Moratorium Adopted	42	7	11
1953	Moratorium Adopted	44	10	2
1954	Moratorium Adopted	43	11	6
1955	Moratorium Adopted	42	12	6
1956	Moratorium Adopted	47	24	8
1957	Moratorium Adopted	48	27	6
1958	Moratorium Adopted	44	28	9
1959	Moratorium Adopted	44	29	9
1960	Moratorium Adopted	42	34	22
1961	(a) Five-power resolution (United States, Australia, Colombia, Italy and Japan) making any proposal to change the representation of China an "important question" requiring a two-thirds majority for approval Adopted	61	34	7
	(b) USSR resolution to oust Chinese Nationalists and seat the Communists Rejected	37	48	19*
1962	USSR resolution to oust Chinese Nationalists and seat Communists Rejected	42	56	12*
1963	Albanian resolution to oust Chinese Nationalists and seat Communists Rejected	41	57	12
1965	(a) 11-power resolution (U.S., Australia, Brazil, Colombia, Madagascar, Nicaragua, Gabon, Italy, Japan, Philippines, Thailand) declaring 1961 vote on "important question" still in force Approved	56	49	11
	(b) 12-power resolution (Albania, Algeria, Cambodia, Congo-Brazzaville, Cuba, Ghana, Guinea, Mali, Pakistan, Rumania, Somalia, Syria) to oust Chinese Nationalists and seat Communists Rejected	47	47	20*
1966	(a) 15-power resolution (U.S., Australia, Belgium, Bolivia, Brazil, Colombia, Gabon, Italy, Japan, Malagasy Republic, New Zealand, Nicaragua, Philippines, Thailand, Togo) declaring China entry motion an "important question" Approved	66	48	7
	(b) 10-power resolution (Albania, Algeria, Cambodia, Congo-Brazzaville, Cuba, Guinea, Mali, Pakistan, Rumania, Syria) to oust Chinese Nationalists and seat Chinese Communists Rejected	46	57	17*
	(c) Italian proposal (with Belgium, Bolivia, Brazil, Chile, Trinidad, Tobago) to appoint special committee to investigate Communist China's position vis a vis UN membership and report to Assembly by July 1967 Rejected	34	62	25*

Year		For	Against	Abstentions
1967	(a) 15-power resolution (U.S., Australia, Belgium, Bolivia, Brazil, Colombia, Gabon, Italy, Japan, Malagasy Republic, New Zealand, Nicaragua, Philippines, Thailand, Togo) declaring China entry motion an "important question" Approved	69	48	4
	(b) 11-power resolution (Albania, Algeria, Cambodia, Congo-Brazzaville, Cuba, Guinea, Mali, Mauritania, Pakistan, Rumania, Syria - Sudan later became the 12th cosponsor) to seat Chinese Communists Rejected	45	58	17*
	(c) Italian proposal (with Belgium, Chile, Luxembourg, Netherlands) to appoint special committee to investigate Communist China's position vis a vis UN membership and report to Assembly during 1968 session (also made an "important question" under Article 18) Rejected	32	57	30
1968	(a) 13-power resolution (U.S., Australia, Bolivia, Brazil, Colombia, Gabon, Japan, Malagasy Republic, New Zealand, Nicaragua, Philippines, Thailand, Togo—Italy later became 14th cosponsor) declaring China entry motion an "important question" Approved	73	47	5
	(b) 15-power resolution to oust Chinese Nationalists and seat Chinese Communists Rejected	44	58	23*
	(c) Italian proposal (with Belgium, Chile, Iceland, Luxembourg) to appoint special committee to investigate Communist China's position vis a vis UN membership and report to Assembly during next session (made an "important question") Rejected	30	67	27
1969	(a) 18-power resolution declaring China entry motion an "important question" Approved	71	48	4
	(b) 17-power resolution to oust Chinese Nationalists and seat Chinese Communists Rejected	48	56	21*
1970	(a) 18-power resolution declaring China entry question an "important question" Approved	66	52	7
	(b) 18-power resolution to oust Chinese Nationalists and seat Chinese Communists Rejected	51	49	25*
1971	(a) 19-power resolution declaring China entry question an "important question" Rejected	55	59	15
	(b) 21-power resolution to oust Chinese Nationalists and seat Chinese Communists Approved	76	35	17

*Two-thirds majority required for adoption

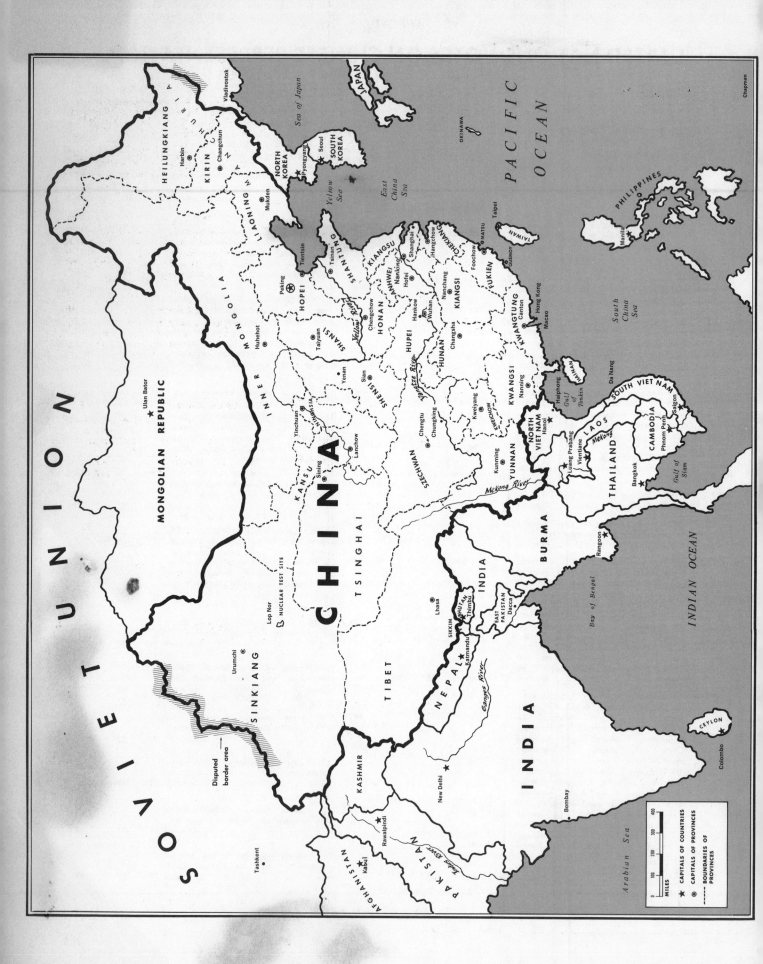